Democratic Partisanship

Democratic Partisanship
Party Activism in an Age of Democratic Crises

Lise Esther Herman

EDINBURGH
University Press

Edinburgh University Press is one of the leading university presses in the UK. We publish academic books and journals in our selected subject areas across the humanities and social sciences, combining cutting-edge scholarship with high editorial and production values to produce academic works of lasting importance. For more information visit our website: edinburghuniversitypress.com

© Lise Esther Herman, 2023

Edinburgh University Press Ltd
The Tun – Holyrood Road
12(2f) Jackson's Entry
Edinburgh EH8 8PJ

Typeset in 11/13 Goudy Old Style by
IDSUK (DataConnection) Ltd, and
printed and bound in Great Britain.

A CIP record for this book is available from the British Library

ISBN 978-1-3995-1185-8 (hardback)
ISBN 978-1-3995-1187-2 (webready PDF)
ISBN 978-1-3995-1188-9 (epub)

The right of Lise Esther Herman to be identified as the author of this work has been asserted in accordance with the Copyright, Designs and Patents Act 1988, and the Copyright and Related Rights Regulations 2003 (SI No. 2498).

Contents

Acknowledgements	vi
List of Figures and Tables	viii
List of Abbreviations	xi
1. The Dual Narrative of Party Crisis	1
2. A Theory of Democratic Partisanship	15
3. Studying Partisanship in Context	44
4. Democracy through the Partisan Lens	65
5. The Cohesiveness of Partisan Identity	97
6. Partisan Respect for Pluralism	132
7. Democracy in Partisan Custody	173
Appendices	197
References	214
Index	237

Acknowledgements

In writing this book, I benefited from the trust, support and friendship of a great number of people. First, this project would have been impossible without the French and Hungarian political activists, journalists, experts and academics that trusted me with this project. I am particularly indebted to the young party members who participated in this study, and especially to those who helped me organise group discussions with their local sections in Paris and Budapest. During my months of fieldwork, I was continuously struck by their enthusiasm, idealism and sense of civic duty. I hope that the respect I have for these qualities comes through in these pages, and that my participants (whose names have been anonymised throughout) will feel I have done due justice to their political engagement.

The European Institute and other services of the London School of Economics and Political Science offered me exceptional administrative and financial support up to 2016. I could not have undertaken this project without being offered a full PhD scholarship by the LSE, which covered both my fees and living costs during the first three years of this project.

I thank Abby Innes and Jonathan White for their unwavering support in the initial stages of this research. Their work and teaching inspired me to become an academic, and their guidance was essential in bringing this work to completion. During my doctoral studies and since completing them, this work benefited from the feedback of many other colleagues I met at the LSE, Sciences Po and the University of Exeter as well as at academic conferences and workshops over the years. I also thank the three anonymous reviewers for their supportive and probing comments, which have helped improve the manuscript in its final stages.

I am so grateful to the talented artist Marcin Gawin for agreeing to illustrate the cover of this book, and for translating my ideas into such a striking image. Many thanks also to Miklós Ferenc, Dániel Polya and Hajnalka Szarvas for agreeing to help me transcribe my Hungarian interviews.

I was graciously given permission to reproduce some copyrighted material for this book. An earlier version of Chapter 2 was originally published in the *American Political Science Review* (Herman, L. E. (2017). Democratic partisanship: From theoretical ideal to empirical standard. *American Political Science Review*, 111(4), 738–54), and part of the content of Chapter 6 was published in the *British Journal of Political Sciences and International Relations* (Herman, L. E. (2020). Can partisans be pluralist? A comparative study of party member discourse in France and Hungary. *The British Journal of Politics and International Relations*, 23(1), 22–42). Many thanks to the publishers for allowing the partial reproduction of these works. Thanks also to the satirical cartoonist Jean Plantureux (aka Plantu) for agreeing to the use of twelve of his drawings as prompts for the French focus groups, and to their reproduction in this book free of charge. Some of my earliest memories of having conversations about public life as a child were prompted by his incisive representation of French politics.

The love of close friends and family in Aix-en-Provence, London, Paris, Budapest and Bristol has brightened my life in these dark times. A very warm thank you to Kamel Boudjemil who, in 2013 during my fieldwork, shared his Parisian home with me. Many thanks to Miklós Ferenc for the many stimulating discussions about my work in Hungary. Finally, to my parents and brother for their support throughout my years of education. I am particularly indebted to my father for the countless and endless discussions about politics we have had since my early teenage years. These conversations awakened the concern for the future of French and Hungarian democracy that is at the heart of this book.

List of Figures and Tables

Figures

1.1:	Distribution of participants according to nationality and party affiliation	10
1.2:	Visual prompts for the French group discussions	12

Tables

2.1:	Dimensions, attributes and indicators of democratic partisanship	40
4.1:	Assessments by French and Hungarian participants of the degree of partisan disagreement on the topics discussed (instances coded)	86
4.2:	Classifications by French participants of the different topics under discussion (instances coded)	88
4.3:	Classifications by Hungarian participants of the different topics under discussion (instances coded)	88
4.4:	Value associated by French and Hungarian participants to political disagreement and agreement (instances coded)	89
4.5:	References by French and Hungarian participants to their positive or negative personal experiences of inter-partisan dialogue (instances coded)	91
5.1:	Dimensions of partisan platforms emphasised by French participants to justify their card classification (instances coded)	99
5.2:	Ideational dimensions of partisan platforms emphasised by French participants to justify their card classification (instances coded)	100

5.3:	References to the topics under discussion by French participants (instances coded)	104
5.4:	Actors emphasised by French participants when justifying their card classification (instances coded)	107
5.5:	Assessments by French participants of the degree of partisan disagreement on the topics discussed (instances coded)	108
5.6:	Arguments used by French participants in their MIXED assessments of partisan disagreement (instances coded)	110
5.7:	References to the topics under discussion by Hungarian participants (instances coded)	113
5.8:	Dimensions of partisan platforms emphasised by Hungarian participants to justify their card classification (instances coded)	118
5.9:	Actors emphasised by Hungarian participants when justifying their card classification (instances coded)	125
6.1:	Praise and criticism by French participants of their own party and their opponents (instances coded)	133
6.2:	Criticism by French participants of their opponents' intentions and practices (instances coded)	134
6.3:	Types of criticism by French participants of their opponents' intentions (instances coded)	135
6.4:	Types of criticism by French participants of their opponents' practices (instances coded)	138
6.5:	References by French participants to the ideas of their opponents (instances coded)	140
6.6:	References by French participants to the ideas of their own party (instances coded)	141
6.7:	Value associated by French participants to political disagreement and agreement (instances coded)	150
6.8:	Praise and criticism by Hungarian participants of their own party and their opponents (instances coded)	153
6.9:	Criticism by Hungarian participants of their opponents' intentions and practices (instances coded)	153
6.10:	Types of criticism by Hungarian participants of their opponents' practices (instances coded)	154
6.11:	Types of criticism by Hungarian participants of their opponents' intentions (instances coded)	156
6.12:	References by Hungarian participants to the ideas of their opponents (instances coded)	159

6.13: References by Hungarian participants to the ideas of their own party (instances coded) 159
6.14: Criticism by Hungarian participants of their opponents' ability to further the common good (instances coded) 164

List of Abbreviations

CEE	Central and Eastern Europe(an)
DK	*Demokratikus Koalíció* (Democratic Coalition)
DL	*Démocratie libérale* (Liberal Democracy)
Együtt	(Together)
Fidesz	*Fiatal Demokraták Szövetsége* (Alliance of Young Democrats)
IKSZ	*Ifjúsági Kereszténydemokrata Szövetség* (Alliance of Young Christian Democrats)
JP	*Jeunes populaires* (Youth for the People)
KDNP	*Kereszténydemokrata Néppárt* (Christian Democratic People's Party)
LR	*Les Républicains* (The Republicans)
MDF	*Magyar Demokrata Fórum* (Hungarian Democratic Forum)
MJS	*Mouvement des Jeunes Socialistes* (Movement of Young Socialists)
MSzP	*Magyar Szocialista Párt* (Hungarian Socialist Party)
RPR	*Rassemblement pour la République* (Union for the Republic)
PRR	Populist Radical Right
PS	*Parti socialiste* (Socialist Party)
SFIO	*Section française de l'internationale ouvrière* (French Section of the Workers' International)
SzDSz	*Szabad Demokraták Szövetsége* (Alliance of Free Democrats)
UDF	*Union pour la démocratie française* (Union for French Democracy)
UMP	*Union pour un mouvement populaire* (Union for a People's Movement)

1

The Dual Narrative of Party Crisis

In May 2006, Hungarian Prime Minister Ferenc Gyurcsány gave a decisive speech at the annual congress of the Hungarian Socialist Party (MSzP). The MSzP had just been granted its second majority in a row and had presided over the country's accession to the European Union (EU) two years beforehand. In what was supposed to be a confidential hearing, Gyurcsány admitted that his party had lacked honesty over the country's financial situation during the most recent electoral campaign and made promises it simply could not keep. The content was leaked by the nationalist broadcast Magyar Radio in September 2006, with the prime minister stating in one key sound bite: 'We lied morning, day and night.' This sparked riots in Budapest at the time, which were violently repressed by state police, as well as mass protests throughout the country.

In the years that followed, opposition party Fidesz continued to use this episode as proof of the MSzP's duplicity, and organised anti-government demonstrations on a regular basis. At the age of nineteen, I stumbled upon one of these gatherings in the summer of 2007 in Budapest. Several hundred supporters of the conservative party stood on Parliament Square, a large majority of whom were middle-aged white men waving the national flag. They demanded the resignation of the prime minister. When I asked one of them to tell me about their reasons, this person answered: 'because those in power are communists'. As a Hungarian citizen who grew up abroad, I walked away puzzled. The MszP had been born out of the ashes of the former Communist Party, but nothing much was left of this heritage. In the early 1990s, it allied with the Alliance of Free Democrats – Hungarian Liberal Party (SzDSz), which itself was founded by left-wing opponents to the pre-1989 socialist regime. Together in government, they orchestrated mass privatisation and market liberalisation in the 1990s and the MSzP was still pursuing market-friendly policies in the 2000s. With so little left of the party's socialist heritage, and so many other good reasons to be angry, I struggled to understand why the party's historical origins was the focus of this man's discontent.

The 2007 financial crisis hit soon after that, with disastrous consequences for the Hungarian economy. Economic mismanagement and political scandal created perfect conditions for the final shattering of the MSzP's political legitimacy and the resounding electoral victory of Fidesz in 2010. Armed with a two-thirds parliamentary majority, the nationalist party proceeded to change the rules of the political game in its favour, carefully dismantling the institutions of liberal democracy that had been in place for the past two decades. In the first years of his leadership, Prime Minister Viktor Orbán also provided some answers to my questions. He presented his illiberal takeover as the true post-communist revolution. The problems of Hungary could all be blamed on the lingering influence of communist elites turned socialist in the 1990s. By putting an end to this influence, Fidesz was also initiating the country's first real break with its Cold War heritage.[1]

Hungary's liberal breakdown struck me as an example of the tenuous relationship between parties and democracy today. While parties fulfil essential democratic functions as agents of representation and actors of the state, there are dramatic consequences when these organisations fail in their responsibilities. I also became aware that how partisans view political disagreement and characterise their own positions and those of their opponents matters to the ways in which they fulfil these democratic functions. This started my personal and intellectual journey to understand the dynamic relationship of partisan identity and liberal democracy in my two countries of origin, France and Hungary. Since then, I have studied what others have said about this relationship, focusing on the normative merits and drawbacks that theorists and political scientists have attached to partisanship over time. I then confronted theory to practice by spending the years 2013 and 2014 between Budapest and Paris, talking to over a hundred party members in party conventions, bars, cafés, community centres and local party sections about their understanding of democratic politics.

This book builds on this work to answer three interconnected research questions about *democratic partisanship*, which I define as the discourses and practices attached to partisan identification, membership and leadership that support liberal democratic regimes. First, *what makes for democratic partisanship* or, in other words, *what norms should we expect democratic partisans to uphold?* Second, *to what extent does partisanship in the real world*

---

[1] For a detailed discussion of this narrative, see Csehi and Zgut, 2020.

resonate with this theoretical ideal? Third, *under what conditions can we expect democratic partisanship to emerge and endure?* This introduction first unpacks the normative judgements that pervade the academic literature on the relationship between political parties and democracy, and what is being lost from these judgements remaining implicit. I then outline how I have gone about answering these questions throughout the book.

Parties under Fire, But What For?

There are two key, seemingly contradictory, developments in the ideational dynamics of Western party systems over the past thirty years: on the one hand, a long-term process of ideological convergence between Left and Right on economic lines, bolstered by the gradual decline of socialist ideology and the emergence of Third Way politics (Berman, 2016; Furedi, 2005; Giddens, 1994, 1998; Mair, 2013a); and, on the other hand, the slow erosion of traditionally dominant parties and the dramatic rise of populist forces. This radical wave has initiated a new cycle of partisan polarisation, opposing pro-system to anti-system forces in national-electoral contests (Bickerton and Invernizzi Accetti, 2017; Hobolt and Tilley, 2018; Lorimer, 2018).

These two trends of convergence and repolarisation have been met with various assessments of their democratic implications. Scholars most concerned with the failure of traditional parties have linked ideological convergence with decreasing rates of citizen engagement and the rise of anti-system sentiment within a large majority of OECD countries (Grzymala-Busse, 2019; Hay, 2007; Mair, 2013a). As party organisations rely less on their members and increasingly on public funding, mass media and public opinion polls for financial and communication purposes, they also lose their ability to act as intermediaries between society and the state (Dalton and Wattenberg, 2000; Ignazi, 2017, pp. 174–232; Katz and Mair, 2009). This is compounded by a structural restriction of the economic policy space since the early 1980s, which limits partisan alternatives and undermines the notion of agency so central to democratic politics (Hay, 2007, pp. 54–60). Scholars have linked these changes in the supply of party politics with the rise of citizen disengagement from the *formal* democratic process since the 1980s in a large majority of OECD countries, evidenced by plummeting voting turnouts, decline in party membership numbers, and drops in levels of declared trust in representative institutions (Dalton and Wattenberg, 2000; Mair, 2013a; van Biezen and Poguntke, 2014). As elites fail in their functions of representation and mobilisation, so citizens retreat from the political sphere, with both processes mutually reinforcing each other to 'hollow out' Western democracy (Mair, 2013a).

But scholarly concern appears to have dramatically shifted in the past decade. The focus is now on the pitfalls of repolarisation fuelled by the increasing success of populist alternatives. In this narrative, political extremism, not citizen apathy, is seen as the greatest democratic threat. The Populist Radical Right (PRR) especially has experienced a stellar trajectory of political success in Europe and the USA since the early 2000s. These forces have not only enlarged their political constituencies but also set the agenda for centre-right parties (Herman and Muldoon, 2018b). In the process, they have repolarised the political mainstream along socio-cultural lines in a number of countries. In multi-party systems such as Italy or Austria, centrist coalitions have engaged with radical right actors (de Lange, 2012), until they themselves became minority partners in populist-led coalitions. In two-party systems such as the USA or the UK, conservative forces have adopted the rhetoric and policies of radical counterparts to the point of becoming their 'functional equivalent' (Mudde, 2016, p. 16; see also Alexandre-Collier, 2018; Grubera and Bale, 2014; Haltinner, 2018).

These tendencies come with their own democratic dangers. Scholars have long linked polarised party systems to governmental gridlock, citizens' dissatisfaction with democracy and, in extreme cases, democratic breakdown (Ezrow and Xezonakis, 2011; Lijphart, 2012; Linz, 1978; Thurber and Yoshinaka, 2015). Contemporary tendencies confirm these general trends, with countries as different as Turkey, Hungary or the USA seeing forms of populist polarisation accompanied by rule of law abuse, human rights infringements, and a general erosion of liberal democratic institutions (Albertazzi and Mueller, 2013; Levitsky and Ziblatt, 2018; McCoy, Rahman and Somer, 2018).

These accounts of party system change are not solely descriptive and analytical, they are also *normative*. In fact, given the positive connotations associated with liberal democracy by the vast majority of Western political scientists, assessments of the democratic character of a given actor or practice almost always include a normative component. As explained by Skinner, democracy is unescapably an 'evaluative-descriptive' term: to use it is 'not only to describe the state of affairs, but also (and *eo ipso*) to perform the speech-act of commending it' (Skinner, 1973, p. 298). Students of political parties and democratic crises do not simply account for *what is*, they also provide a critical analysis in light of what they believe *ought to be*.

Different empirical assessments betray contrasting democratic ideals. From concerns around citizen disengagement and ideological convergence transpire a prioritisation of popular sovereignty, participation and meaningful political choice. This is the properly *democratic* dimension of liberal democracy. Scholars who emphasise populist polarisation and associated risks of institutional breakdown generally place greater value on political stability, as well as respect for human rights and the rule of law. These elements correspond more closely to the *liberal* dimension of liberal democracy. Contemporary preoccupations over the democratic performance of parties carry the legacy of radically different traditions in democratic theory: participatory and agonistic on the one hand, liberal, institutional and elitist on the other (for an overview of these distinctions, see Mouffe, 2000; Pateman, 2007 [1970]).

Often these normative assumptions remain implicit, one reason for this being that the party literature seldom engages with debates in contemporary political theory, normative democratic theory especially (Allern and Pedersen, 2007; Katz, 2006; van Biezen and Saward, 2008). Much empirical work on political parties relies on the minimalist theories of democracy that flourished in the 1950s and 1960s, theories that claimed to deal in facts and description rather than values and prescription (Gerring and Yesnowitz, 2006; Pateman, 2007 [1970]; Skinner, 1973). An important body of political theory has taken partisanship as an object of normative enquiry in the past decade (see below and Chapter 2), but party studies are still largely disconnected from these theoretical debates. In practice, this results in a situation where the basis and criteria for assessing the democratic contribution of political parties is left largely under-theorised. With some noteworthy exceptions (Allern and Pedersen, 2007; Crum, Alvaro, and Overeem, forthcoming; Ignazi, 2017), the literature insufficiently spells out the democratic ideal at stake when partisanship is cast as either conducive to, or impinging on, the democratic performance of a given regime. The presumed end-result of changes in partisan appeals and organisation, for instance the disengagement or radicalisation of citizens, is taken instead as evidence of their problematic nature.

There is a lot to gain from reversing this trend. Because the minimalist outlook on democracy is so widely endorsed, it acts most often as an *implicit* theoretical framework that is not itself subject to falsification (Shapiro and Green, 1994). As a result, performance indicators often lack thorough justification and escape counter-argument. A more solid engagement with democratic theory would allow the reasons why one ascribes the adjective 'democratic' to the practices of political parties, or to their consequences, to be made explicit.

The pitfalls of normative ambivalence are most apparent when key terms are used for political purposes in academic and journalistic circles. Consider the concepts of populism or polarisation, which respectively purport to be descriptive of given political phenomena. In practice, they carry predominantly negative connotations: both populism and polarisation are associated with various forms of democratic dysfunction, from poor political debate to democratic backsliding (McCoy et al., 2018). Yet most definitions of either concepts also include features that could be defined as positive for democracy – in some understandings, polarisation may increase policy choice for citizens (Dalton, 2008; Lachat, 2011), while populism can help shake up the status quo, mobilise citizens and enhance their sense of political agency (Mouffe, 2018). By using the same terms to describe phenomena with widely different democratic implications, rather than an explicitly normative vocabulary, we run the risk of associating negative connotations with political phenomena that simply do not warrant it. Maiguashca and Dean (2017, 2018) illustrate this problem by analysing the widespread academic and journalistic depiction of former British Labour leader Jeremy Corbyn as a populist. While this term was often used as a way to delegitimise his brand of politics, their close analysis of Corbyn's discourse and practices provides little evidence that he meets the defining characteristics of populism (Maiguashca and Dean, 2017, 2018). The normative ambivalence of academic concepts can easily be weaponised for political purposes.

But there are more positive reasons for party scholars to engage with normative political theory. It opens new avenues for political research, directing us towards research questions too often side-lined. Minimalist democratic theory has shaped the ways in which parties are studied: as institutions of the state and electoral machines rather than as intermediary institutions performing affective and symbolic functions within civil society. With political parties conceived 'merely [as] coalitions of individuals seeking to control government', their values and policies serve first and foremost 'to maximise their share of the popular vote, or to perhaps create a minimum winning coalition of parties' (Vassalo and Wilcox, 2006, p. 414). Relying on such frameworks, party scholars also implicitly endorse the idea that, in a modern, representative democracy, nothing more can be expected from parties than the perpetuation of a competitive struggle for the attention of free, independently minded voters. In doing so, they deprive themselves of the means to formulate theoretically informed assessments of the extent to which parties, *beyond* the fulfilment of minimal functions, might meet more demanding democratic ideals.

Bridging the Divide between Theory and Empirics

This book contributes to bridge the divide between normative political theory and the study of political parties, to the benefit of both perspectives. Relying on a framework of analysis derived from contemporary theories of democratic partisanship, I conduct an exploratory study of partisan identity in France and Hungary – two countries that make for ideal-typical cases of some of the key pathologies of contemporary party politics. This study not only contributes to party studies by providing a theoretical framework to assess the democratic merits of partisanship, but also adds to political theory by confronting existing normative principles with empirical manifestations of partisan discourse. The following sections provide an overview of the book's structure and key findings.

The framework of democratic partisanship

I draw on the work of democratic theorists to answer my first research question: *what makes for democratic partisanship* or, in other words, *what norms should we expect democratic partisans to uphold?* Chapter 2 presents my conclusions, building on and contributing to existing theories of democratic partisanship. Since the mid-2000s, a number of democratic theorists have taken the traditional institutions of representative democracy as objects of normative theorising. Their works analyse the functions that representation plays in democratic societies and the conditions under which claims to representation can be deemed democratic (Disch, 2011, 2015; Disch, van de Sande, and Urbinati, 2019; Dovi, 2007; Mansbridge, 2003; Saward, 2010; Urbinati, 2006; Young, 2000). Within this larger body of work, scholars have addressed the place and contribution of parties and partisanship in democratic societies from an explicitly normative perspective (see Bonotti, 2011, 2012, 2014, 2018; Herman, 2017; Herman and Muirhead, 2020; Muirhead, 2006, 2014; Muirhead and Rosenblum, 2006, 2012; Rosenblum, 2008, 2014; White, 2014, 2015a, 2015b; White and Ypi, 2010, 2011, 2016; Wolkenstein, 2015, 2016a, 2016b, 2016c, 2018, 2019). This literature seeks to rehabilitate partisanship as a normative category, and thus account for what 'good partisanship' entails in democratic societies.

This scholarship defines the nature and content of the responsibilities that partisans should exercise in their political functions. It is also anchored in an analysis of how parties have contributed historically to the emergence of representative democracy, and an understanding of the failings of parties to live up to their potential today (for a comprehensive overview, see Ignazi, 2017). But this scholarship falls short of providing guidelines to explore the extent to which specific, real-world instances of partisanship resonate with normative ideals.[2] Chapter 2 consolidates the many attributes that the literature ascribes to democratic partisanship into a single theoretical model and makes a specific form of partisanship, partisan *discourse*, amenable to empirical study on this basis. This results in a portable framework which I intend for application to the speech acts of *mainstream* partisan actors, those with sufficient political clout to regularly lead majorities or take part in them. It is the proximity of mainstream parties to political power that grants them specific normative responsibilities.

I develop two specific standards for democratic partisanship. First, mainstream parties should campaign on the basis of claims that display the general quality of *ideological cohesiveness*. To be cohesive, parties should articulate their idea of the common good with a specific programme of government, both of which should be clearly differentiated from the values and policies of their opponents. I link this quality to the function of parties as intermediaries between citizens and the state, and more broadly their capacity to further popular self-rule and therefore the *democratic* dimension of liberal democracy. Second, mainstream parties should display a form of *respect for political pluralism* both in their attitudes towards political opposition and in their attitudes towards political disagreement. This quality is linked to the responsibilities of parties to safeguard constitutional essentials, the rule of law and human rights, and therefore the *liberal* dimension of liberal democracy. These two general characteristics are broken down into more specific criteria, making mainstream partisan discourse amenable to analysis under this framework.

This leads to my second research question: *Is democratic partisanship a realistic ideal? To what extent do theoretical ideals resonate in the real-world of party politics?* This interrogation touches on the very nature of partisanship

---

[2] As developed in detail elsewhere, these theories present two main limitations as a basis for empirical study (Herman, 2017). They are insufficiently refined and therefore require further operationalisation in order to serve as benchmarks to analyse partisan discourse. But they are also insufficiently comprehensive, as the principles of democratic partisanship are dispersed across the literature, with no single author offering a comprehensive series of principles that partisans should uphold to be considered as democratic. The theoretical framework for this book seeks to address both of these limitations.

and, more broadly, of liberal democracy. While political theorists have emphasised the important contribution that partisans can make to democratic life, there also exists a long tradition of suspicion towards the intransigent and divisive character of the partisan passion (Rosenblum 2008). One objective of this research is to investigate whether stringent democratic standards are in fact attainable by real-world partisans. More specifically, I am interested in whether partisanship can be *both* cohesive and pluralist: Do partisans who defend strong viewpoints necessarily express more disrespect for opposing positions? Are these two qualities antagonistic or complementary?

Studying French and Hungarian party activists

I answer these questions by focusing on specific partisan actors: young party members in France and Hungary. My fieldwork took place within the youth sections of four mainstream party organisations: in France the *Parti socialiste* (PS) and *Union pour un mouvement populaire* (UMP),[3] in Hungary the *Magyar Szocialista Párt* (MSzP) and its 2014 electoral allies, and the *Fiatal Demokraták Szövetsége-Kereszténydemokrata Néppárt* (Fidesz-KDNP).[4] These parties qualified as mainstream at the time of study in 2013 given they constituted the main alternatives for the exercise of political power in both countries.[5] The empirical study relies on participant observation and the testimonies of 117 party members participating in a series of twenty-eight group discussions in Paris and Budapest in 2013 (see Figure 1.1 for a breakdown of participants by party affiliation).

---

[3] The UMP changed its name to *Les Républicains* on 28 May 2015. In this book I will refer to the party as UMP, the name it endorsed at the time of my interviews.

[4] The fragmentation of the Hungarian opposition to Fidesz in 2013 justifies my adoption of a loose definition of the mainstream Left. My sample therefore includes MSzP activists, but also members of Együtt 2014 and *Demokratikus Koalíció* (DK). These last two political organisations were led by former MSzP politicians (Gordon Bajnai and Ferenc Gyurcsány), and ran with the MSzP under the banner Összefogás 2014 in the 2014 Hungarian general elections. The Fidesz and KDNP are formally two separate parties, but in practice their permanent alliance means they act as two branches of the same organisation. Throughout the book, I use the simplified labels 'MSzP' and 'Fidesz' to describe left- and right-wing mainstream groups respectively in Hungary.

[5] As discussed in Chapter 2, *mainstream* refers to the position parties occupy in the political system rather than to their degree of ideological moderation. As discussed in Chapter 7, it is debatable whether the MSzP specifically would still be considered a mainstream party today given its systematic disempowerment through Fidesz-led institutional reform in the past decade.

Figure 1.1 Distribution of participants according to nationality and party affiliation

Chapter 3 discusses what we can learn from studying these specific cases, as well as explains some of my ontological, epistemological and methodological choices. I apply the framework of democratic partisanship to the discourse of a specific type of partisan: the party member. The discourse of activists is less structured than that of party elites and more engaged than lay voters', but it reveals the norms within which the party socialises citizens and key insights into the democratic life of their country. This research adds to the expanding field of party membership studies, exploring how systemic changes are perceived by party activists and how these changes contribute to shape partisan discourses and practices (Marlière, 2007; van Haute, 2011; Weltman and Billig, 2001). Comparing party member discourse across the Left–Right political spectrum allows the study of specific expressions of partisanship within a broader context of political competition, and as they relate to other such expressions.

The group discussions in France and Hungary were structured around a semi-experimental methodological design. I conducted these myself in the participants' respective mother tongues and used twelve cards as discussion prompts – with each card illustrating separate areas of public policy (see Figure 1.2 for the cards used in France).[6] As discussed in Chapter 3, I asked party members to establish a classification of the cards according to the political salience of the illustrated issues, and then encouraged them to justify their classification to each other. In this process, partisans would account for their own party's positions on these topics and for their opponents' stances. This provided the raw material to explore the cohesiveness and pluralism of their discourse when I subsequently analysed the transcripts.

Chapter 3 also makes clear how I intend to answer my third and last research question: *Under what conditions can we expect democratic partisanship to emerge and endure?* Throughout my analysis of the group discussions, I pay specific attention to how party members interpret their past, and find the important role played by historical legacies in the emergence and endurance of democratic partisanship. I also focus on how they view their present, and identify the internationalisation of domestic politics as a key structuring factor in their discourse. The theory and methodology chapters (Chapters 2 and 3) provide templates for future studies of partisanship. While the research in this book focuses on the discourse of party members in two specific countries, these frameworks can be replicated to study other actors within mainstream party organisations, specifically the official discourse of political elites, but also partisan identity in different national contexts.

The empirical practice of democratic partisanship

The following three, empirical chapters (Chapters 4, 5 and 6) offer insights into the interrelation between macro-level party system change and the evolving nature of partisan identities at the micro-level. I find strong variation in the perception party members have of their own party system and in the extent to which their discourse resonates with liberal democratic norms.

Chapter 4 explores the relationship between parties and democracy in France and Hungary from a variety of perspectives. The secondary

---

[6] The cards used for the French group are illustrated with satirical drawings by Plantu (Jean Plantureux), published in various issues of the French newspaper *Le Monde* in the late 2000s and early 2010s. The images for the Hungarian focus groups, not reproduced here because of file quality issues, were illustrative pictures under Creative Commons licence. In Chapter 3, I discuss the reasons for, and implications of, using different types of visual prompts in both countries.

Card 1: Public service reform;

Card 3: Religious and/or national minorities;

Card 5: Unemployment and employment policy;

Card 7: Industrial and/or agricultural policy;

Card 2: EU politics;

Card 4: Gender minorities and social change;

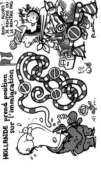
Card 12: 'Legal and illegal immigration'

Card 8: Taxation, social policy and redistribution of wealth;

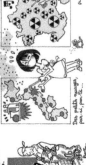
Card 11: 'Sexual minorities and social change';

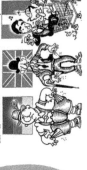
Card 6: Public morality;

Card 9: Public debt finance and deficit management;

Card 10: Environmental politics ; Card

Figure 1.2 Visual prompts for the French group discussions (© Plantu)

literature paints both political landscapes in stark contrasts. In France, a long-term convergence between the PS and UMP led to citizen apathy and, ultimately, to the near-disappearance of these parties after 2017 (Lefebvre and Sawicki, 2006). Scholars of Hungarian democracy depict an extreme form of populist polarisation between the conservative Fidesz party and socialist MszP, linked to on-going constitutional abuse and democratic backsliding since 2010 (Enyedi, 2016; Herman, 2016; Palonen, 2009). Following this review of the case specific literature, I move to explore the perspective of party members on these changes. I find important overlaps in scholarly and partisan assessments: activists in France, on the Left especially, see ideological convergence as a democratic loss, while Hungarian party members yearn for more appeased and constructive forms of political debate.

The two following chapters (Chapter 5 and 6) focus on the democratic norms party activists uphold, analysing how they balance the two attributes of democratic partisanship outlined in Chapter 2: ideological cohesiveness and respect for pluralism. Differences *between* the two countries are the most stark: French partisans are more cohesive in their identity, but also more systematically respectful of their political opposition; Hungarian party members, in contrast, struggle to single out the value systems or policy proposals that distinguish parties, and instead perceive morality as a key partisan divide. The latter also express strong disrespect for opponents, and their discourse has little resonance with the norms of political pluralism.

In both countries, important differences are also apparent across the political spectrum: the Left is less cohesive than the Right, but also more pluralist. PS partisans express the most respect for opponents among all four groups, and Fidesz partisans the most radical brand of anti-pluralism. Conversely, while UMP participants have the most ideologically cohesive discourse, MSzP activists are the least capable of justifying their party's position. On this basis, I develop a fourfold typology of contemporary partisan pathologies: *ideological dissonance* (PS), *ideological confusion* (MSzP), *benevolent holism* (UMP) and *intolerant holism* (Fidesz).

Chapter 7 returns to my initial research questions: How realistic is the theoretical ideal of democratic partisanship? Can partisans meet the two conditions of cohesiveness and partisanship? Under what conditions? I show that theoretical standards have strong, real-world relevance. Democratic forms of partisanship are not a naive and unattainable ideal, but a political practice with a firm grounding in empirical reality. The relative strength of cohesiveness and pluralism in France suggest that these two dimensions can work hand in hand, while ideologically vacuous and intolerant forms of partisanship in Hungary are also self-sustaining. The two pillars of democratic partisanship are complementary rather than clashing ideals in the discourse of partisans. The semi-inductive approach to party member discourse developed in this book therefore enriches the concept of democratic partisanship, specifying its components and their interrelation. My results provide normative thinkers with a better understanding of the normal and acceptable failings of partisanship, and, conversely, of the points at which these failings become problematic.

My findings also suggest that democratic forms of partisanship are only likely to emerge and endure under very specific conditions, with a history of open political competition and relaxed constraints on governmental agency facilitating democratic forms of competition. The conditionality of democratic partisanship invites political theorists to consider the cultural foundations of their own normative assumptions but does not justify lowering our standards. I argue that partisans who aspire to be democrats should exercise their individual agency in support of liberal democracy, and this even in challenging circumstances.

At the close of this book, I return to the macro-level trends that first motivated this study. There are clear parallels between the micro-level of partisan identity and broader changes at the level of party systems. The pathologies of partisanship at the micro-level largely mirror the failures of these organisations at the macro-level: an identity crisis on the Left stifling its capacity to mobilise citizens, and an ethical crisis on the right compromising its capacity to uphold fundamental liberal norms. I also argue that, much as weak cohesiveness and anti-pluralism are interdependent in partisan discourse, so party cartelisation and populist polarisation are intimately connected, and can only be addressed in concert. European politics are simultaneously affected by the decline of substantive, Left–Right oppositions and the rise of affective, populist politics. Far from being at odds with each other, these dynamics are intrinsically linked. Partisans from the Left and Right with democracy at their heart face vastly different tasks in this context: the former to rebuild cohesive ideologies that will mobilise citizens and muster the respect of opponents, the latter to refrain from the illiberal temptation of anti-pluralism. Ultimately, the endurance of liberal democracy in a populist era may depend on renewed adversarial relations between forms of partisanship that are both cohesive *and* pluralist.

2
A Theory of Democratic Partisanship

A suspicion of political parties characterises much Western political thought (Ball, 1989; Hofstadter, 1969; Ignazi, 2017, chs. 1 and 2; Rosenblum, 2008).[1] From Bolingbroke's criticisms of the evils of 'faction' in the eighteenth century to Rawls's contemporary dismissal of the 'great game of politics' (Muirhead and Rosenblum, 2006), parties have long been targeted as self-serving entities that defend the interests of a few and unnecessarily divide the political community. Such distrust has only been reinforced in the past decades. While traditional centre-right and centre-left parties appear increasingly out of touch with the demands of citizens, more radical actors capitalise on popular grievances to subvert democratic institutions.

Alongside this suspicion, however, exists an equally strong understanding that parties are among the most essential actors of representative systems of government (Kitschelt, 2006; Sartori, 1976). They are present and indispensable at every step of the electoral process: organising and raising funds for campaigns, offering citizens platforms capable of aggregating their dispersed preferences, and providing a means for the effective translation of electoral majorities into governing coalitions. They are also pivotal agents of democratic government, controlling the political agenda, forming majorities in parliament to support the government in power and, when in opposition, keeping majorities in check.

These two propositions are only seemingly contradictory: it is because parties have important democratic responsibilities that they cause so much damage when they fail. To this extent, partisanship is a double-edged sword

---

[1] An earlier version of this chapter was originally published in the *American Political Science Review* under the following reference: Herman, L. E. (2017). Democratic partisanship: From theoretical iudeal to empirical standard. *American Political Science Review, 111*(4).

for liberal democracy. If the endurance and vitality of this political system depends to a large extent on partisans fulfilling certain key functions, then the pathologies of partisanship bring about their own democratic perils. Parties can exercise the power they dispose of for the best – engaging citizens and promoting norms of tolerance and institutional forbearance – or for the worse – fuelling apathy and the radicalisation of political passions. Democracy is in partisan custody.

What, then, should democrats expect from partisans? And how can we evaluate the extent to which real-world partisans meet these expectations? This chapter draws on existing theories of democratic partisanship to answer these questions. I understand *partisanship* as the *array of practices and discourses attached to party identification, membership or leadership in support of a shared understanding of the public good*. Within this broad understanding of partisanship, the scope of this specific book is more limited. This chapter puts forward empirical standards designed to explore how partisan *discourse* contributes to liberal democracy.[2] These standards are then applied to the discourse of a specific set of partisan actors: young *party members* from the mainstream Left and Right in France and Hungary.[3]

Partisanship can be labelled as democratic when it makes a distinct contribution to both the *democratic* and the *liberal* dimensions of liberal democracy. The *democratic* dimension relates to the classic notion of popular self-rule, which requires the engagement of citizens with, and their participation in, the political process of representative government. The *liberal* dimension relates to the preservation of minority rights and political pluralism in an otherwise majoritarian system of political decision-making. Partisans have a responsibility to support both pillars of liberal democracy.

This chapter consolidates the different attributes of democratic partisanship scattered across the literature within a single theoretical framework. This concept is structured around two key dimensions that respond

---

[2] The democratic contribution of partisan *discourse*, which this book focuses on, does not operate in isolation from partisan *practice*, the other central component of partisanship and an expanding topic of theoretical and empirical inquiry (see specifically the work of Fabio Wolkenstein on deliberation within political parties). The mode of organisation of political parties, their procedures of internal decision-making and the types of decisions they make are all fundamental components of their democratic contribution. While this study mostly focuses on partisan discourse, I interpret my results in Chapter 7 in light of the actions of the political parties under study and their broader democratic performance.

[3] In Chapter 3 I discuss issues of representativeness, and what we can learn about partisanship in general by studying the discourse of party members specifically.

to the above-defined pillars of liberal democracy: *ideological cohesiveness* and *respect for pluralism*. First, a cohesive partisan discourse aggregates dispersed issues of political relevance into a normatively grounded, coherent programme of government. Cohesive partisanship, at its best, offers citizens reasons to engage with representative politics, and thus makes a distinct contribution to the *democratic* dimension of liberal democracy. This dimension corresponds to the function that theorists have ascribed to parties as intermediaries between citizens and the state, and thus as effective agents of political representation enabling popular self-rule (Bonotti, 2011, pp. 20–2; Muirhead and Rosenblum, 2006, p. 104; White and Ypi, 2010, 2011, 2016, pp. 8–32, 55–101).

Second, democratic partisan discourse is *pluralist*. It vehicles respect for a multiplicity of legitimate interpretations of what constitutes the common good, and awareness that the partisan's own interpretation cannot be imposed on the polity as a whole. In displaying such respect for the principles of political pluralism, parties make a distinct contribution to the *liberal* dimension of liberal democracy. This dimension corresponds to the function that theorists have ascribed to partisans as both promoters of norms of political tolerance in democratic societies, and guardians of the institutions of limited government (Bonotti, 2011; Muirhead, 2006, pp. 22–5; Rosenblum, 2008, pp. 362–8; White and Ypi, 2016, pp. 142–64).[4]

Crucially, I intend the standards of democratic partisanship defined below to apply *only* to the ways in which *mainstream* partisans self-identify and interact with *other mainstream partisans*. By mainstream political parties, I understand those that have the potential to exercise political power, and thus to form a majority in parliament or be partners in a governmental coalition – even if they may be in opposition at regular intervals. My use of the term 'mainstream' is concerned with the position of parties in the political system, *not* their degree of ideological moderation; in this understanding, a party may be mainstream *and* radical. The focus on mainstream parties stems from the idea that proximity to political

---

[4] As discussed in Chapter 3, in focusing on discourse I remain agnostic on the reasons why individual partisans abide by these norms or reject them. These are likely to be both diverse and complex: in part to remain in line with their own sense of right and wrong, but also to fulfil their party's expectations and follow what they think voters expect to hear from them. Regardless of their reasons, partisans that abide by democratic norms in their discourse contribute to their diffusion, and thus to the perpetuation of liberal democracy as a way of life. Consequently, I endeavour to use the vocabulary of discursive practices throughout this chapter (to display, demonstrate, show, express, etc.) rather than the lexicon of deep-seated attitudes (to believe, think, be convinced, be committed, etc.) when referring to democratic forms of partisanship.

power increases the responsibility of partisans to uphold democratic norms. The greater the power parties exercise, the greater the damage they are capable of doing to citizens' faith in collective agency, and to the integrity of democratic institutions. Different standards from the ones developed below are likely to apply to marginal parties that do not share the responsibility of government, but also to the ways in which mainstream partisans treat opponents at the margins of the political spectrum.[5] It follows from this that all partisans at all times need not approximate the ideal below for democracy to endure. As discussed in Chapter 3, partisan elites have greater normative obligations than members, who themselves have greater responsibility than regular voters (Bonotti, 2012).

The first part of this chapter further defines key concepts, and makes explicit my prior assumptions on the relationship between mainstream partisan discourse and liberal democracy. Next, I outline in turn the two key dimensions of democratic partisanship, detailing their corresponding attributes and associated indicators for the analysis of French and Hungarian partisan discourse in subsequent chapters. Finally, I discuss the potential tensions between the principles of cohesiveness and pluralism, and how the empirical study of democratic partisanship can clarify their interrelation.

On Liberal Democracy and Partisanship

Three key theoretical assumptions structure the relationship between partisan *discourse* and liberal democracy. I first assume that liberal democracy is more than a procedural arrangement and constitutes, instead, a distinct political ethos or way of life. This view is in line with a long-established tradition in political philosophy (Cruickshank, 2014; Galston, 2002, 2005; Hallowell, 1954; Kateb, 1981; Lefort, 1988; Macedo, 1990; Mouffe, 2000; Rosenblum, 1989; Ryn, 1978). It also resonates with cultural institutionalist understandings of democracy held by political scientists (Dryzek and Holmes, 2002; Hall and Taylor, 1996; Herman, 2016; Miller, White and Heywood, 1997; Plattner and Diamond, 1996). According to this

---

[5] For instance single-issue parties (e.g. marijuana legalisation parties), or movements built on negative identification (e.g. anti-fascist movements) may lack cohesiveness according to the criteria set out below, yet they may still fulfil other, essential democratic functions appropriate to their position in the party system – bringing new policies to the forefront of public debate, or denouncing illiberal tendencies within society, for instance. Similarly, the standard of pluralism need not necessarily apply to the ways in which mainstream parties treat marginal political forces that explicitly reject democratic institutions.

view, democracy rests on its members sharing 'implicit norms determining notions of just and unjust, good and evil, desirable and undesirable, noble and ignoble' (Lefort, 1988, pp. 2–3). Procedural norms codified in law are respected because they resonate with more informal norms that are 'inscribed in shared forms of life' (Mouffe, 2000, p. 68). This collective adherence is fluid rather than static: to persist, it requires renewing and reinforcing in the daily practices and discourse of citizens.

This 'thick' understanding of democracy contrasts with the minimalist approach still dominant in party studies. In such frameworks, parties are first and foremost rational actors motivated by vote-seeking, office-seeking and policy-seeking goals (Strom, 1990). Democracy is sustained by political competition among these actors within well-designed institutions, the latter providing rational partisans with positive and negative incentives to comply with the rules of the political game (Przeworski, 1999; Schmitter and Karl, 1991). In the minimalist understanding, democratic institutions do not require virtue from partisan actors, and instead contain within themselves the conditions for their own perpetuation (for a full version of this argument, see Herman and Muirhead, 2020). In contrast, to understand democracy as a way of life is also to admit that it requires the active support of committed agents. Democratic institutions are not self-standing, they endure because the principles underlying them are defended, promoted and diffused by an array of actors in society, including the media, schools and, as defended in this book, political parties themselves. The discursive norms of democratic partisanship can therefore be conceived as a central feature of the political culture that sustains democratic constitutional settlements.

My second, related assumption is that political representation, especially as performed through partisan claims, has a creative role in shaping the self-understanding and attitudes of constituents. In line with the representative turn in political theory, I conceive of political representation as an on-going interaction between representatives and constituents in which the identities of both partisans and citizens are mutually and continuously constituted (Saward, 2010; Urbinati, 2000). Partisans do not simply mirror the pre-existent and fixed political preferences of voters, because the groups to be represented never offer themselves as homogenous, predefined entities with clear and encompassing sets of interests (Young, 2000, p. 126). Excluding strict imperative mandates, a degree of interpretation of what voters demand is not only a possibility open to the representative agent – it is inseparable from the act of representing itself. The representative claims of parties therefore play a crucial role in the emergence of political identities: they 'give form' to these by putting forth normative ideals that a multitude of citizens with disparate ideas or interests can converge on and identify with (White and Ypi, 2010).⁶ This lends political parties, and mainstream parties specifically, significant influence on the contours of public deliberation: as Schattschneider suggested over half a century ago, 'the definition of the alternatives is the supreme instrument of power' (Schattschneider, 1960, p. 66).

Third, and relatedly, I assume that parties are not only the bearers of pre-existing structures, responding to a set of incentives created by the constitutional settlement within which they operate, but that they are also shapers of their institutional environment. In other words, democratic institutions are largely endogenous to the political process itself and result from complex decision-making processes that involve mainstream parties. Historically, these have not only had a key role in making these procedures at the birth of first-wave democracies, but also in the subsequent democratisation of constitutional settlements (Alexander, 2001, pp. 263–4; Renwick, 2010). Conversely, partisan majorities can use procedures provided by the democratic framework itself to undermine democratic institutions, an increasingly common method of democratic backsliding often referred to as *abusive legalism* (Bermeo, 2016; Levitsky and Way, 2020).⁷ For democracy to endure, partisans therefore need to do more than simply fulfil the *legal* obligation of complying with the rules of the game. They should also comply with more intangible, moral obligations: to refrain from systematically exploiting legal loopholes available to political parties, and from changing the rules of the game in their favour when given the chance (Herman and Muirhead, 2020).

Taking these three assumptions as a starting point, the discourse of *mainstream* political parties affects the functioning of liberal democracy because of their key role as *citizen representatives* and *state actors*. If liberal democracy is conceived as a way of life, nourished by the normative dispositions of its members, the fact that parties that have access to power support these norms becomes crucial to the endurance, and flourishing,

---

⁶ These assumptions about the nature of political representation resonate beyond political theory. The contextualist turn in public opinion and political psychology studies provides significant evidence that the opinions of citizens shift according to the ways in which political parties frame issues (Broockman and Butler, 2017; Chong and Druckman, 2007; Ciuk and Yost, 2016; Slothuus and Bisgaard, 2021; Sniderman and Theriault, 2004).

⁷ Constitutional lawyers have used various other terms to designate this same phenomenon, for example 'stealth authoritarianism' (Varol, 2015), 'autocratic legalism' (Scheppele, 2018) or 'abusive constitutionalism' (Landau, 2013).

of democratic regimes. The position of mainstream parties in the public sphere – with privileged access to financial resources, media attention, law-making and key administrative positions – lends them significantly larger amounts of political power than more marginal parties and, therefore, greater capacity to directly affect the stability and quality of democracy. In their functions as *citizen representatives*, mainstream parties hold considerable influence on the self-representation of citizens and their commitment to democratic norms. In their functions as *actors of the state*, mainstream partisans have the power to shape democratic institutions themselves, either through abusing power or deepening existing constitutional settlements. Democratic forms of partisanship matter because they condition the ways in which partisans will fulfil these essential functions.

Arguably, mainstream parties have an even greater transformative power in relatively newly formed democracies such as Hungary, which this book takes as a case study (Enyedi, 2016; Herman, 2016). The attempts of parties to represent citizens and mobilise them around competing platforms have a particularly strong influence on the stabilisation of political identities in democratising societies, characterised by Jowitt as 'genesis environments' with a strong 'potential to generate novel ways of life' (Jowitt, 1992, p. 266). The institutional and legislative framework of newly formed democracies is also likely to be more easily subject to change given their weak consolidation, granting mainstream parties considerable power of influence on the changing rules of the democratic game (Grzymala-Busse, 2007).

None of this is to say that a democratic form of partisan discourse is sufficient to constitute a liberal democracy: partisans cannot create a democratic or an undemocratic society from scratch. More specifically, the institutional and cultural context within which partisan discourse is deployed sets limits to its transformative power. First, the performative dimension of partisan representation is necessarily exercised within certain limits: although partisans occupy a privileged position in the public sphere, representation remains a creative dialogue. Parties interpret and draw on the demands of citizens, while citizens in turn reappropriate, reject or validate the representative claims of political parties. To this extent, the boundaries of collective memory will have a bearing on the claims that find 'cultural resonance' within a given population, and which partisans will adopt (Gamson, 1992, p. 135; Saward, 2010, pp. 75–7). Second, institutions that guarantee political and civil rights provide a necessary framework for liberal democracy, which may then be supported or undermined by partisan discourse and practices. In this regard, some institutional designs may act as stronger bulwarks against abuse of power than others, with limitations to constitutional amendments and judicial review as key (albeit in many contemporary cases insufficient) checks to abusive legalism.

In short, the extent to which mainstream partisan discourse is democratic depends on not only the good will or intrinsic morality of individuals, but also the environment in which they evolve. Partisans are core political actors with sufficient agency and power to contribute over time to the transformation of democracy, but they are also the bearers of previously existing structures (P. A. Lewis, 2002, p. 22; see also Haughton, 2005, pp. 7–12; Sibeon, 1999). As developed in Chapter 3, democratic partisanship might be influenced over time by a wealth of contextual factors which I separate into two main categories: political culture and exogenous shocks. Within this framework, one of the objectives of this book is to formulate informed hypotheses on what explains variations in democratic partisanship across countries, but also across parties within a single country.

The following framework outlines how the discourse of mainstream partisans affects the *democratic* and *liberal* dimensions of liberal democracy. It builds on and contributes to the work of a number of democratic theorists who have taken an interest in the normative dimension of partisanship. First, *ideological cohesiveness* conditions citizens' willingness to engage with political affairs, and thus, more broadly, the extent to which liberal democracy approximates the ideal of popular self-rule. Second, partisan *respect for pluralism* will influence citizens' support for the principles of minority rule and political pluralism, as well as reveal partisan attachment to existing constitutional settlements.

Ideological Cohesiveness: The Democratic Condition

Parties play an essential role in engaging citizens with public life, and thus fostering the *democratic* dimension of liberal democracy. I assume that the involvement of constituents in the political process is essential to the proper functioning of representative democracy. It ensures that, even when citizens delegate responsibilities to their representatives, political leadership remains accountable. Democratic representation requires that constituents organise and discuss issues of political relevance in anticipation of upcoming moments of authorisation and discuss them again in recollection of these moments (Mansbridge, 2003; Urbinati, 2006; Young, 2000). Only with the active participation of the represented can representative government claim to be 'a form of people's self-rule'

(Kateb, 1981, p. 371). To this extent, representative democracy should not be singled out from other democratic forms – direct or deliberative – as a regime that can do away with the engagement of its citizens outside of election periods. As stressed by Urbinati, 'elections [...] make responsible and limited government, but not representative government' (Urbinati, 2006, p. 224).

In line with White and Ypi, I understand civic engagement as an affective orientation that disposes individuals towards feeling concern for their political community and towards taking action in order to contribute to the common good (White and Ypi, 2010, p. 809). Citizens engage with the political process when they hold normatively grounded convictions and identify with a group that shares these convictions, when they believe that there are political goals that deserve to be pursued in common (White and Ypi, 2010, 2016). If engaged citizenship requires a certain understanding of the common good, this understanding is always partisan *in the minimal sense*. The engaged citizen does not necessarily identify with a party *stricto sensu*, but the type of conviction that leads to engagement does involve taking sides and does involve standing with others. First, political conviction discriminates among the causes that are worth fighting for, and rests on a partial interpretation of foundational values. The engaged citizen resembles Mill's 'one-eyed man', convinced 'that some principle or cause in the political world is right and something else wrong, something is better and something else is worse' (Muirhead, 2014, p. 99). Second, defending one's convictions in the public realm is not a solitary enterprise – it involves sharing with others this partial understanding of the common good (Muirhead, 2014, ch. 5; Rosenblum, 2008, pp. 340–8). To prompt engagement, normative goals have to be pursued with the idea that it is a matter for 'us' to do so, that there is a collective responsibility to pursue these goals which are in some way 'ours' (White and Ypi, 2010, p. 812).

As discussed by Nancy Rosenblum, dispelling the myth of 'independence' as good citizenship also highlights the civic value of partiality and collective loyalty (Muirhead, 2006, p. 723; Rosenblum, 2008, ch. 7). Independents' rebuttal of partisan commitments puts these citizens outside, rather than above, public life, depriving them of the passions that drive citizens to inform themselves and take part in collective action. Their absence of loyalty will likely lead to 'weightlessness', 'detachment' and 'unconcern for power' rather than more astute and informed reasoning (Rosenblum, 2008, p. 351). And if independents stand only for themselves, there is little reason for them to engage with public life.

Empirical studies show that independents are less knowledgeable about politics, spend less time informing themselves and are less capable of taking in new political information; they are also generally less interested in politics, and less likely to vote or take part in civic life (Blais, 2006; Keith et al., 1992).

These conditions for political engagement, however, do not exist prior to the process of representation. As Muirhead emphasises, 'somewhere the variety of individual sentiments, interests and convictions needs to be collected [. . .] (A) group large enough to claim democratic legitimacy does not exist spontaneously [. . .] It must be created' (Muirhead, 2006, p. 719). The 'bilingualism' of political parties, with one foot in society and the other in the state, puts them in a privileged position to fulfil this creative role (Muirhead and Rosenblum. 2016, p. 103). As institutions of the state, mainstream parties have access to financial assets, media attention and political power that social movements, for instance, do not. As civil society organisations, parties use these resources to mobilise existing members, organise support and generate new sympathies. If the partisan enterprise is particularly creative, it is also because of the form it takes: an agonistic clash of opposing views. In this process, parties not only make claims to represent citizens, they also 'create the terms of contest' and thus the necessary conditions for public deliberation over rival understandings of the common good.

Parties are therefore well placed to spark civic engagement among the broader public. This, however, does not mean they make good use of their privileged position in the public sphere. The disaffection with representative politics in established and emerging democracies today is enough to demonstrate that parties can fail to perform their function of intermediation (Hay, 2007; Mair, 2006, 2013a). Given that parties have a unique responsibility in generating political loyalties, it remains necessary to isolate the conditions under which they can effectively do so.

The general argument made by theorists is that parties should display a form of cohesiveness in their claims to represent citizens, and thus campaign on the basis of a discourse that aggregates dispersed issues of political relevance into a normatively grounded, coherent programme of government. At its best, partisanship does not only unite a community of citizens across different social spaces but also across time, grounding political commitment in the struggle of past generations and offering this struggle a political future (White, 2015a; White and Ypi, 2016, pp. 122–42). This understanding of cohesiveness entails that democratic partisanship cannot be defined solely according to the ideas and policies it opposes: mainstream partisans at their best make instead a positive contribution to political debate by offering constituents a distinct alternative of government.⁸ In the following sections, I draw on normative political theory to isolate three attributes of partisan cohesiveness, and further operationalise indicators for each of these attributes. These will later serve to explore whether French and Hungarian partisan discourses resonate with the standard of ideological cohesiveness.

Attribute A: Normative grounding

First, an ideologically cohesive partisan claim has a solid normative grounding. This means mainstream parties account for the principles that underlie the exercise of political power, and for the ends that justify this exercise. It demands from parties that they stand for a distinct vision of the common good, rooting their approach to matters of common concern in rival interpretations of the meaning of fundamental principles such as equality or freedom.⁹ Partisanship at its best locates the particularistic appeals of given sectors of society in a broader understanding of the political world, coherently connecting its different aspects across time, space and subject matter. This partisan enterprise is directed towards the demos as a whole and is therefore fundamentally distinct from what factions are. Indeed, the latter are designed to further the interests of particular groups in society and exhibit 'no concern to justify [their] program to the community in toto' (White and Ypi, 2011, p. 383).

Normative grounding is a key condition for partisanship to support the democratic dimension of liberal democracy, and thus incite citizen engagement with politics. By weaving individual concerns together in an overarching narrative, parties contribute to citizens making sense of their own grievances not as strictly personal dissatisfactions but as issues of political and therefore collective relevance. In the words of White and Ypi, parties provide citizens with the tools to formulate 'a critical

---

⁸ As for every aspect of the normative ideal of democratic partisanship, this applies to *mainstream* partisanship – that is, identification to parties that exercise political power, habitually lead governmental majorities or take part in them (see pp. 17–18). For instance, anti-fascist organisations may not be cohesive given they are mostly built in opposition to fascist ideas and movements, yet this would not be an essential criterion to judge their democratic contribution if they do not habitually exercise power.

⁹ This normative condition lies at the heart of one of the very first definitions of party. In the late eighteenth century, Burke accounted for parties as 'a body of men united, for promoting by their joint endeavours the national interest, upon some particular principle in which they are all agreed' (Burke, 1990 [1770], p. 86).

appraisal of their joint political institutions, [...] to form judgments on matters of common concern and to articulate such judgments in a way that could appeal to the understanding of all' (White and Ypi, 2010, p. 811). In this sense, principled partisanship contributes to the emergence of a broader community of commitment and enables the exercise of collective political agency.

Normative grounding also means that political action is justified according to some principles that citizens can, at a minimum, accept as reasonable. Such acts of justification are necessary to ensure that coercive power is being exercised in a non-arbitrary fashion, and, more generally, to safeguard the legitimacy of the decision-making process (Chambers, 2010). This requires that parties make the rationale that motivates their policies explicit, or, in other words, that they spell out the values, interests and visions of the 'good society' their legislation intends to further (Bonotti, 2014; White and Ypi, 2011). Beyond the role normative principles play in legitimising political action, a higher order of reasons is necessary for making party programmes and policies intelligible to citizens and to win the support of constituents. As Muirhead emphasises, 'the arcane and lawyerly details of alternative policies [cannot] excite passions, generate loyalties, or sustain lasting commitments' (Muirhead, 2014, p. 67).

To identify empirically the normative grounding of partisanship, I pay attention to two features of political discourse. A first indicator is that partisans insist on the *problems or objectives* that their actions intend to address, the 'matters of common concern' that should be considered collectively because they result from social linkage. The health, education and security of citizens may be seen, for instance, as 'common goods', and are among the societal objectives that partisans wish to achieve regardless of their position on the political spectrum (Galston, 2013). Normative grounding also requires partisans to establish the relative importance of these objectives according to their particular understanding of the common good.

> *Indicator 1:* Cohesiveness entails that mainstream partisans justify their engagement by making explicit the matters of common concern (problems or objectives) that their party intends to address. For instance, a mainstream partisan may position unemployment as one of the most important societal problems that their party intends to address.

A second indication is that partisans put forth a particular *worldview*, and therefore refer to the fundamental principles that define the common good at large. While some of these – justice, equality or freedom – are common to most democratic constitutional frameworks, their order and emphasis may differ from one to another.[10] Cohesive partisans will take these principles as given and offer different interpretations of their meaning, relative importance and implications. These particular interpretations are generally grounded in long-lasting traditions of thought and thus informed by comprehensive doctrines such as, for example, socialism or conservatism.[11]

> *Indicator 2*: Cohesiveness entails that mainstream partisans make explicit the values and fundamental principles that their party intends to further. For instance, they may justify their party's programme in the name of furthering a certain idea of freedom, interpreted as the absence of constraints.

Attribute B: *Programmatic substance*

A cohesive partisan discourse also displays programmatic substance: it provides citizens with the sense that normative goals can be advanced by exercising political power. This is what White and Ypi have termed the 'executive' condition for political engagement: demonstrating the practical relevance of abstract normative commitments by addressing particular grievances through policymaking (White and Ypi, 2010, pp. 817–18). There are a number of reasons why it is crucial that parties demonstrate the possibility for citizens' normative goals to be realised through political action. First, they are the only political actors that dispose directly of the coercive power and taxing capacity of the state. While social movements may offer normative objectives, they cannot enact direct changes in legislation (ibid.). Second, normative thinking

---

[10] Even agonistic theories of democracy, which give a central role to political contestation, recognise that democratic political communities entail a 'certain amount of consensus' and, more specifically, 'a shared adhesion to the ethico-political principles of liberal democracy' (Mouffe, 2000, p. 103).

[11] In her definition of political ideas, Schmidt makes a similar distinction, separating the level of 'public philosophies' from that of 'programmatic beliefs' (Schmidt, 2008). 'Public philosophies', according to Schmidt, are the 'ideas, values, and principles of knowledge and society' that undergird 'policies and programs' (ibid., p. 306). As for 'programmatic beliefs', they 'operate in the space between worldviews and specific policy ideas' and include 'the problems to be solved by such policies; the issues to be considered; the goals to be achieved' (ibid., p. 306).

without practical outlet is insufficient to engage citizens with the political process. As emphasised by Muirhead and Rosenblum, 'when principles of justice do not seem to have a connection to our aims and purposes, even reasonable principles could not be rational for us personally, as concretely-situated individuals' (Muirhead and Rosenblum, 2006, p. 103). Partisans should demonstrate the practical relevance of their normative commitments and therefore give constituents reasons to maintain their loyalty.

A relevant indicator for programmatic substance is that partisans clearly outline their programmatic orientations and specific policy proposals. Cohesive partisans will explain *how* they intend to further their particular understanding of the common good and thus provide citizens with a well-defined bundle of policies and measures.

> *Indicator 3:* Cohesiveness entails that mainstream partisans explain how they intend to further their particular understanding of the common good with their actions in government. In practice this entails that:
>
> - When in opposition, mainstream partisans present a well-defined bundle of policies and measures that makes for a clear, alternative programme of government. For instance, a partisan who defends a negative understanding of freedom will not solely vouch to liberalise the job market but suggest a series of specific measures of liberalisation.
> - When in government, mainstream partisans show how their measures and policies will impact the political community in a way that furthers their specific understanding of the common good. For instance, a partisan may show how specific measures of market liberalisation will impact society and the economy in a way that furthers their vision of the good society.

A second, relevant indicator for evaluating programmatic substance is the ways in which partisans talk about their own political agency. Cohesiveness entails that partisans will communicate that their actions have consequences and that they can make a difference, rather than insist on their lack of choice or agency (Hay, 2007, p. 66). In this last case, partisans give citizens little reason to believe that their normative goals can be realised, and this will likely breed resignation or animosity.

> *Indicator 4:* Cohesiveness entails that mainstream partisans demonstrate their ability to exercise political agency in their discourse. In practice, this means that:

- Mainstream partisans present specific political actions as resulting from a political choice between alternatives that can be justified from a normative perspective (see Indicator 1).
- Mainstream partisans refrain from presenting specific political actions as the only possible choice available to governments, for instance as a decision solely dictated by external factors.

Attribute C: *Capacity for differentiation*

Finally, partisan cohesiveness requires differentiation from the position of opponents. In other words, parties need to offer citizens *distinct* normative goals and policy proposals. This is essential for citizens' engagement with the political process for several reasons. First, positioning with regard to a political 'other' is necessary for parties to assert their commitments, and mobilise citizens on this basis. This squares with the post-structuralist notion of a 'constitutive outside', according to which all forms of identity are constructed through differentiation (Mouffe, 2000, p. 33). Partisan identities strong enough to mobilise civic passions are thus adversarial in nature: they define themselves not only with regard to what they are, but also with regard to how they diverge from other partisan identities.

The most obvious argument for partisan differentiation is that it offers citizens a meaningful choice between political alternatives. Only when offered a plurality of options can voters find an alternative closer to their own interests and choose a different majority if their expectations are disappointed. This is a core idea of minimalist theories of democracy, which cast the free competition of political parties for citizens' votes as a defining feature of the democratic regime (A. Downs, 1957; Przeworski, 1999; Schumpeter, 1956 [1942]). It also echoes the classic ideal of 'responsible party government', according to which citizens can only hold parties accountable if these spell out clear alternatives of government (American Political Science Association, 1950; Mair, 2013b; Schattschneider, 2009 [1942]). Differentiation therefore also creates obligations for the opposition, which should 'contain within itself the potential of an actual alternative government' with 'a sober attempt to formulate alternative policies which it believes to be capable of execution' (Hofstadter, 1969, p. 4).

Differentiation is necessary not only for parties to gain support, but also to justify to citizens their claim to the exercise of political power. White and Ypi show that parties make an 'important contribution to political justification' precisely because they are more likely than other political agents to make claims that are both *comparative* and *adversarial* (White and Ypi, 2011, p. 385). Political justification should be comparative because 'to justify a political principle, an act of public policy, or a political program is to show what makes it preferable to alternatives' (ibid.). Further, the *quality* of political justification is dependent on its potential for being challenged by competitors, thus demanding an adversarial context. To offer reasons that are likely to convince citizens of the legitimacy of their choices, political parties must therefore compare and contrast them with those of opponents.

A good indicator for partisan differentiation is the extent to which partisans justify their claim to the exercise of political power in a comparative fashion. Partisans in government will be tempted to ignore the current opposition and focus only on their own programme, while partisans in opposition will tend to solely criticise the government without making clear what policies and measures it would enact in its place. Both should instead show how their platform is preferable to the alternative suggested by opponents, and thus adopt a comparative form of political justification.

> *Indicator 5:* Cohesiveness entails that mainstream partisans justify their claims to political power in a comparative fashion. In practice, this entails that:
>
> - In opposition, mainstream partisans not only criticise the policies and particular understanding of the common good of the party in government, but also outline how their own understanding of the common good differs and what their own party would do in place of their opponents.
> - In government, mainstream partisans not only defend their own policies and understanding of the common good but outline in the process how these differ from those defended by past governments and the current opposition.

Respect for Pluralism: The Liberal Condition

The *liberal* dimension of liberal democracy ensures the preservation of the rule of law and minority rights in an otherwise majoritarian system of political decision-making. At the individual level, liberalism posits the moral equality of members of the polity, as well as their liberty – minimally conceived as freedom from external restraint and state coercion (Berlin, 1969; Constant, 2010 [1819]). These principles not only protect the civil rights of individuals, but also open the door to citizens exercising their political rights to contest, inform and compete for the exercise of political power and influence (Dahl, 1971, pp. 3, 202). To this extent, the principles of equality and freedom also apply to the multiplicity of associations of citizens that compose the democratic polity, including not only parties but also media outlets and advocacy groups, such as trade unions, NGOs and other interest groups. These ideas are given institutional expression through a variety of legal and constitutional arrangements that create checks on majoritarian governments, ensure the separation of powers, and protect individual rights. Crucially to the topic of this book, constitutions also guarantee the freedom and fairness of electoral processes, ensuring that parties compete on equal terms for votes and, through this, for political power.

Democratic partisanship plays a key role in the functioning of liberal democracy so understood. As central actors of representative government with a unique position between civil society and the state, mainstream parties have privileged access to power. This lends them a considerable amount of influence on the contours of public opinion and on the continued integrity of democratic institutions. When partisans mobilise citizens on the basis of holist appeals or berate democratic procedures in their discourse, they also erode the norms that sustain liberal democracy as a way of life. In this case, liberal democracy's formalised rules and procedures are also far more vulnerable and susceptible to being undermined (Herman and Muirhead, 2020). These dangers are well illustrated by the ways in which populist majorities today in countries as diverse as Hungary, Poland, Turkey or the USA tinker with the rules of the political game to favour themselves, and this often without using force or fraud (Bogaards, 2018; Cinar, 2019; Norris, 2017; Pech and Scheppele, 2017; Sözen, 2019). If, subject to a sufficient majority, mainstream partisans have the power to hollow out democratic institutions, then something other than self-interest must ensure that they refrain from doing so. To this extent, partisans must be 'active, avowed, intentional agent' in support of the liberal democratic regime (Rosenblum, 2008, pp. 124, 363).

This brings me to the second main dimension of democratic partisanship: respect for political pluralism. According to the pluralist worldview, there exist reasonable disagreements over how to interpret the common good, and over the means to reach it. A partisan who shows respect for political pluralism acknowledges that multiple such understandings are worthy of expression in the public sphere. In turn, pluralist partisans reject *holism* in their discourses and practices, or the idea that the People are essentially *one* and that there is therefore only one legitimate way of furthering its interests (Rosenblum, 2008, pp. 124, 363).[12]

---

[12] Importantly, I am agnostic as to what pluralist discursive practices reveal about the moral worth of individual partisans, or their deep-seated values. Instead, I see pluralist partisanship as *avowed adherence* to political norms that sustain a specific and contextual, liberal democratic way of life. In practice, partisans are likely to have mixed motives for expressing respect for pluralism, including strategic ones. For a full discussion of this point, see Chapter 3.

Respect for pluralism is an endorsement of the most basic principle of liberal democracy: that the political universe is characterised by a plurality of legitimate claims to the common good, and that, consequently, authority devolved through elections is necessarily and always of a provisional nature. As argued by Lefort, 'the revolutionary and unprecedented feature of democracy [is that] the locus of power becomes *an empty place* [. . .] it is such that no individual and no group can be consubstantiated with it' (Lefort, 1988, p. 16). At the heart of this mutation of symbolic power is a moral revolution, 'instituted and sustained by the dissolution of the markers of certainty' (Lefort, 1988, p. 19). Power cannot be permanently occupied in a world characterised by indeterminacy, where no claim to the good is accepted as complete and definitive. Pluralist partisanship is therefore essential to the preservation of liberalism, acting as the single-most important ethical brake on strong majorities using their power to indulge in abusive legalism and shape institutions in their own interest (Herman and Muirhead, 2020). Conversely, there is a close relationship today between the increasingly common use of abusive legalism as a tool for liberal democratic backsliding, and an increasingly anti-pluralist political climate (Müller, 2016, 2017). Pluralist partisanship in the political mainstream therefore forms the bedrock of constitutional settlements. When such commitments are absent among those who exercise power, liberal democratic institutions are at direct risk of manipulation, erosion and, in the worst cases, breakdown.[13]

Partisans with pluralist discursive practices defend their position, seeking to persuade others but never to impose their views. They accept that political disagreement over the *meaning* and *implications* of common principles is both ineliminable in a modern liberal democracy and central to its perpetuation. To this extent, they do not question, in their discourses or practices, the fundamental moral indeterminacy of democracy. They accept that power can only be occupied for a limited period of time. In other words, pluralist partisans 'do not want or expect the elimination of political lines of division' precisely because they are committed to the

---

[13] As acknowledged above, the design of institutions certainly plays a role in the extent to which and rate at which power can be abused. However, no constitutional settlement is void of loopholes, and therefore all are vulnerable to different degrees. The USA today provides a striking example of a country where institutions were designed to resist abuse of power, yet constitutional manipulation at the level of the states is rife, and political violence a reality. Major first-wave democracies, including France and the UK, provide far lower levels of institutional protection against abuse (for a detailed version of this argument, see Herman and Muirhead, 2020).

'system of regulated rivalry that defines liberal democracy' (Rosenblum, 2008, p. 364; p. 362). They fight, while accepting the impossibility of a final victory, without aiming for their struggle to end future contestation and bring about a permanent consensus. They argue for the superiority of their claims, but do not assert that these are the only legitimate claims that can be defended. They pursue their particular goals 'without threatening the fundamental values and institutions of the framework itself' (Sartori, 1976, p. 16).

In the following sections, I isolate three attributes of pluralist partisan discourse and explain why these particular traits contribute to sustaining the liberal dimension of liberal democracy. I focus on the ways in which partisans relate to those they disagree with, as pluralist partisanship implies a voluntary, 'reciprocal positive regard' in the discourse of opponents that treat each other as equals in an inclusive and pluralist political community (Gutmann and Thompson, 2010, pp. 1129–30).[14] These guidelines relate to the norms of political discourse that mainstream partisans should adopt towards their *main opponents*, so their mainstream right or left counterparts.[15] Each attribute of pluralist partisanship is broken down into a number of indicators, which are then applied to the analysis of French and Hungarian partisan discourse in the following chapters.

Attribute D: Practice-focused criticism

How partisans criticise their opponents is a key indication of their pluralist inclinations. Rivals who respect their adversaries refrain from engaging in what Gutmann and Thomson have coined 'motive-cynicism': raising doubts on the integrity of the reasons opponents have to say or do something (Gutmann and Thomson 2020). Typical of this type of negative

---

[14] Such respectful attitudes in the face of political disagreement are a central feature of both agonistic and deliberative approaches to democracy (Knops, 2007). For the former, a 'shared adhesion to the ethico-political principles of liberal democracy' means that our opponent is 'no longer perceived as an enemy to be destroyed, but as an "'adversary" that is, somebody whose idea we combat, but whose right to defend those ideas we do not put into question' (Mouffe, 2000, pp. 101–2) Deliberative approaches also view 'reciprocity' as a key condition for democratic subjects to deliberate in the face of moral disagreement, a condition that involves viewing opponents as both 'competent subjects' and 'moral and political equals' (Gutmann and Thompson, 1996, p. 17).

[15] It is more controversial whether these norms also apply to the ways in which mainstream parties treat fringe political actors, although there is also a case to be made for this. Mouffe, for instance, argues it is both ethically problematic and strategically inefficient for mainstream parties to disrespect far-right ones and cast them as outside of the sphere of common political morality (Mouffe, 2005a).

rhetoric are accusations that opponents are moved by their own private or political interest. These may range from simple references to the vote-seeking attitude of opponents to more serious charges of being motivated by material gain.

Partisans need not ignore that their opponents strategically target voters or that a measure of corruption exists in all democracies.[16] Respect for political pluralism does not amount to naivety. It is rather a recognition that, if the motives of those who engage with politics, including their own, are always mixed, then choosing to focus on the integrity of their opponents' motivation is both hypocritical and destructive of healthy deliberation. Not only are attacks on motives often grounded in assumptions rather than facts, but they also prevent constructive criticism of opponents' discourse and practices that should form the basis of partisan debates. This leads to the following indicator for pluralist respect:

Indicator 6: Pluralist respect entails that mainstream partisans refrain from engaging in 'motive-cynicism' when they criticise political opponents, and thus from raising doubts on the integrity of political opponents in general, or on the reasons that motivate their opponents to do or say something in particular. In practice, this entails that:

- Mainstream partisans do not criticise the decisions of opponents on the basis that these are solely designed to advance their political interests. For instance, a partisan criticising their opponents' decision to raise the minimum wage on the basis that it is motivated only by the desire to gain votes would be engaging in motive-cynicism.[17]
- Mainstream partisans refrain from picturing the decisions of opponents as solely designed to advance their personal interests. For instance, a partisan criticising their opponents' decision to lower taxes on wealthy incomes on the basis that it favours the economic interests of their own circle would be engaging in motive-cynicism.

---

[16] Refraining from motive-cynicism is undoubtedly more complex in a context where opponents engage in rampant corruption or abuse of power: to demand from democratic partisans that they honour opponents who are blatantly disloyal in their practices may seem unreasonable. This dilemma is discussed in Chapter 7 in light of the Hungarian case which provides a textbook example of these dynamics.

[17] These types of accusations focusing on the 'political' interests of opponents are all the more problematic that the central functions of political parties is to represent their constituencies' interests for electoral advantage.

Instead, pluralist partisans will criticise opposing positions and policies on the basis of their own account of the common good. Pluralist partisans show how decisions taken by their opponents may come to undermine widely accepted societal goods in light of their own understanding of fundamental principles. Such forms of criticism remain compatible with a pluralist understanding of the political world. Democratic partisans take a stand for a specific understanding of fundamental principles, without denying that there exists a plurality of legitimate interpretations of their meaning, hierarchy and implications.

Indicator 7: Pluralist respect entails that mainstream partisans will criticise their opponents' positions by highlighting their limitations with regard to advancing the common good. In practice, this entails that:

- Mainstream partisans will criticise the decisions of adversaries on the basis of their limitations in advancing widely shared societal objectives. For instance, a pro-choice partisan could criticise anti-abortion policies for undermining the well-being of women in society.
- Mainstream partisans will use the hierarchy they establish between fundamental principles as a basis for criticising the decisions of adversaries. For instance, a partisan criticising their opponents' decision to raise taxes on high incomes may do so on the basis that it compromises the economic freedom of citizens.

Attribute E: Acknowledging principled opposition

Second, pluralist partisans acknowledge the principled nature of opponents' positions, even if this entails criticising these principles. They should assume that, even if they disagree with their rivals' stances, these 'act not only for their own political gain but also out of a desire to do what they think is right' (Gutmann and Thomson, 2010). To take as a starting point the 'mixed motives' of opponents is thus to see that, while those we disagree with are partly moved by the desire to win elections and gain office, opponents are also committed to advancing a set of principles they believe in. This is a straightforward sign of respect, to the extent that principled commitment carries intrinsically positive connotations: to say that a politician stands by their principles is recognition of political merit.

This recognition also entails an understanding that the 'common good' is essentially plural. If disagreement persists despite a joint commitment to the common good, it is because opponents have different understandings of fundamental principles and their practical implications. As Connolly insists, principles such as freedom or equality are 'essentially contested' precisely because they are both appraisive – that is, valued as social goods – and internally complex (Connolly, 1993, pp. 10, 40). These characteristics entail that no single agent can ever account for them in such a way that all will agree. Any identity built around a given interpretation of these principles will exclude other identities built on diverging interpretations, and thus cause disagreement.[18] By criticising opponents' understandings of shared principles, partisans also acknowledge the essentially contested nature of these concepts, and thus the ethical necessity of political pluralism and partisan disagreement.

> *Indicator* 8: Pluralist respect entails that when mainstream partisans explain the reasons why they disagree with opponents, they evoke differences in values, worldview and understanding of shared principles. For instance, a partisan supporting same-sex marriage may recognise that opponents prioritise a traditional idea of family and marriage over the equal rights of sexual minorities, all the while criticising this position.

Attribute E: Recognising a good in common

Finally, respect for political pluralism involves allegiance to a non-partisan and supra-partisan idea of the political community. This means not only that the loyalty of partisans to the political community should have precedence over their allegiance to the party, but also that they should refrain from equating allegiance to their party with allegiance to the community. In other words, partisans should be dedicated to an idea of the political community that includes all parties yet transcends them. The dedication to the political community, in all its plurality and complexity, is what acts as a break on the selfish drives of partisan conviction. As Rosenblum emphasises, ethical commitments 'arise from "identification" with the political community and feelings of belonging: we are affiliated and therefore morally obligated, not vice-versa' (Rosenblum, 1998, p. 52). Ryn goes even further to equate ethical conscience with communal allegiance. According to him, 'community can emerge only in a society where

---

[18] Theorists of deliberative democracy have also stressed the unavoidable persistence of such forms of moral disagreements, deliberation only making possible the mutual understanding necessary for finding common solutions to practical problems (Gutmann and Thomson, 1996).

the forces of egotistical interests are tempered by concern for the common good. In disposing us against what is merely arbitrary and selfish, ethical conscience disposes against what separates us from others' (Ryn, 1978, p. 83).

The political community starts with the idea of the common good. What makes the political community is what we share with others that transcends particular group interests and our defence of particular convictions. Following Galston, we can identify three separate components of the 'common good' in democratic societies (Galston, 2013). The first refers to the existence of 'matters of common concern', issues that should be considered collectively because they result from social linkage such as the health, education and security of citizens. Second, the idea of political community is grounded in a series of fundamental principles that define the common good *at large*. Such principles are generally listed in the preamble of a democracy's constitution. While some of these – justice, equality or freedom – exist in most democratic constitutional frameworks, other principles are particular to certain constitutional arrangements. Finally, the institutions of democracy may also be seen as a common good. They provide the framework within which, and procedures with which, collective decisions can be made and implemented, disputes settled, and the voices of minorities protected. Liberal democratic institutions are both supra-partisan and non-partisan: they put every party on an equal level, and thus ensure that partisan contestation remains open and the place of power 'empty'.[19]

That partisans consider these different components of the common good as foundational of the political community at large is a key component of their respect for pluralism. First, this entails that they refrain from engaging in *holist* political appeals. In other words, partisans will not picture the common good as a unitary, immutable and uncontroversial notion that their party alone defends. They do not claim any 'mastery of the foundations of society', and therefore do not argue that they alone can defend the democratic political community and represent its fundamental principles (Mouffe, 2000, p. 21). Populist political discourse – where the speaker insists they represent the people's will as a unitary whole – is by this measure at odds with pluralist forms of partisanship. This would also be the case for extreme forms of technocratic appeals according to which

---

[19] This is also why constitutional drafting and major constitutional amendments are generally seen to require the assent of a multiplicity of parties. To be accepted by all, rules should be seen as belonging to the common and not as favouring one particular group over another.

both societal goals and the best way to achieve them can be determined by experts, and are therefore not a matter for legitimate political debate within the political community at large.[20] In contrast, pluralist partisans do not confuse the common good with their own understanding of it.

> *Indicator 9:* Pluralist respect entails that mainstream partisans do not engage in holist political appeals. In practice, this entails that:
>
> - Mainstream partisans refrain from claiming that their party alone can truly represent the political community. For instance, a partisan who asserts that only their party can speak for the nation and defend its values and traditions engages in a holist political appeal.
> - Mainstream partisans refrain from claiming that there exists a single way of reaching widely accepted societal goals. For instance, a partisan who pictures unemployment as a problem for which there is only one correct solution, the one their own party advocates, engages in a holist political appeal.

Second, partisans can only respect their opponents if they see them as oriented towards the common good, and therefore as part of the political community. This amounts to a belief that adversaries are committed to addressing widely accepted societal problems (sickness, poverty, crime), and are guided by a concern for fundamental principles such as freedom, equality and the preservation of democracy's 'procedural minimum' (Galston, 2013). The two previous attributes of pluralist partisanship, practice-based criticism and acknowledging principled opposition, are in line with this belief in the morality of opposition. While it may be too much to ask from partisans that they explicitly recognise their opponents' orientation towards the common good, they should at least refrain from picturing opponents as opposed to the common good, and thus outside of the sphere of common morality. Gutmann and Thomson give the example of pro-life activists that depict pro-choice activists as being 'in favour of killing babies' (Gutmann and Thomson, 1996, p. 80). If opponents aim to destroy those objectives, principles and institutions widely understood as goods in common, then they are fundamentally immoral. This also means they fail the very basic condition for being included in a political discussion and are, de facto, illegitimate to govern.

---

[20] A number of scholars have highlighted this anti-pluralist affinity between populism and technocracy (Bickerton and Invernizzi Accetti, 2017; Caramani, 2017).

Indicator 10: Pluralist respect entails that mainstream partisans refrain from picturing their opponents as fundamentally opposed to the common good. In practice, this entails that:

- Mainstream partisans do not picture morality as a dividing line of politics, describing their own camp as fundamentally good and their opponents as fundamentally evil. For instance, they will avoid calling their opponents fascists because they are in favour of restricting immigration.
- Mainstream partisans do not picture their opponents as opposed to addressing widely shared societal objectives. For instance, they will not claim that their opponents do not care about addressing crime because they advocate for alternatives to prison sentences.
- Mainstream partisans do not claim their opponents are opposed to widely shared, common principles. For instance, they will refrain from claiming that their opponents want to destroy individual freedom because they advocate for high taxes on the wealthy.

A Realistic Ideal?

This model of democratic partisanship is avowedly normative rather than descriptive. In other words, I do not conceive of cohesiveness or pluralism as default characteristics of real-world mainstream partisanship in liberal democracies. These are instead standards that real-world partisans can live up to, but also fail to uphold. Far from being apologetic of real-world parties, theories of democratic partisanship offer tools for a constructive criticism of their actual doings.[21]

Normative does not, however, mean utopian. This framework is grounded in principles of political philosophy but also in an understanding of the role that parties have played in the history of first-wave democracies.

---

[21] It is noteworthy that theorists on both sides of the Atlantic insist most on those characteristics of partisanship that they see missing in their own political environment. American theorists, such as Russell Muirhead or Nancy Rosenblum, are especially aware of the dangers of extreme partisan polarisation and widespread disrespect for political opponents, and their work is therefore more directly centred on the importance of partisans upholding a pluralist ethic. On the other hand, European authors such as Jonathan White or Léa Ypi show more concern for the failings of parties to put forward meaningful and clearly differentiated platforms and are consequently also more directly concerned with partisan political justification and efforts at citizen engagement.

Table 2.1: Dimensions, attributes and indicators of democratic partisanship

	DIMENSIONS	ATTRIBUTES	INDICATORS
DEMOCRATIC PARTISANSHIP	Ideological cohesiveness	A. Normative grounding	1. Justifying political engagement by referring to broad societal problems and objectives that actions intend to address
			2. Justifying political engagement by referring to the fundamental values and doctrines that actions intend to further
		B. Programmatic substance	3. Justifying how particular understanding of the common good are furthered through policies and planned actions in government
			4. Demonstrating agency in political discourse
		C. Capacity for differentiation	5. Justifying normative commitments and policy proposals in a comparative fashion
	Respect for pluralism	D. Practice-focused criticism	6. Refraining from engagement in 'motive-cynicism' when criticising political opponents
			7. Criticising opponents' practices by highlighting their limitations in advancing the common good
		E. Acknowledging principled opposition	8. Recognising that disagreements are grounded in different worldviews, values and understandings of shared principles
		F. Recognising a good in common	9. Refraining from engagement in holist political appeals
			10. Refraining from picturing opponents as morally corrupt or intent on destroying the common good

In the nineteenth and early twentieth century, party systems socialised the citizens of Western Europe and the USA into mass democracy, and they helped structure the ways in which we still understand politics (Campbell, Converse, Miller and Stokes, 1960; Rokkan and Lipset, 1967). The gradual institutionalisation of party systems throughout the modern era is also inseparable from the emergence of a pluralist worldview and the side-lining of holist understandings of the common good (Daalder, 2002; Ignazi, 2017, pp. 24–31; Sartori, 1976, pp. 19–27). It is precisely because, in the words of Schattschneider, '[t]he political parties created democracy and modern democracy is unthinkable save in terms of parties', that it is reasonable to be demanding of them (Schattschneider, 2009 [1942], p. 1). My theoretical framework seeks to highlight the potential of *actual* partisanship to contribute to a democratic way of life. Both philosophical principles and historical insight serve to develop standards of what partisans can do at their best.

While explicitly normative, the theoretical framework presented here does not make a claim to universality. It builds on a contextualist understanding of liberal democracy, according to which 'the normative dimension inscribed in political institutions [. . .] always refers to specific practices, depending on particular contexts, and [. . .] is not the expression of a universal morality' (Mouffe, 2005b, p. 121). This contrasts, for instance, with the Rawlsian liberal tradition according to which there exist principles that would be considered acceptable by any *reasonable* person, and which can form the basis of an ideal of justice (Rawls, 2001, 2005). To put it bluntly, the purpose of this book is not to defend liberal democracy as a form of government that every partisan should necessarily promote. I intend, instead, to isolate the conditions under which partisan discourse effectively contributes to the specific type of regime that is liberal democracy, and therefore the norms that partisans who are also liberal democrats (in the primary sense) should hold themselves accountable to.

These caveats notwithstanding, some may apprehend this theoretical framework with suspicion. While political history gives us reasons to believe that some partisans, at certain moments in time, might have approximated the ideal, it also provides many examples of the uncompromising nature of partisanship. There are legitimate questions, especially, on the compatibility of ideological cohesiveness and respect for pluralism. Since the eighteenth century, political thinkers in Europe and the USA have, with few exceptions, presented partisanship as a form of factionalism breeding unnecessary political divisions (for a detailed overview, see Ball, 1989; Hofstadter, 1969; Rosenblum, 2008, pp. 23–163). Still today, the a priori commitment of partisans to a given political identity sits uncomfortably with the 'ideal speech' situation of deliberative democrats, involving actors with flexible positions capable of compromise for the sake of the public good (Gundersen, 2000; Muirhead, 2010). At first glance, Rawlsian political theory also distances 'high' political liberalism from the 'great game of politics', partisanship being associated with forms of partiality, irrationality and intransigence at fundamental odds with a pluralist worldview (Bonotti, 2014, 2018; Muirhead and Rosenblum, 2006, p. 99). Until very recently, liberal political theorists excluded partisanship from their considerations precisely because they considered it as a form of loyalty that undermines the respectful, constructive and open-minded attitude required to enter the deliberative process (van Biezen and Saward, 2008).

While theorists of partisanship have argued that partisans *can* adopt the pluralist attitudes best fitted to sustain liberal democracy, they also emphasise a trade-off between partisan conviction and pluralist ethics. Muirhead, for instance, depicts an antagonistic relationship between cohesiveness and pluralism, where belief in the superiority of a set of partisan claims puts one at risk of desiring their complete triumph. He stresses that partisan loyalty brings with it 'permanent moral danger', because 'in transcending self-interested strategic reason, loyalty threatens to become immune to reason and judgement. It can become a form of unthinking stubbornness that brings with it a kind of closure – closure to fact, to principle, and to consequences' (Muirhead, 2014, p. 116). Some empirical studies support the contention that partisanship risks intransigence. In their comparative study of abortion debates in Ireland, Suiter et al., for instance, find that citizens in deliberative settings are more able to approximate the ideal-speech situation than partisans; in turn, strategic electoral incentives in parliamentary settings are less conducive to high deliberative quality (Suiter, Farrell, Harris, and Murphy, 2021). This is supported by studies in cognitive-psychology research, according to which political reasoning comes with a range of biases that limit partisans' capacity to see the other side (Chambers, 2018, p. 38).

From an alternative position, the adoption of a value pluralist outlook may be too much to ask from those who hold principled convictions. This is much the position defended by John Stuart Mill at his time, according to which the 'salutary effects' of political disagreement will be visible to the 'disinterested bystander', not the 'impassioned partisan' (Mill, 1991 [1859], p. 58). Respect for pluralism might in fact be counterproductive to partisans pushing other democratic goods. By undermining the partisan's belief that they are in the right, by excessively tampering their assertiveness, a pluralist outlook could deprive them of the necessary tools to convince others of their claims. A number of authors suggest that pluralist ethics might limit the capacity of politicians to fulfil more essential political functions – with trade-offs between respect for opposition on the one hand, and political accountability or the substantive weighing of arguments on the other (discussed in Bächtiger and Beste, 2017). Like Mill's one-eyed man, partisans cannot, and perhaps should not, be completely lucid. They need to be blind in some respect in order to fulfil more essential democratic functions: providing citizens with clear governing alternatives, and therefore with the means to keep them accountable.

To what extent, then, does the stringent ideal of democratic partisanship find resonance in the real world of party politics? Can partisans uphold *both* an ideologically cohesive identity and the pluralist orientations that are essential to liberal democracy? In the following chapter, I outline how my study was designed to answer these questions.

3
Studying Partisanship in Context

I understand *partisanship* as the array of practices and discourses attached to party identification, membership or leadership in support of a shared understanding of the common good. The focus of my empirical study, however, is solely on the *discourse of French and Hungarian mainstream party members within the context of focus groups* – specific instances of partisanship. This choice assumes that party member discourse in these specific contexts is significant and can be studied as a critical case for understanding mainstream partisanship within these societies. It also assumes that, by studying partisanship in two given countries, France and Hungary, we can learn about the more general conditions under which democratic partisanship is likely to flourish. This chapter provides justification for these claims.

The first part discusses methodological considerations, highlighting the relevance of studying activists to understand their party organisation, and why I chose to study partisanship in the context of group discussions specifically. Second, I dive into some ontological and epistemological issues, discussing how I interpret instances of partisans upholding democratic norms: What does this say about the partisans themselves and their political environment? I explain why I refrain from inferences about the moral worth of individual partisans throughout this book, and instead understand democratic discourse as largely a function of the context within which partisans evolve. Structural limitations on the individual agency of partisans, I argue, opens the gate to understanding the conditions under which democratic partisanship is likely to emerge and endure. Finally, I show why France and Hungary are particularly interesting cases to study democratic norms in party discourse, and the way they are shaped by context.

Facilitating Party Member Discussions

I designed discussion guidelines for the focus groups with two, seemingly contradictory objectives in mind: first, to minimise my influence on the process as much as possible, specifically to diminish the risk of leading discussions and prompting certain types of responses; and second, to obtain data that would be comparable across different focus groups, and that would help address my research question. It was particularly important to avoid asking party members direct questions about the cohesiveness of their ideology or their respect for pluralism. Instead, I settled for general discussions about politics where partisans could account for their own positions as well as their opponents'.

Different steps of this process are highlighted below. I first discuss why I look at party members specifically and address the thorny question of whether their discourse is representative of what their party stands for. I then move to the advantages of studying partisanship in the context of group discussions and provide an overview of my discussion guidelines. I also account for how the theory of democratic partisanship (Chapter 2) served as a framework to analyse the discussion transcripts through computer-assisted coding.

Why study party activists?

My focus on party members assumes that democratic norms within 'the party on the ground' (grassroots membership) tells us something about their absence or presence at the elite level ('the party in central office' and 'the party in public office') (Mair and Katz, 1998), but also among party supporters at large. One of the main reasons to doubt this assertion is that activists are known to hold more radical positions than either elites or party supporters – a rule known as the 'law of curvilinear disparity' (May, 1973). My comparative research design offsets this issue to some extent. Even if my participants were more radical than the elites or supporters of their own party, there would still be relevant comparisons to be had in terms of the *relative* cohesiveness and pluralism of partisan norms across different organisations and domestic contexts. But I also object to the claim of party member unrepresentativeness for a number of more fundamental reasons.

The discourse of activists, the 'party on the ground', will not mirror like-for-like the public face of the party (Mair and Katz, 1998). However, democratic norms at the grassroots level do provide important information about what the party stands for. As 'the most tightly knit connection between party elites and voters' (Poguntke, 2002, p. 9), members perform the major function of linking both levels in a 'two-way interaction' (see also Crouch, 2004, pp. 70–1; Lawson, 1980, ch. 1). Because of this, they are the citizens most actively socialised and mobilised by the upper echelons of party hierarchies. Difficulties among activists to provide a cohesive discourse about the party's values and actions, for instance, also constitutes a failure of the party to socialise and mobilise its own members and, by extension, its most faithful advocates among lay citizens. In this specific example, lack of cohesiveness from party members is a proxy for the party's weak capacity to educate citizens more generally. But this failure to socialise members also has a direct democratic impact, as weakly cohesive activists are less likely to successfully mobilise less ideologically inclined citizens.[1]

As compared to lay supporters, party members have a greater moral responsibility to uphold democratic standards than lay supporters (Bonotti, 2012), because they more actively and voluntarily embrace their status as partisans. External observers can hold higher standards for activists than for lay supporters or regular voters. Elites exercise more power, and, to this extent, there would be an even stronger normative case for studying democratic partisanship among their ranks. However, this comes with its own set of difficulties. Party leaders are likely to be more polished and contrived in their expression, given they have routine experience of public speaking and are subject to far greater public scrutiny. Party elites would also have been unlikely to agree to participate in this study in comparable numbers (117 participants across both countries) – thereby ultimately limiting the significance of my findings.[2]

There is also a distinct rationale for studying *young* activists, which this study focuses on. Because political socialisation happens early in the life cycle, older cohorts may hold ideas that will lose their present-day

---

[1] It follows from this that I contest the idea of a necessary trade-off between parties successfully mobilising their members on the one hand and their voters on the other (Katz, 2014). This presumes that members are necessarily more radical than supporters, a claim for which we have mixed evidence in the European context (see end of this section). The 'trade-off' argument also rests on the idea that, to be successful, parties should passively represent the tamer pre-existing attitudes of lay voters whereas there is much evidence that parties also contribute to shape these attitudes (see Introduction and Chapter 2). Finally, we know that parties with a strong organisation, a notion which includes the reach and extent of its local anchorage, do better electorally in the longer run (Art, 2011; Bolleyer and Bytzek, 2016; Dinas, Georgiadou, Konstantinidis and Rori, 2013).

[2] In Hungary specifically, recruitment proved particularly cumbersome (see Chapter 4) and might not have been successful if my focus were on party elites. Based on the anecdotal evidence of fellow colleagues, Fidesz elites are particularly hard to convince and have been more likely to refuse participation in social science studies than other party rulers in the region.

relevance with generational renewal (Hooghe and Stolle, 2003; Hyman, 1969). Relatedly, young members are the depositary of the future of parties and therefore of partisanship. At the most prosaic level, it is among their ranks that future party elites will emerge (Bruter and Harrison, 2009a, pp. 211–22; 2009b, pp. 1284–5). These last points are particularly relevant in post-communist countries, where young partisans represent the first generation socialised within a formally democratic system. In this regard, they are both the children of a period of political transition in which parties have been crucial and a cohort that holds responsibility for the future consolidation of democracy.[3]

Finally, more rather than less evidence is required on the ideological positioning of European party activists, especially among younger cohorts. While May's law has received some empirical backing, especially in the US context (A. Abramowitz, 2010; A. I. Abramowitz, 2012; Fiorina, 1999; Sunstein, 2002), the evidence for European party systems is scarcer and tends to be mixed. A number of studies show that party members are subject to divergent ideological and electoral incentives, and that in many cases they display positions close to those of a loyal voter (Gallagher and Marsh, 2004; Narud and Scare, 1999; Norris, 1995). This is becoming increasingly true in the European context, where the very distinction between a party member and a supporter is breaking down given the multiplication of new party affiliation categories and the rise of what Scarrow has termed 'multi-speed membership organisation' (Scarrow, 2015). My research provides much needed data on the perspectives of party members in this changing context.

The importance of sociable interaction

In choosing the methodology for this study, I assumed that political norms are best studied not as fixed and attached to an individual, but as resulting from a process through which meaning about public affairs is constructed in common with others. In this sense, the group is not merely an opportunity to study a collection of individual opinions: if this was my aim, one-on-one interviews would have been more appropriate. Group discussions allow instead the exploration of socially

---

[3] Party memberships are relatively younger in Eastern Europe compared to Western Europe, and young people play an essential role in the current evolution of Central European party systems (in the case of Hungary, see Saltman, 2014; see also Scarrow and Gezgor, 2006).

shared knowledge and places of dissensus, reasoning and argument, and, more generally, how political meaning is constructed within different cultural contexts (Belzile and Oberg, 2012, p. 467; Marková, 2007; White, 2011b, pp. 40, 45). Focus groups diminish the constraints imposed by the research setting itself, allowing partisans to define in conversation the terms of their participation in the study. This is less likely to be the case in individual interviews, where the power of the moderator over the conversation is greater (Steiner, Bächtiger, Spörndli and Steenbergen, 2004, p. 54; White, 2011b, p. 45), and even less so in survey participation, as questionnaires more easily foreclose participants' answers (Bourdieu, 1993).

I designed the study to encourage this dimension of sociable interaction and offer participants as much room as possible to choose how to represent themselves. First, it was particularly important that participants be able to use their mother tongue in these discussions. This was not only so participants could express themselves as fluidly as possible, but also because I assume that political norms within a given political community are embedded in language. I therefore recruited activists, moderated discussions and analysed transcripts in the French and Hungarian languages respectively.[4]

Second, the discussions were purposefully conducted with a limited number of participants, a minimum of three and a maximum of six, a setting which has been shown to spur discussions of greater depth while also being more inclusive (see Gamson, 1992; Krueger, 1998, p. 73; White, 2011b).

Third, I delegated part of the recruitment of participants to single party members, who then mobilised other activists within their peer group – a technique known as 'snowballing'.[5] This ensured that there were pre-existing social ties among party members, and that they were used to talking politics together. As important sites of secondary political socialisation for my participants, peer groups provided an ideal space for studying the construction of shared political norms. I also purposefully organised discussions in bars or cafés familiar to the group, which set a more informal and relaxed tone for these conversations.

Finally, the discussion protocol itself minimised my influence in these discussions and enhanced partisan interaction.

---

[4] I completed these tasks myself, but delegated the transcription of the Hungarian interviews to three different research assistants in Hungary (see Acknowledgements).

[5] See Chapter 4 for a comparative account of the recruitment process in both countries.

The use of visual prompts

After brief presentations, I gave each participant an identical series of twelve cards, every card matching a different area of public policy. Ten out of the twelve topics were identical in both countries:

Card 1: Public service reform
Card 2: EU politics
Card 3: Religious and/or national minorities
Card 4: Law and order
Card 5: Unemployment and employment policy
Card 6: Public morality
Card 7: Industrial and/or agricultural policy
Card 8: Taxation, social policy and redistribution of wealth
Card 9: Public debt finance and deficit management
Card 10: Environmental politics.

Two more cards were specifically tailored to the political context of each country at the time. The country-specific cards where, in France 'Sexual minorities and social change' and 'Legal and illegal immigration' (Cards 4 and 6 from left to right in Figure 1.2) and in Hungary 'Institutional reforms' and 'The nation in politics'.

Cards were illustrated with different types of images in both countries: in France, satirical drawings (see Figure 1.2); in Hungary, descriptive symbols or photographs corresponding to each theme, for example a recycling symbol for 'Environmental politics', or a Hungarian flag for 'The nation in politics'.[6] These differences in the type of visual prompts used require some justification.

In choosing illustrations for each policy theme, my intention was to enhance the playful dimension of discussions and encourage a more relaxed atmosphere for participation. Given each participant had the same twelve cards, distinct imagery allowed them to identify the theme other participants were talking about at different points in time. These illustrations also had to satisfy an important criterion of neutrality: to be perceived as such by participants and therefore maintain my position as an impartial researcher.[7] Given the context of partisan cartelisation

---

[6] The Hungarian cards are not reproduced in this book because of low image quality.
[7] In Chapter 4, I discuss how my position as a neutral academic observer was perceived by participants – with trust in France and with suspicion in Hungary. I also analyse what these divergent perceptions of impartiality reveal about the political context of both countries.

in France and hyper-polarisation in Hungary (see Chapter 4), these two conditions were best satisfied in different ways.

For the French discussions, I chose a series of drawings by satirical illustrator Plantu (also known as Jean Plantureux), found through online research but initially published at different points in time in the centre-left newspaper Le Monde. Despite the journal's political orientation, Plantu's indiscriminate attacks on politicians from both sides of the political spectrum, as well as the fact that he is one of France's most respected contemporary satirists, means he is largely perceived as transcending partisan divides. This allowed me to select a set of drawings with a balance of political positions, taking issue with both mainstream parties. As intended, these images acted as a helpful icebreaker and set a positive tone at the beginning of each discussion.

For the Hungarian discussions, I chose more neutral images with a Creative Commons licence, also found through online research. The cards similarly encouraged a livelier atmosphere and created useful points of reference to different topics. More importantly, these illustrative images ensured a form of neutrality that could not have been achieved using satirical images. After some extensive research, I could not find a Hungarian equivalent to Plantu, critical of both sides of the political spectrum yet also respected by both camps. This is reflective of Hungary's hyper-polarised political context which, to a large extent, prevents political neutrality: since 2010, reactions to the Fidesz government tend to go from complete rejection to adamant support, with very little space in the middle ground.[8] Standard images related to the twelve policy themes ensured the cards fulfilled their purpose, facilitating discussions while projecting impartiality.

I have no evidence that using different types of image in both settings fundamentally influenced the outcome of this research. The images were presented as mere illustrations of the topic under discussion and were very seldom the direct object of commentary from my participants. While it is plausible that the French cards created a lighter atmosphere in the first few minutes following the card distribution, the discussion guidelines were otherwise consistent in both settings and led to very comparable discussion structures across national boundaries.

---

[8] As measured through perceptions of polarisation, Hungary shifted from the fifth to the second most polarised European polity between 2004 and 2014 (Vegete, 2019, p. 80).

Guidelines for the discussions[9]

Once each party member had the twelve cards in hand, I asked participants to rank them, *according to the degree of disagreement these different issues generate between their own party and their main opponents*. They were asked to establish this ranking on their own rather than in discussion with others. Once they had finished this task, the discussions lasted for approximately one hour and were divided into three parts.

Part 1 (approximately 40 minutes): In the first and main part of the discussion, party members discussed why they had decided to rank the cards as they did. I instructed them to start discussing the topics they saw as generating the least disagreement within their party system, and to progressively shift towards discussing the more polarising topics. Throughout the conversation, they discussed each card in turn and offered justifications for why they saw different topics as either generating consensus or conflict.

In most cases, this protocol generated quasi-autonomous group discussions from which I could step back altogether. Participants picked up on the guidelines, and after five to ten minutes of discussion switched from one topic to another without being prompted. This method also offered activists considerable freedom to define the terms of the discussion. They decided on how to organise the cards, the order and length at which they discussed them, and their interpretation of the different topics. Most importantly perhaps, they chose how to define inter-partisan agreement and disagreement, and therefore the measure by which to classify the cards.

Part 2 (approximately 15 minutes): Once the last, most conflictual theme had been discussed, I encouraged participants to step back and express a normative judgement on partisan disagreement in their political system. I asked whether they thought there existed the right balance between areas of agreement and disagreement between political parties. Conversely, I prompted them to reflect on whether either more disagreement, or greater consensus, would be preferable according to them, and why.

Part 3 (approximately 5 minutes): The concluding questions related to participants' personal experiences of encounters with political opponents. I would ask whether participants had opportunities to discuss politics with people of different political opinions than their own, in what circumstances these encounters occurred, and how well they generally went.

---

[9] For a verbatim account of the discussion guidelines, see Appendix 1. For other examples of focus group studies using visual prompts, see Gamson, 1992; Meinhof, 2004; White 2011.

Democratic partisanship as a framework for empirical analysis

In addition to minimising my influence on the structure of these discussions, this methodology served another, essential purpose: to collect comparable data on how partisans perceive political disagreement, and on the extent to which their discourse resonates with the two dimensions of democratic partisanship. The protocol described above gave participants a lot of autonomy, but also ensured this autonomy was exercised within clearly defined boundaries. The cards acted as a visual reminder of the guidelines and kept discussions on-track without requiring my intervention. A common framework also ensured the comparability of discussion content across all twenty-eight groups, while ensuring my core research questions were addressed.

Taking democratic partisanship as a theoretical framework, the textual analysis was concerned with how partisans position themselves and their platform vis-à-vis other actors, here their political opponents (Harré and Moghaddam, 2003; Harré, Moghaddam, Cairnie, Rothbart and Sabat, 2009). More specifically, I focused on the set of characteristics partisans attributed to their own party (self-positioning) and to their opponents (other-positioning) when discussing agreement and disagreement on the twelve policy areas represented by the visual prompts (Harré and Van Langenhove, 1999, pp. 20–1). This provided a gateway for analysing the dimension of *cohesiveness*, mostly concerned with how partisans define their own party identity, and the dimension of *respect for pluralism*, focused on the ways in which opponents are characterised.

The twenty-eight group discussions were transcribed verbatim and analysed through a process of computer-assisted coding. Coding in qualitative analysis is the process by which codes, or keywords, are associated with portions of text – a word, a sentence or a paragraph – throughout the data. In this context, a code is generally 'a word or short phrase that symbolically assigns a summative, salient, essence-capturing, and/or evocative attribute' to the portion of data it is associated with (Saldaña, 2013, p. 3). The coding scheme was designed in light of my theoretical framework, with specific indicators attached to the different attributes of cohesiveness and pluralism (see summary in Table 2.1). Relying on NVivo, a computer-assisted qualitative data analysis software (CAQDAS), I applied the same codes repeatedly to the self- and other-positioning of party members in group discussions. The occurrences and co-occurrences of specific codes then allowed for the identification of recurrent patterns and themes in the data, as well as variations in these patterns across different groups of speakers: French and Hungarian party members, but also left- and right-wing activists within each national context. Appendix 2 contains my codebook, with a detailed description of all of the codes referred to throughout the empirical analysis.

The results of this coding process are presented in two different forms over Chapters 4, 5 and 6. Cross-tabulation tables highlight key variations in the frequency of different codes across countries and parties. While the numbers are too small to conduct significance tests, these descriptive statistics give a sense of the magnitude of differences in the patterns of speech of partisan groups. This quantitative data is complemented with an analysis of multiple extracts from the transcripts, which provide qualitative evidence for the different trends identified.

Interpreting Partisan Discourse

When party members meet or fall short of the standards of democratic partisanship, what does this say about them and their political environment? The following section situates this book within the interpretive tradition of political study and, within this framework, theorises the relationship between partisan discourse and the wider context in which partisans evolve. I aim to avoid what I call the fallacy of pure ethical motive or, in other words, I am careful not to explain democratic partisan discourse with reference to the personal qualities of individuals. I interpret democratic partisan discourse instead as a function of structural factors, specifically political culture and exogenous events. This provides the framework within which I explain variations in democratic partisanship across parties and countries later in this book.

The fallacy of pure ethical motive

In exploring how partisan discourse resonates with democratic norms, I remain intentionally agnostic on the personal reasons that motivate the discourse of individual partisans. In other words, I suspend judgement on partisans' hidden motives, psychological dispositions or internal moral compass. This also means I do not aim to capture 'honest' political discourse, stripped of rhetoric or political strategy. There are several reasons for this.

First, social scientists have very imperfect methodological tools to access the hidden motivations or 'deep beliefs' of individuals (White, 2009). As highlighted below, these reasons will be necessarily mixed, and often obscure to participants themselves – let alone the researcher as an external observer. Second, it is unreasonable to expect pure ethical motivations from partisans. Machiavelli's legacy guards us against applying the standards of private ethics to those choosing to pursue political power (Thompson, 1987). In this specific case, partisans cannot be studied independently from their desire to persuade others and obtain political power. Even theorists who insist on the virtues of partisanship do not deny that politicians have mixed motives, and therefore that they are at least partly driven by their own personal ambition (Muirhead, 2014, p. 18; Muirhead and Rosenblum, 2006).

Finally, it is unnecessary for partisans to have pure ethical motives to fulfil their obligations within a liberal democratic framework. I read democratic partisanship not as an expression of individual value, but as *avowed adherence to a specific and contextual, liberal democratic way of life*. A partisan could, in principle, campaign on the basis of a perfectly pluralist discourse not because they believe in their own words, but because they evolve in a context where this is expected of them. Participants in this study will have aimed to give a certain image of themselves to their party organisation, as represented by their fellow partisans, but will have also directed their discourse towards the outside world, as represented by myself (the researcher) and you (the reader). What is interesting here is precisely what party members understand as appropriate political discourse in this context, and therefore what they chose to say in front of these audiences – rather than the reasons why they chose to say it. Regardless of their motivation, partisans who abide by democratic norms in their discourse contribute to their diffusion, and thus to the perpetuation of liberal democracy as a way of life. It also remains reasonable to expect relative (albeit imperfect) alignment between partisan discourse and partisan practice, even where democratic partisanship is a product of social conformism and not deep commitment. If partisans feel compelled by their peers to express respect towards opponents, for instance, it also proceeds that they are less likely to publicly undermine their opponents through institutional manipulation.

The role of structural factors in democratic partisanship

While I do not focus on the personal reasons that motivate individual partisan discourse, I am interested in the structural conditions that enable both democratic and undemocratic forms of partisanship. It will be clear at this point that I view partisans as agents of democratic change. They have sufficient power to contribute, over time, to the gradual transformation of the structures within which they function.[10] This may be to the

---

[10] For a detailed discussion of this point, see Chapter 2.

benefit of liberal democracy, when they mobilise citizens or consolidate liberal institutions; or to its detriment, when they fuel apathy or engage in abusive legalism. This is why the norms of democratic partisanship matter to liberal democratic regimes: they condition the ways in which partisans exercise their communicational and institutional power.

Yet, partisans are also bearers of pre-existing structures: they evolve in context, not in a vacuum. The extent to which partisans are ideologically cohesive or committed to pluralism depends to a large extent on the constraints and incentives offered by their environment. As emphasised by Lewis, '[while] actors are the only efficient causes or sources of activity in the political world, social structures are material causes that influence political affairs by conditioning the course of action that actors choose to pursue' (P. A. Lewis, 2002, p. 22; see also Haughton, 2005, pp. 7–12; Sibeon, 1999). The forms of causality I posit between democracy and partisanship are therefore of an 'emergent' or 'immanent' nature, a process in which material factors, events, discourse and practices affect one another in a loop-like fashion (Gofas and Hay, 2007). Events trigger ideas and discourse about them. These ideas and discourse are shaped by pre-existing social, economic and political structures. In turn, ideas and discourse give meaning to the ways in which individuals react to triggering events. Finally, these actions give rise to new events, which gradually modify pre-existing structures over time.

One objective of this book is to identify contextual factors favourable to democratic partisanship, and others that act as constraints on its emergence or persistence. Partisan discourse is a precious source of evidence in this regard, as it provides a window on how partisans *create* and *negotiate* meaning about their political environment. In this regard, I follow the interpretative tradition in political studies, which posits that the meaning individuals give to their environment conditions how they act and, ultimately, the ways in which they in turn influence the society they live in (Yanow and Schwartz-Shea, 2006). This explains the central focus this book places on the interactions between partisans and their milieu, with structural factors acting both as constraints and opportunities for the production and negotiation of democratic meaning (Gamson, 1992; Pateman, 1971; Swidler, 1986; White, 2009).

In Chapter 7, I focus on variations in discursive practices across different contexts and analyse how structural factors help explain these variations. More specifically, I pay attention to two categories of relevant factors in my analysis: first the role of political culture, or how the array of signs, symbols, ideas and memories carried by the history of a given polity shape the discourse of partisans in the present; second, the role of exogenous factors – political, economic or social events and phenomena that parties do not fully control yet need to respond to.

I adopt a *semiotic* understanding of political culture, according to which culture functions as a 'toolkit' available for actors to make use of in discourse and practice (Gamson, 1992; Pateman, 1971; White, 2009). The symbolic political resources offered by history, what Nora has termed a polity's 'lieux de mémoire' (Nora, 1996), give sense to partisanship beyond the defence of circumstantial and transitory interests. The boundaries of collective memory will thus have a bearing on the types of discourse that resonates within a given population, and which partisans will consequently adopt. In their discourse, partisans are therefore both empowered and limited by their cultural context. Gamson, for instance, writes about the 'cultural resonance' of particular political claims, arguing that 'some frames have a natural advantage because their ideas and language resonate with a broader political culture' (Gamson, 1992, p. 135).[11]

Within one and the same polity, rival parties are likely to draw on different cultural resources to build their own claims. This also means that they are constrained in different ways by the cultural context they have in common. Indeed, partisanship itself is intricately bound with political memory (White, 2015a). Rival partisans are likely to ground their commitments and build their appeals on resources provided by the history of their own political family: the types of ideas that their camp has promoted since its inception, and the personalities, events, achievements, hymns and symbols that have shaped the political tradition they are committed to (Marlière, 2007; Muirhead, 2014, pp. 128–30; Rosenblum, 2008, p. 355; White, 2015a).

Exogenous factors are another source of constraints and opportunities for partisan discourse that this book focuses on. Under this umbrella term, I understand the political, economic and social phenomena that happen outside of the full control of parties and that partisans need to respond to (Berezin, 2009). Socio-economic crises, terrorist attacks, political scandals, natural disasters, the actions of political allies or opponents, and the decisions of international organisations would fall under this category. These events or series of events prompt partisans to take a stand, but also act as building blocks for their political discourse. Exogenous factors may also cover more diffuse,

---

[11] Saward makes a very similar point, insisting that 'the cultural moment [...] sets the limits or parameters for the aesthetic possibilities' of representative claims, as these 'tap into existing understandings of what might make for a successful (i.e. accepted) representative claim in a given context' (Saward, 2010, pp. 75–7).

structural and long-term processes that affect the doings of party governments, such as financial globalisation, global warming, long-term trends of immigration or regional integration. In such cases, the response of political entrepreneurs to external events can act as critical junctures, creating new cleavages and, ultimately, new political parties (Kriesi et al., 2012; Rokkan and Lipset, 1967). In my empirical analysis, I aim to uncover how different types of events can either facilitate or inhibit the extent to which partisans uphold the standards of democratic partisanship.

Finally, this framework assumes an interaction between how cultural resources and exogenous factors impact democratic partisanship. Partisans make sense of events thanks to the cultural toolkit available to them. This means the same event can affect the democratic merits of partisan groups in very different ways, depending on whether it activates issues that are particularly salient for a given party. For instance, a right-wing party in Western Europe, given its cultural inheritance, may find it easier to develop a cohesive discourse in response to an Islamist terror attack than its left-wing counterpart. Second, external factors are to a large extent cultural resources in the making: as they are appropriated by parties, they are also progressively integrated into partisan culture itself. In the example above, right-wing reactions to terrorist attacks might, over time, contribute to shift aspects of conservative political identity towards intolerance of Muslim minorities. While no event in itself determines the response of partisans, certain events will be more or less favourable to rival partisans developing cohesive or pluralist responses.

It is the task of Chapter 7 to unpack how cultural resources and external events shape expressions of partisanship in the two countries under study. Crucially, this study is exploratory rather than deductive in nature. Given both my interpretive lens and the small-n nature of this study, I do not aim to verify predetermined hypotheses about democratic partisanship – for instance whether either culture or exogenous factors have a greater impact on its emergence. Instead, I assume a priori that the factors above matter. What I aim to uncover is how partisans make sense of their specific political context, and consequently how the democratic identities of French and Hungarian partisans are shaped by this environment. Through a close study of the ways in which party members interpret specific dimensions of their immediate context, I formulate conclusions on how this context, in turn, informs their representation of the world. Further research would be necessary to verify the generalisability of my findings beyond the cases under study.

Comparing Parties across Borders

The comparative dimension of this study, with a focus on both Left and Right in countries with a vastly different democratic history, is essential to complete the above task and explore how context informs specific expressions of partisanship. My research focuses on mainstream right and left political forces in France and Hungary – mainstream parties defined as those with a realistic claim to political power, habitually leading governmental majorities or taking part in them.[12] These include the French *Party socialiste* (PS) and *Union pour un mouvement populaire* (UMP), and the Hungarian *Magyar Szocialista Párt-Együtt* (MSzP-Együtt) and *Fiatal Demokraták Szövetsége-Kereszténydemokrata Néppárt* (Fidesz-KDNP).[13] In 2013, at the time the data was collected, the PS was in government under the presidency of François Hollande (2012–17). In Hungary, Fidesz had a two-thirds majority in the Hungarian Parliament with Viktor Orbán at the helm (2010–14).

From a normative perspective, there are legitimate reasons to apply a liberal democratic framework to the analysis of partisanship in both countries.[14] Despite divergent democratic histories, democracy is a foreign concept for neither states: they both have a history of liberal democratic government, with constitutional continuity from 1946 to today in France, and from 1989 to 2011 in Hungary. Both countries have also voluntarily entered a contract with the EU which entails they uphold liberal democratic principles of government. Specific obligations fall on mainstream parties in both contexts. These have all participated, to different extents, in deepening their country's integration into the EU – thereby regularly renewing their liberal democratic contract. Mainstream parties more generally carry a responsibility to uphold democratic norms: their capacity for agenda-setting, policymaking and institutional reforms grants them significant power, thereby creating democratic obligations. There is therefore a legitimate claim to hold all four political forces accountable to democratic standards.

Moving beyond these normative arguments, there are also good empirical reasons to focus on mainstream parties in France and Hungary. These countries and parties display a number of traits that justify their inclusion

---

[12] For a discussion of my definition of mainstream parties and its implications, see pp. 17–18.
[13] For a discussion of the relationship between Hungarian mainstream parties and their allies, see p. 9, fn. 4.
[14] Wolkenstein has provided an interesting discussion of the conditions under which the concept of liberal democracy (and democratic backsliding specifically) can be applied to non-Western contexts such as Hungary (Wolkenstein, 2022).

in this study. Similarities in party system dynamics and international context facilitate the comparison of all four parties, while variations in historical legacies opens the door to exploring how political culture shapes the democratic expression of partisanship.

Institutional incentives and party system dynamics

When I conducted this study in the mid-2010s, similar institutional incentives in both countries resulted in comparable patterns of competition between mainstream parties – thereby facilitating their comparison. The French and Hungarian electoral systems have a strong majoritarian component counterbalanced with some degree of proportionality. In France, a two-round majoritarian system prevails for both presidential and parliamentary elections, encouraging many parties to compete in the first round but only producing one winner in the second round. Since the beginning of the Fifth Republic in 1957, this electoral system coupled with semi-presidentialism produced two main centre-right and centre-left parties capable of pre-selecting winning presidential candidates and leading parliamentary majorities, but only in alliance with secondary, satellite parties. In Hungary, a two-round, mixed-member system structured the party system from 1989, voters casting two ballots in each round to elect a share of members of parliament through a majoritarian system and the other with a measure of proportionality (Benoit, 1996).[15] This also contributed to create two relatively stable party blocs (Benoit, 2003), with the MSzP and Fidesz as sole organisations capable of heading governmental coalitions – also with the help of smaller parties.

In short, both party systems were characterised in 2013 by forms of bipolar multi-partyism: alternation between two main governmental parties, alongside a series of secondary, satellite parties on their left and right flanks that act as minor coalition partners. In the two decades preceding data collection, all four of the parties studied (Fidesz, MSzP, PS and the UMP) alternated in power, experiencing periods in government and

---

[15] The last general elections in Hungary prior to my 2013 fieldwork were held under this mixed-member electoral system, in 2010. The two-thirds Fidesz majority which emerged from this ballot orchestrated an electoral reform in 2012. The mixed-member system was preserved, but with some major changes which ultimately favoured Fidesz in the 2014 and 2018 elections: a single-round instead of two, the number of seats reduced from 386 to 199, and a radical redrawing of electoral constituencies (Political Capital, 2013).

periods in opposition.¹⁶ These four parties also had similar experiences of governing with a minor coalition partner, while none have had to share power with a major opposition party – a 'grand coalition' scenario which is not uncommon in PR systems. At the time of data collection, all four political groups therefore met the criteria to be defined as 'mainstream' according to the definition proposed in Chapter 2.¹⁷

In addition to facilitating comparison between mainstream parties in both countries, these similarities keep constant some core institutional incentives with a likely impact on the two qualities of democratic partisanship. Electoral systems specifically impact the incentives offered to both parties and voters, the resulting shape of the party system and, arguably, the types of virtues upheld by partisans themselves (Bonotti and Weinstock, 2021). Proportional representation systems give a voice to political minorities, encourage power sharing and are generally considered to fulfil best the principle of democratic fairness (see Beitz, 1989; Christiano, 1996; Ganghof, 2016; McGann, 2006, 2013; van der Hout and McGann, 2009). To this extent, these systems may also offer partisans an incentive towards more *respect for pluralism* – that is, avowed acceptance of alternative understandings of the common good. At the same time, proportionality may push parties towards compromises with adversaries that undermine 'a politics of principled commitment' (White, 2021, pp. 334–7; see also Lardeyret, 2006; Hodgson, 2021), and therefore possibly weaken the *cohesiveness* of partisan ideologies. Conversely, majoritarian systems may foster adversarial forms

---

[16] It is noteworthy that Hungary has displayed more robust, bipolar patterns of party competition up to 2010 as compared to many other CEE countries (Grzymala-Busse, 2002, 2007). This trait has been considered as particularly favourable to the rooting of parties in society, with comparatively lower electoral volatility, higher levels of party identification, and higher turnout rates than most other post-communist democracies (Casal Bértoa and Mair, 2010; P. G. Lewis, 2006; Rose and Mishler, 1998; Sikk, 2005). Partisanship is thus likely to be more meaningful in Hungary, and more comparable to partisanship in France, than in many other post-communist countries that have shown less regularity in their patterns of party competition over the last twenty years.

[17] Given political developments in France and Hungary since my fieldwork in 2013 (discussed in Chapter 4), it is debatable whether all four parties would still be considered as mainstream today. The electoral scores of the PS, LR and MSzP have plummeted to such an extent that they have not taken part in any governmental coalitions since 2010 in Hungary and 2017 in France. The French party system is still in considerable flux and could see the return of these parties, while the MSzP's disempowerment may be more entrenched given changes to the institutional environment brough about by Fidesz since 2010. As discussed in Chapter 7, there would be valid concerns around applying the standards of democratic partisanship to MSzP today given its lack of access to political power.

of politics that do not necessarily favour pluralist respect, but do encourage more cohesive partisan ideologies (Meisburger, 2012; Shapiro, 2018; White, 2021, pp. 337–8).

Given France and Hungary are at neither of these polar opposites, I consider that partisans in both countries are subject to mixed institutional incentives that do not disproportionately favour either of the two dimensions of democratic partisanship. This allows me to set aside electoral systems as a potential explanatory factor for variations in democratic partisanship across cases, and focus instead on exploring the other, more subtle intervening variables I am interested in: political culture and exogenous factors.

Political culture and exogenous factors

I chose countries with contrasting historical legacies to explore the role of political culture in democratic forms of partisanship. The roots of mainstream parties in both countries are sharply contrasted. In France, partisan identity is informed by a century-long history of open political competition. Certainly, the history of French democracy is tumultuous, non-linear and has been interrupted by regular periods of authoritarianism from the 1793 revolutionary terror to the Vichy regime of 1940. It nevertheless includes prolonged periods of relatively free party competition in the past 200 years: under the Third Republic from 1870 to 1940, and under the Fourth and Fifth Republics from 1944 up to the contemporary period. During this period, the general categories of 'Left' and 'Right' (White, 2011a), born in eighteenth-century revolutionary France, have retained a strong, albeit changing, significance (Gauchet, 1996). Since French parties have been free to compete for the votes of citizens for a long period of time, specific traditions, symbols, personalities, policies and values have settled, and progressively become attached to both registers.

In contrast to France, Hungary's history of political competition was neither free nor fair up to the early 1990s. While the country saw several liberal and democratic uprisings between 1848 and 1956, these all resulted in a quick relapse into authoritarian rule (for an overview, see Kende, 2004; Molnár, 2007). The interwar period gave Hungary its independence following Habsburg domination but was marked by the authoritarian regency of Miklós Horthy (1920–44). Hungary experienced a brief Second Republic from 1946 to 1949, only to be ruled by another foreign power, the USSR, for an additional forty years. During this extended period of time, forms of partisanship still existed, with historical cleavages rooted in the first half of the twentieth century. The current Centre Right finds its political roots in a Hungarian tradition of nationalism and conservatism, most clearly embodied by Horthy's rule between 1920 and 1944 and gone underground following the communist takeover of 1946. On the other hand, the current Centre Left has its origins in a Hungarian tradition of socialism on the one hand, and of liberal-cosmopolitanism on the other. While both of these strands of left-wing thought were repressed until 1946, socialism was imposed as Hungary's official ideology in the second half of the twentieth century.

There is, then, a great difference between the political resources that French and Hungarian partisans dispose of. In France, the meaning of partisanship was, in most part, built in a historical context of open political competition. Both camps had to learn to compete in open elections, and therefore to be in power, cede power and be in opposition. In Hungary, partisanship was constructed in authoritarian contexts, in which only one of two political traditions was allowed to dominate. I explore how partisans carry and navigate the memory of past political competition, but also, more broadly, of how historical legacies either enable or constrain democratic expressions of partisanship in both countries today.

As for exogenous factors, defined as the political, economic and social events or phenomena that happen outside of parties' control, a multiplicity of relevant variables may come into play. One task of the empirical analysis is to highlight which specific events or phenomena are recurrent in partisan discourse and inform expressions of partisanship. But one common element of context worth mentioning is the internationalisation of domestic politics over the past three decades. As Kriesi has highlighted, globalisation exposed post-industrial nation-states to three types of competition: economic, with a face-off between sectors exposed to outsourcing and those sheltered from it; political, with the development of alternative sources of supranational sovereignty limiting the role of the nation-state; and cultural, with an increased porosity of national borders to the movement of people (Kriesi et al., 2008). These changes matter not only because they fundamentally changed the sociological make-up of European electorates and their core attitudinal characteristics, but also because they impacted the ways in which parties govern. The economic policy space available to mainstream political actors, specifically, has considerably shrunk (Hay, 2007, pp. 123–53). Worldwide, the opening of national economies and financial globalisation reduced the impact of state investments and made it difficult to collect tax revenue from increasingly multinational economic players. The acceleration of European integration from the late 1980s onwards, a process that pools the national sovereignty of EU Member States in a bid to develop greater collective resilience to these trends, adds other limitations to the agency of Member States. With the Single Market in 1986 and Maastricht Treaty in 1992, strong restrictions were also established on the state subsidisation of firms and authorised size of budgetary deficits. Maastricht laid out the roadmap to a common currency which, ultimately, deprived Eurozone states of monetary tools. In parallel, the social safety nets built in the postwar years of the welfare state gradually eroded while dividends soared, leading to a slow rise of inequalities from the 1970s onwards in the large majority of OECD countries (Piketty, 2014).

Both France and Hungary have been strongly impacted by these changes, albeit to different degrees. While interventionism is central to the culture of the French state, opening borders and European integration have strained its capacity to intervene in an economic context of continuous downturn. Like other post-communist countries, Hungary was faced with the imperative to complete a parallel economic and political transition in record time (Offe, 2004), with pressure from international creditors such as the IMF and political organisations such as the EU (Barr, 2005; Roland, 2001). The 2008 financial crisis also affected state agency in both countries, with stringent budgetary requirements agreed upon at EU level and Hungary specifically having to accept a $25 billion loan from the IMF, World Bank and EU. These forms of economic and political globalisation are widely accepted as having restructured Western and Eastern European party systems in the past decades, displacing traditional allegiances to left- and right-wing parties and catalysing the birth of partisan organisations along a new, 'transnational cleavage' (Kriesi et al., 2012; Marks, Hooghe, Nelson and Edwards, 2006). Given the importance of these developments, a central focus of Chapter 7 will be on how party members make sense of processes of globalisation and European integration in their discourse, and how these exogenous factors inform democratic expressions of partisanship.

This chapter has set the scene for addressing, in the remainder of this book, two key research questions: *To what extent does real-world partisanship resonate with the two pillars of democratic partisanship – ideological cohesiveness and pluralist respect?* and *Under what conditions can we expect democratic partisanship to emerge and endure?* Having defended an interpretive approach to politics, I contend that democratic partisanship is less dependent on personal virtue than it is a function of the wider environment in which party members evolve. Studying party member discourse in the context of group discussions reveals the norms within which party organisations socialise activists and which parties more generally seek to promote. Partisan discourse also provides important indications of the wider structural factors, such as political culture or external events, which contribute to its shaping. Having now outlined the theoretical and methodological foundations for this study, in the next four chapters I apply these frameworks to the analysis of French and Hungarian partisanship.

4
Democracy through the Partisan Lens

How well have French and Hungarian parties performed on standard criteria for democratic performance in the past decades? In this first empirical chapter, I assess democratic party politics in France and Hungary from a number of complementary perspectives. The case-specific literature provides essential context to interpret the perspectives of party members in the remainder of this book. With the theoretical framework of democratic partisanship in mind, key similarities and differences between the cases emerge. Polar opposites in their democratic pathologies, they also show striking parallels in some key party system dynamics.

Moving on from existing academic knowledge, I then focus on some key empirical findings. My initial experience of fieldwork, observing party members in action and recruiting them as participants, taught me invaluable lessons on the very different ways in which French and Hungarian party members approach politics: from a place of curiosity and openness in France; from a place of suspicion and sometimes fear in Hungary. The last section takes a first dive into the group discussions, with a focus on how activists portray the interplay of party politics and democracy in each national context. Their claims strongly resonate with normative assessments in the literature: in France party members value disagreement and desire clearer distinctions between programmatic offers, while in Hungary activists call for greater consensus and a more appeased dialogue between mainstream parties.

Party Politics in France and Hungary

The literatures on democratic party politics in France and Hungary depict vastly different political landscapes. These two cases make for near ideal-typical examples of the broader pathologies affecting party politics in new and old European democracies: cartelisation leading to citizen disengagement in France, and polarisation leading to breakdown in Hungary. Upon closer look, however, parallels also emerge. Left- and right-wing political organisations in both countries show distinct weaknesses: while the Left in both countries is failing its *democratic* functions, suggesting a *lack of ideological cohesiveness*, the Right in both countries is more clearly failing its *liberal* function, suggesting a *lack of respect for pluralism*.

France: Mainstream party failures in an ageing democracy

French politics illustrate the cartelisation of mainstream politics common to long-standing, first-wave democracies, along with its nefarious consequences. Ideological convergence between the long-standing *Parti socialiste* (PS) and *Union pour un mouvement populaire* (UMP) has triggered citizen apathy and, ultimately, the marginalisation of these parties after 2017 (Lefebvre and Sawicki, 2006). Left and Right nevertheless experienced different types of democratic failings in past decades, from the PS's incapacity to adapt to a changing economic context, to the UMP giving in to the temptation of adopting the ideas and policies of the radical Right.

Citizen disengagement and defiance

France experienced regular alternations of power after the decline of the powerful Communist Party in the mid-1980s. The PS, created during the 1969 Alfortville Congress as successor to the *Section française de l'internationale ouvrière* (SFIO), won its first post-war majority in 1981, a second in 1988, a third in 1997, and a fourth in 2012. Its main centre-right opponent, the UMP at the time of my interviews, was created in November 2002 out of an alliance between the Gaullist *Rassemblement pour la République* (RPR) and two other parties of the Centre Right, *Démocratie libérale* (DL) and the *Union pour la démocratie française* (UDF) (Haegel, 2012). The Centre Right has had a post-war parliamentary majority in the periods 1986–8, 1993–7 and 2002–12. A third, centrist option has governed under Emmanuel Macron's *En marche!* party since 2017, although his politics are largely perceived as right-wing by French citizens (CEVIPOF, 2018, 21 January; Le Monde, 2018, 5 May; Motet, Darame and Carriat, 2021, 8 March). Over the past decades, the two former parties experienced the fate of many others in Europe: organisational and ideational change weakening their capacity for citizen mobilisation and leading to their near disappearance from 2017 onwards. While sudden, this collapse was long in the making.

French parties never had very large memberships compared to other Western European countries, but the relative share of party members has considerably declined over time – from close to 7.5 per cent of registered voters in 1950 to only 2 per cent by the mid-2000s (Scarrow, 2015, p. 70).[1] Abstention rose spectacularly over the same period, from a low point of 16.8 per cent in the first round of the 1978 parliamentary elections, to records of 51.3 per cent and 52.3 per cent in 2017 and 2022 respectively (Centre d'observation de la société, 2022). Abstention has also risen in the first round of presidential elections, from 15.2 per cent in 1965 to 25.1 per cent in 2022 (ibid.). The share of those lacking confidence in politicians also rose, from 55 per cent in 1985 to 75 per cent in 2001 (Balme, Marie and Rozenberg, 2003). Not only do political parties stand as French citizens' least trusted political institutions (Cheurfa and Chanvril, 2019), but France displays one of the worst records in the EU on this measure: only 7–10 per cent of French respondents trusted parties in the period 2013–19, against 14–19 per cent in the EU as a whole (Eurobarometer Interactive, 2020).

In parallel, the country witnessed a dealignment of voters' preferences with mainstream offers. The share of those who self-identify as centre-right, centrist or centre-left declined in the late twentieth century, while those who declare to be far-left or far-right have become more numerous (Marthaler, 2010, p. 92). Socialist and communist voters from working-class backgrounds flocked to the far-right *Rassemblement national* (RN; previously *Front national*) in the 1990s and 2000s (Mayer, 2013, pp. 170–1). Born in 1972, the RN's political weight has grown to such an extent in the past thirty years that many commentators speak of a 'tripolarisation' of the French party system (see, e.g., Ehrhard, 2016, pp. 96–102; Martin, 2015). The Front national has increased its share of the vote in almost every election since Marine Le Pen took over the party presidency in 2011 (for an overview, see Mayer, 2013, Startin, 2022).[2]

Organisational change and cartelisation

Defiance towards mainstream political parties affects most advanced democracies today (Dalton and Wattenberg, 2000; Mair, 2013a; Norris,

---

[1] The decline in absolute membership numbers is more contested: while Scarrow finds a rise in absolute numbers over the same period, Mair establishes a 64.5 per cent decline from 1978 to 1999 (Mair, 2006, p. 43; Scarrow, 2015, p. 71).
[2] Note the exception of a temporary dip in the RN's vote share during the 2007 presidential and parliamentary elections – discussed further below.

2010). Some explanations centre around the effects of macro-level, structural change on the political preferences and levels of engagement of citizens – so-called 'demand-side' theories (Hay, 2007). Rising levels of education, changing patterns of media consumption and new cleavages born out of globalisation create a context that favours anti-political sentiment and a demand for more radical political options (Bornschier, 2018; Kriesi et al., 2008; Norris, 1999). Yet scholars also point out how mainstream parties themselves have contributed to their own demise (Hay, 2007; Mair, 2013a).

The cartel-party thesis is a relevant blueprint for understanding changes in the supply of mainstream party politics in France, and their consequences (Katz and Mair, 1995, 2009). Katz and Mair's argue that, to survive in a changing electoral context, mainstream parties in Western Europe have colluded organisationally and ideologically since the 1980s. In France, as elsewhere, this has entailed a growing reliance on public funds. In 1988, new party finance laws gave a disproportionate advantage to the bigger political players in France. Between 2008 and 2013, for instance, the PS and UMP collected 61 per cent of the funds going to a total of twenty-eight main parties (François and Phélippeau, 2018, pp. 280–1).

In parallel, French parties have relied less and less on activists, the 'party on the ground', and increasingly on high civil servants as a pool of recruitment for leadership positions (Katz and Mair, 1995). Over the years, the French political class has grown increasingly homogenous in its socio-economic origin, education, career path and ethos (Birnbaum, 1994; Kreuzer and Stephan, 2003). Characteristically, while the prestigious *École nationale d'administration* (ENA) awards only eighty to ninety diplomas a year, half of all French presidents, a third of prime ministers, and one out of seven ministers on average have been graduates since 1958 (ibid,). Elected officials can also hold multiple offices simultaneously, which contributes to the predominance of lifelong political careers and a lack of diversity in individual trajectories. Together with heavy state funding, this results in a situation where French parties 'look more like state agencies based on politicians rather than supporters or citizen members' (François and Phélippeau, 2018, pp. 280–1).

Financial and administrative collusion also contributed to limit the diversity of political positions on offer within the political mainstream.[3]

---

[3] The number of partisan organisations, however, has risen: from twenty-eight to 381 between 1990 and 2012 (François and Phélippeau, 2018). Contrarily to the predictions of Katz and Mair, there is evidence that, even if increased party funding favours mainstream players, it also provides incentives for the birth of new parties (Scarrow, 2006).

Grassroots parties tend to be assertive ideologically and more geared towards policy than office or vote share – conversely state funding conditioned to vote share encourages parties to target the median voter, and thus dilute their appeals (Strom, 1990). Political professionalisation is also a vector of ideological convergence, with common trajectories leading to increasingly similar viewpoints among the French political class. Convergence on economic policy is evidenced by different available measures of ideological change. On the 200-point Manifesto Research Group (MRG) Left–Right scale, the distance between the PS and their mainstream right opponents shrank from 58.3 to 25.0 points between 1977 and 2002 (Marthaler, 2010, p. 87). Voters perceive this ideological convergence, yet are increasingly less likely to self-declare as centrist – suggesting that policy convergence is an additional factor distancing mainstream parties from citizens (Marthaler, 2010, p. 92).

Ideological change from Left to Right

Notwithstanding these common trends, mainstream parties in France have undergone different forms of ideological change on either side of the political spectrum. In France and elsewhere, globalisation has most clearly forced programmatic shifts within the social-democratic family (Callaghan, Fishman, Jackson and McIvor, 2009). Given left-wing ideology is fundamentally premised on the necessity for the state to rectify inequalities through intervention (Bobbio, 1995; Lukes, 2003), the restriction of state agency creates a unique challenge for these political parties. The impact of globalisation was harshly felt by the *Parti socialiste* in France, early on in its experience of political power (Goetschel and Morin, 2007; Lefebvre and Sawicki, 2006; Marthaler, 2010). In 1983, two years after having conquered political power for the first time since the 1930s, the PS disavowed its radical campaign promises. It chose a politics of austerity, and orchestrated mass privatisation and deregulation at a scale so far unprecedented in France. Multiple periods of cohabitation from the mid-1980s onwards, where the president and parliamentary majority do not share the same partisan affiliation, contributed to further reinforce common governing practices among mainstream parties.

In the past three decades, the PS has been deeply divided between its left wing, arguing for continued state intervention in the economy, and its Third Way, reformist division. Examples of these internal rifts include a party split over the 2005 referendum campaign on the European constitutional treaty, or the lack of cohesive support for the 2007 presidential candidate, Ségolène Royal (Blier, 2008; Crespy, 2008; Wagner, 2008).

Between 2012 and 2017, a sizable left-wing minority in the PS majority parliamentary group regularly voiced opposition to François Hollande's policy choices (for an example, see Bekmezian, 2014). This did not stop the party's market-liberal drift, with a more recent right-wing turn on socio-cultural issues as well (Cos, 2017). Under Hollande's presidency, France adopted tougher law and order and immigration legislation – for example citizenship withdrawal for bi-nationals convicted of terrorist activity. This resonates with a more global trend of social-democratic parties adapting to (what they perceive as) increasingly conservative public opinions (Bale, Green-Pedersen, Krouwel, Luther and Sitter, 2010; Wagner and Meyer, 2016).

LR has also experienced a right-wing drift since the late 1990s, in part to find new topics of differentiation with the Centre Left, in part to regain voters lost to the Radical Right (Berezin, 2013; Godin, 2013; Haegel, 2012, pp. 239–97). A shift to tougher positions on socio-cultural issues was most clearly embodied by Nicolas Sarkozy as minister of the interior under Jacques Chirac, and then president (2002–7 and 2007–2012). During this time, France became the first country in Europe to ban full-face veils in public spaces. During the 2007 electoral cycle, Sarkozy's hard stance was successful at limiting the success of the *Front national*. This temporarily comforted those who defend accommodation as an efficient strategy of the mainstream against radical parties (Meguid, 2008). In the longer run, however, this ideological shift proved counterproductive: not only did the *Front national* bounce back in 2012 and achieve unprecedented electoral scores in 2017 and 2022, but the UMP largely contributed to legitimise its ideas within society at large. Centre-right voters have consistently adopted more conservative positions on socio-cultural issues over the past decade (Fourquet and Gariazzo, 2013; Kantar-Sofres-One Point, 2017; TNS-Sofres, 2015). By 2017, these positions were very close to those of *Front national* voters (Gougou and Persico, 2017, pp. 317–18). Once again, developments in France mirror parallel changes elsewhere in Western Europe, where conservative parties radicalise their policy stance to win back voters. As in France, this strategy has comforted the agenda-setting power of radical right parties, without fundamentally challenging their ownership of key issues linked with cultural globalisation (Bale, 2003; Herman and Muldoon, 2018b; Krause, Cohen and Abou-Chadi, 2022; Meijers and Williams, 2020).

The electoral and organisational failure of French mainstream parties

The April 2017 elections can be seen as the logical end-point of these long-term trends. For the first time in the history of the Fifth Republic, neither mainstream party achieved a sufficient score to make it into the second round of the presidential election – a failure that was repeated in 2022. The PS candidate, Benoît Hamon, dropped below 10 per cent of the vote in March 2017 opinion polls, while centre-right candidate François Fillon, plagued by corruption scandals, consistently remained in third position. They were overtaken by Emmanuel Macron, a former PS minister of finance who founded the centrist party *En marche!* in April 2016, and by Marine Le Pen, who remained ahead of all other contenders in the polls until the final week of the campaign. The April 2017 presidential election gave the FN their best result yet, with 21.3 per cent of the vote in the first round and 33.9 per cent in the second round, nearly doubling its 2002 score. A month later, in May 2017, the PS and LR (previously UMP) obtained together only a third of seats in the French National Assembly. These trends have only deepened in 2022: the former dominant parties totalled 6.5 per cent of the vote in the first round of the presidential elections, while the second round confirmed the realignment of the French party system around centrist and far-right forces.

Both centrist organisations have faced significant financial and membership losses. Ironically perhaps, party finance rules that previously linked vote shares to funding, and therefore consolidated their position, have backfired. Both parties had to downsize significantly and sell their Parisian headquarters. The PS and LR also lost many high-profile politicians to *En marche!* (Legrand and Billard, 2017; Mourgue and Wesfreid, 2019). Among the 156 members of the PS's national bureau in 2015, 63 per cent left, and 30 per cent joined other parties (Bachelot, 2020). The *Mouvement des jeunes socialistes* (MJS), which this study focuses on, also collapsed when 300 local cadres along with 25 out of 30 members of the national board, stepped down in March 2018 to join *Génération.s.*, Benoit Hamon's new movement. Finally, the 2017 election cycle led to a further decline in membership numbers for both parties. PS membership nearly halved from 71,000 to 37,000 between 2015 and 2018 (Bachelot, 2020). As for LR, the number of fee-paying numbers dropped from 238,208 in 2015 to 58,000 in 2019 (Vigogne, 2020). While the future of these two parties is still uncertain, they are certainly undergoing one of the most profound crises in their history.

Both parties have failed as political organisations, but in the battle of ideas the Right as a larger political family has been much more successful than the Left. In line with a broader European trend, the French political spectrum has shifted rightwards in the past two decades. French voters not only self-position more to the right in 2021 than they did in 2017, but they are also more likely to perceive Islam as a threat, to reject immigration and to prioritise economic liberalism over social intervention (Delage, 2021). This is also apparent in electoral terms. Left-wing parties have drastically diminished their political representation, from winning majorities in the early 2000s to minor representation in the late 2010s. The Left has also failed to bring candidates into the second round of the 2017 and 2022 presidential elections. These shifts translate to the make-up of the French National Assembly, with left-wing parties occupying less than a third of total seats in the 2017 and 2022 legislatures.

Hungary: A young democracy threatened by populist polarisation

Hungary presents a very different political context, where populist polarisation has directly eroded relatively young democratic institutions. Much as in France, however, failure to mobilise and ideological incoherence have been most apparent on the Left, while a lack of respect for minority rights and constitutional settlements has characterised the Right.

From post-communist poster child to authoritarian backsliding

From 1989 to 2010, Hungary boasted two relatively stable party blocs (Benoit, 2003), with the MSzP and Fidesz as sole organisations capable of heading governmental coalitions. The MSzP was born out of the early conversion of the Hungarian Communist Party to social democracy in October 1989 (Grzymala-Busse, 2002, 2003; Kitschelt, Markowski, Mansfeldova and Toka, 1999). It achieved a majority in coalition with the *Szabad Demokraták Szövetsége* (SzDSz) in 1994, and then on its own in 2002 and 2006. The Fidesz was founded in 1988 as a party of anti-communists and liberal democrats. It soon replaced the *Magyar Demokrata Fórum* (MDF), in government from 1990 to 1993, as the main conservative political force in the party system. Fidesz governed Hungary from 1998 to 2002, in coalition with the Christian-democratic *Kereszténydemokrata Néppárt* (KDNP). Since 2010, this coalition has achieved three supermajorities (in 2014, 2018 and 2022), facilitated by institutional reforms tilting the level playing field in its favour.

The empirical studies of the early 2000s put Hungary within the bloc of democratisation frontrunners in the region, along with the Czech Republic, Estonia and Slovenia. With some exceptions (e.g. HZDS in Slovakia), mainstream parties in Central Europe preferred to follow rather than subvert the rules of the democratic game. By the mid-2000s, all future EU members had fulfilled Huntington's two-turnover test for democratic consolidation, undergoing two peaceful turnovers of ruling parties in transparent and fair elections (Huntington, 1991). Most displayed party systems with increasingly regular patterns of competition. Ex-communist parties seemed willing to reform (Bozóki and Ishiyama, 2002; Ishiyama, 1999), and radical-right parties lacked the broad support to be serious democratic threats (P. G. Lewis, 2001, p. 203; Millard, 2004, pp. 119–27).

The Hungarian case, especially, was considered a model of democratic consolidation. The country experienced one of the smoothest transitions to democracy in the region, developing a range of viable opposition parties as early as 1988 (Hungarian Parliament, 1989; Szikinger, 2001). The Hungarian Communist Party held its last congress and converted to social democracy that same month. The first democratic elections followed in May 1990, initiating a first peaceful alternation of power, with the centre-right MDF scoring 43 per cent of votes (Rothschild and Wingfield, 2000). By the late 1990s, Hungary displayed what many scholars classified as the most institutionalised party system in Central and Eastern Europe (CEE): strong elite competition, regular alternation between two main parties, and a rather robust institutional framework (Casal Bértoa and Mair, 2010; Grzymala-Busse, 2007; P. G. Lewis, 2006). Further, Hungary was a front runner in meeting the Copenhagen criteria for EU accession, conditions which included respect for the rule of law and human rights (Herman and Saltman, 2014). Relatively smooth accession negotiation, led by Fidesz from 1998, made Hungary part of the EU's first round of eastern expansion in 2004 (Batory, 2008).

These positive trends came to a halt after 2010. With 52.36 per cent of the vote and a supra-majority in Parliament, the party Fidesz engaged in what scholars have named *abusive legalism*, using procedures provided by the democratic framework itself and consistent with a nominal respect for the rule of law to undermine the integrity of democratic institutions (Herman and Muirhead, 2020; Scheppele, 2018). The most controversial measures have included a Media Law effective since early 2011; a new constitution applicable since early 2012; five major constitutional amendments to this fundamental law between 2012 and 2014; and a large number of organic laws that can be changed only with a new, supra-majority (Bánkuti, Halmai and Scheppele, 2012; Dani, 2013). These resulted in important challenges to the rule of law, including the Constitutional Court being dispossessed of its power of oversight, the Election Commission and new Media Authority being packed with Fidesz loyalists, and electoral district boundaries redrawn to the advantage of the ruling party.

At the time, Fidesz's measures attracted criticism from many independent international organisations for threatening the independence of the judiciary, the freedom of the press and the impartiality of electoral monitoring bodies (see Council of Europe, 2013; European Parliament, 2013; Norwegian Helsinki Committee, 2013; US Commission on Security and Cooperation in Europe, 2013). Since then, Hungary's democratic performance has continued to decline. On the Freedom House seven-point Nations in Transit (NIT) scale, for instance, Hungary collapsed from a high 5.61 to a low 3.96 since 2010, shifting from a Consolidated to a Semi-Consolidated democracy status in 2015, and officially becoming a Hybrid regime in 2020 (Freedom House, 2020).

Polarisation and right-wing radicalisation

Retrospectively, the academic consensus around the successful democratisation of Hungary appears ill-founded. Its main fault is to have focused on the most formal and institutional aspects of the country's regime (Herman, 2016). Political competition was robust, but the party system also showed signs of acute polarisation as soon as 2002 – a particularly favourable ground for democratic breakdown (McCoy et al., 2018). Political debates were predominantly structured around issues of identity, the Right defending a form of nativist nationalism, and the Left adherence to European values and institutions (Palonen, 2009). These socio-cultural divisions considerably widened in the 2000s. Drawing on the European Elections Survey (EES), Vegetti shows that, when comparing citizens' perception of polarisation, Hungary shifts from the fifth to the second most polarised European polity between 2004 and 2014 (Vegetti, 2019, p. 80). This was accompanied by an increasingly poor quality of political deliberation, with strong antagonisms and an inability to compromise building on both sides of the political spectrum.

The Fidesz and MSzP have different responsibilities in this state of affairs. The conservative party experienced a rightward shift from the mid-1990s onwards, gradually adopting a primarily national-conservative platform (Fowler, 2004). Its 1998 victory was won thanks to this agenda, with an emphasis on the importance of religion, tradition and family (Bozóki and Kriza, 2008; Palonen, 2006). But the party's defeat in the 2002 elections triggered a change towards an even more radical form of right-wing nationalism. Party leader Viktor Orbàn accused his opponents of having rigged the results and claimed that 'the nation cannot be in the opposition' – contesting in clear terms the legitimacy of opponents to rule (Müller, 2011, p. 6). Over time, this rhetoric became substantially more populist, Eurosceptic and conspiracist. Orbàn claimed increasingly frequently to be the sole defender of the Hungarian people against an alliance of anti-national elites (Csehi, 2019; Csehi and Zgut, 2020; Enyedi, 2015a). In parallel, the party started championing a form of economic patriotism in industrial and agricultural issues (Centre for Fair Political Analysis, 2013; Tavits and Letki, 2009).

Fidesz's capacity for citizen mobilisation grew substantially during this period. In opposition from 2002 to 2010, the party became one of the most socially embedded party organisations in post-communist Europe (Enyedi, 2015b; Enyedi and Linek, 2008; Greskovits, 2020). Fidesz increased its membership numbers from 10,000 in 1995 to 40,300 in 2010, only declining to 36,800 in 2015 (Kovarek and Soós, 2017, p. 188; Saltman, 2014, pp. 105–6). In parallel, local party branches increased from 400 to 1,050 between 2001 and 2005 (Enyedi and Linek, 2008, pp. 462–3). This contrasts with the substantial decline of MSzP's ageing membership, from 50,000 in 1990 to 20,000 in 2015 (Kovarek and Soós, 2017, p. 188).

Fidesz also encouraged, funded and coordinated the Civic Circles movement, a network of right-wing local associations, organisations and media. As summarised by Greskovitz, civic circles were responsible for organising 'cultural, educational, charity, leisure, and contentious activities' along conservative and religious lines (Greskovits, 2020, pp. 251–2). While many civic circles were not officially registered, there were over 11,000 circles and 163,000 known members at its peak – a number that exceeds the membership of all other Hungarian parties taken together (ibid, p. 252). Civic Circles organised 4,800 official events between July 2002 and April 2006 alone, in a country of fewer than 10 million inhabitants (Greskovits, 2020, p. 250). Fidesz also coordinated a number of spectacular actions, such as several mass rallies of over 100 000 participants in 2006, as well as four large-scale petitions collecting close to a million signatures (Enyedi and Linek, 2008, p. 464).

These strategies played a crucial role in the party's impressive electoral success in 2010, a gain of over 10 points compared to the previous 2006 parliamentary elections. This provided the party with the power to carry out sweeping institutional reforms. Since then, Fidesz has belied academic expectations about the tempering effects of governmental incumbency on populist forces (Hegedüs, 2019). It has further radicalised its discourse and practices, with Orbàn openly defending the need 'to abandon liberal methods and principles of organising a society' and to build an 'illiberal state' in Hungary (Orbán, 2014). The party has also consolidated its popular support. By June 2020, after winning two-thirds majorities in three elections in a row, 60 per cent of committed voters in Hungary still expressed a preference for Fidesz over other parties (Medián, 2020). Crucially, the share of Hungarians expressing trust in political parties as a whole has also increased during this period, from about 14 per cent to 30 per cent between November 2013 and November 2019 (Eurobarometer Interactive, 2020).

The structural weakness of the Left

Fidesz's resounding electoral victories also signal the failure of the MSzP to play its role as main opposition force. In 2010, the former Communist Party achieved a mere 19.3 per cent of votes, losing 24 points since 2006. The party never recovered from this fall. After the election, sections of the MSzP splintered and formed two alternative parties: the *Demokratikus Koalíció*, led by Ferenc Gyurcsány, and *Együtt 2014*, also headed by an ex-MSzP-nominated prime minister, Gordon Bajnai (Saltman, 2012). While the three parties reached a coalition agreement on 14 January 2014, following an arduous cycle of negotiations started in April 2013, their common platforms still only convinced 25.9 per cent of voters in the spring 2014 elections. By 2018, most of these parties could not agree on a common platform and ran separately, resulting in a score of 11.31 per cent for the MSzP. By June 2020, only 4 per cent of regular voters expressed a preference for the MSzP over other parties (Medián, 2020).

Long-term, structural weaknesses have affected the party's ability to build an effective opposition to Fidesz in recent years. The party largely failed to redefine an already thin ideological corpus following Hungary's accession to the EU and had few ammunition to counter Fidesz's radical national conservatism. In the early 1990s, the MSzP was eager to prove that it embraced the Western 'way of life' and positioned itself as a defender of the country's future within the EU (Grzymala-Busse, 2002, 2003; Kitschelt et al., 1999). In power from 1994 to 1998, it orchestrated the end of the socialist economy. As in most other Central European countries, the reformed Communist Party adopted a free-market approach to economic policy, involving mass privatisation and liberalisation, resulting in a sharp increase in inequalities (Evans and Whitefield, 1993, 1995; Grzymala-Busse, 2003; Kitschelt, 1995; Kitschelt et al., 1999; Tavits and Letki, 2009). In practice, very little has distinguished the economic policies of Hungarian parties from one another (Vegetti, 2019, p. 86). While this consensus ultimately contributed to deliver EU accession in 2004, the party largely failed to produce an alternative vision once this goal was reached.

This ideational weakness made the party particularly vulnerable to a series of crises in the 2000s. Following the April 2006 elections, the press unveiled several scandals involving the MSzP and its former coalition partner, the SzDSz (Müller, 2011). The most detrimental affair surfaced in September 2006, when a speech given by Prime Minister Ferenc Gyurcsány was leaked by the nationalist Magyar Rádio. Speaking in front of the MSzP congress in May, he admitted that his party had lied about the country's financial situation during the electoral campaign. This sparked mass protests in Hungary and riots in Budapest, and has since been brandished regularly by Fidesz as unquestionable evidence of its opponents' duplicity. The 2007 financial crisis hit only a year later, with disastrous consequences for the already weakened Hungarian economy. The MSzP government had to accept a rescue package from the IMF, given the accumulation of large state deficits since the early 2000s, and to adopt a tight regime of austerity, with important cuts to social and unemployment benefits. Economic mismanagement and corruption scandals thus created the perfect storm for a resounding electoral defeat in 2010 and durably shattered the MSzP's political legitimacy. These failures largely contributed to Fidesz maintaining its two-thirds majority in the past decade, and to Hungary becoming a much-cited example of modern democratic backsliding (Bermeo, 2016).

Democratic partisanship in France and Hungary

From the comparative overview above, I draw some cautious, preliminary conclusions on the democratic performance of the four parties under study. In France, both parties have struggled to fulfil their *democratic* function, as shown by their growing failure to represent and mobilise French citizens in recent years. Based on the framework of democratic partisanship, this may correspond to a deficit in *ideological cohesiveness*: a growing incapacity to coherently articulate distinct programmes of governments based on a specific interpretation of foundational values. This issue, however, is clearly exacerbated on the Left, which struggles to adapt its century-old ideology to an increasingly globalised political context and has more radically decreased its political representation overall. A similar imbalance is apparent in Hungary where, in recent years, the MSzP has demonstrated greater difficulties than its conservative counterpart, Fidesz, to put forward a coherent programmatic offer and mobilise citizens on this basis.

In both countries, the right-hand side of the political spectrum displays different types of weaknesses. Crucially, they struggle to uphold the *liberal* function I ascribed to political parties: the safeguarding of minority rights, individual freedoms and party pluralism more broadly. These trends may cautiously be associated with deficits in *respect for pluralism*, and in turn a willingness to impose holist partisan views onto the community as a whole. In France, this is apparent in LR's adoption and legitimisation of views promoted by the populist Radical Right. This issue is exacerbated in Hungary, where Fidesz's illiberalism has led to a radical dismantling of the country's constitutional settlement.

Based on a close reading of secondary literature, these conclusions remain to be substantiated with primary data. The original research in the remainder of this book triangulates these results, exploring how changes at the macro-level of party systems translate at the micro-level of party member discourse. Are similar variations on the two dimensions of democratic partisanship apparent from party member discourse?

An Academic in the Partisan Arena

Many of these developments were ongoing when I started my fieldwork in 2013. Living between Paris and Budapest, I gained first-hand experience of how partisans understand their political context. I talked to dozens of party members in party conventions, bars, cafés, community centres and local party sections about their political views. During this time, I conducted the twenty-eight two-hour-long discussions with activists analysed in this study.[4] With four to six participants in each focus group, a total of 117 young partisans made this research possible, in their vast majority members of the youth branches of the parties under study. In France, these included the PS's *Mouvement des jeunes socialistes* (MJS) and the UMP's *Jeunes populaires* (JP). In Hungary, the MSzP's *Societas* as well as members of allied, centre-left organisations, Fidesz's youth section, *Fidelitas*, and the allied KDNP's *Ifjúsági Kereszténydemokrata Szövetség* (IKSZ).[5]

Differentiated experiences of fieldwork

I learned a lot about my subject simply *being* in the field to recruit participants for this study. Participation observation, or 'exposure to or involvement in the day-to-day or routine activities of participants in the researcher setting' (Schensul and LeCompte, 1999), was not my main

---

[4] In total, I organised twenty discussions in France and eighteen in Hungary – but only seven UMP groups. I therefore cut down the total sample to twenty-eight to have a comparable number of groups from each party and country. I selected the groups I would study before analysing the transcripts, putting aside those with features that made them outliers: with party sympathisers rather than members, far shorter in length or with fewer (two to three) participants.

[5] For a breakdown of participants by party organisation, see Figure 1.1.

method of research. My differentiated experiences in both partisan circles still proved a precious source of evidence. Recruiting participants was uncomplicated in France, difficult in Hungary. How party members reacted to my efforts at recruitment and to my presence in their political circles gave me some first, invaluable lessons on how they conceived of their role, and how they understood politics more generally.

To recruit participants, I first sent emails to the heads of all local sections of the youth party organisations in Paris and Budapest, those in charge of a specific geographical district. These emails provided details on myself and my institutional affiliation to the London School of Economics, my research interest in how party members in France and Hungary understand democratic politics, as well as a broad overview of the guidelines for discussion (see Chapter 3 and Appendix 1). The emails also guaranteed participants, full anonymity,[6] and invited intermediaries to meet beforehand. I also participated in different types of political events, from a local town hall meeting in Paris's 18th arrondissement to the MSzP 2013 national congress. For every group, one activist recruited three to five party members in their political circle – a snowballing method that ensured participants were familiar with one another.

My initial contacts with French and Hungarian local party sections generated very different responses. In France, my attempts proved particularly successful. Out of eighty-nine individual activists contacted, forty-one answered my email, and twenty accepted to help me organise a group discussion. The interviews were then all conducted within a period of two months. This was a good turnout, especially given I offered no financial incentive to participants (this is common in many focus group studies; see, e.g., Duchesne and Haegel, 2004; Gamson, 1992; Perrin, 2006; White, 2011b). In all but one case, intermediaries did not think it necessary to meet with me before helping me organise a discussion. None of these intermediaries knew me beforehand, and I was never introduced to potential interviewees via pre-existing, common acquaintances. In only three cases did one group trigger the recruitment of another, with participants suggesting other activists I could contact.

In Budapest, I had to send twice as many emails to organise a similar number of discussions. I contacted 191 party activists, sixty-seven answered but only eighteen of these exchanges led to a group interview. This process also required twice the amount of time, four months instead

---

[6] Participant names have been changed throughout this book, and any other identifying information removed. I did not collect information on gender identity or pronouns, and use they/them to refer to all participants.

of two in France. It also involved more personal networking. six out of the eighteen willing intermediaries asked to meet me beforehand, and for fourteen of these eighteen interviews, introductions by third parties were necessary. These included a minority of previously interviewed activists, but mostly external actors to the youth organisations: journalists, scholars, political analysts and higher-profile politicians.

The politics of impartiality

The attitude of French and Hungarian party members towards my research was also very different. In France, party members appeared to participate out of curiosity, or willingness to share their experiences as party members. In their emails, many showed enthusiasm to take part in a facilitated political discussion. Others shared that they saw my academic interest as validation of their civic action.

In Hungary, on the other hand, participants seemed to expect not only validation but also a platform from which their partisan message would be given visibility. Fidesz participants especially showed signs of considering the study as a way of communicating their viewpoint to the West. In their interactions with me, they regularly positioned themselves as ambassadors of their own party, with a duty to correct misrepresentations of their government's actions. Some explicitly offered this argument as a reason for participation. Conversely, however, fear that their message could be misrepresented to a Western audience might have contributed to the greater difficulty I had recruiting participants in Hungary. Such suspicion by Fidesz activists would be understandable. By 2013, the party's institutional reforms had already come under considerable fire from EU institutions and the Western press. According to one journalist I met at the time, Fidesz was so concerned with maintaining its image abroad that no party official in Budapest had accepted interview requests by a foreign correspondent since the 2010 elections.[7] Later on, colleagues of mine also shared difficulties they encountered trying to interview Fidesz officials as compared to other CEE political leaders.

---

[7] According to this source, Fidesz officials favour giving interviews in Brussels, or abroad, for several reasons. First, this shields them from the attention of the national press and allows Fidesz to maintain a double-discourse that is more conciliatory abroad than within domestic politics. Second, in contrast to foreign correspondents in Hungary, foreign journalists abroad are less likely to speak Hungarian or specialise in Hungarian politics – which also makes them potentially less critical.

While resistance was weaker among MSzP recruits, I was also faced with a certain level of suspicion from potential participants on the Left. Some openly voiced fear to my intermediaries that I might be an undercover journalist, an informer for the Fidesz government, or perhaps even a spy from *Demokratikus Koalíció* (DK), one of their party's electoral allies![8] Again, left-wing party members had empirical ground for such fears. In Hungary, leaks in the media by investigative journalists and members of the opposition regularly spark political scandals. Party members know that their rivals will go to great lengths to destroy their reputation. Considering the next parliamentary elections were held approximately six months after my fieldwork, potential participants may have worried about an involuntary leak of important information, or that I would twist their words in recounting them.

This situation made my position as an impartial researcher more difficult to negotiate in Hungary as compared to France. In both countries, it was crucial that I avoided taking sides in my interactions with them. In line with the discussion guidelines (Chapter 3), I aimed to strike a balance between transparency and ensuring participants would not pre-empt my findings in a way that might bias them. I stressed the cross-national nature of my study and that I was also talking to their opponents. I also made clear my focus on how party members understand democratic politics, and my lack of interest in compromising pieces of information about their organisation. In France, my position as an academic observer was easily accepted, and few participants gave me the impression that they were expecting me to take sides. But in Hungary, these guarantees were insufficient: it became quickly apparent that participants wanted clearer proof that I was sympathetic to their cause.

These dynamics considerably slowed down my research in Hungary, especially with Fidesz activists. Following my first wave of emails, I obtained more positive responses from the Right than the Left of the political spectrum. I had already planned a couple of groups with Fidesz activists when, approximately two weeks after my arrival, I received an unsolicited email from a national-level official in the *Fidelitas* youth organisation, asking me for information about the study – which I provided. When I received no further answer from this stranger, it became clear my response had not been to their satisfaction. Over the following two days, I received cancellation notices

---

[8] The slow process of recruitment among young socialists, however, also seemed to result from a great amount of organisational inertia, and the smaller size of the network of young party members in this ageing reformed communist party.

from four out of five of the Fidesz activists who had previously agreed to meet. They provided various excuses, but all suggested I write to the central office of the youth organisation for further help. One activist was more explicit about their need for hierarchical approval, stressing that they 'cannot give out an opinion without the leaders' permission'. A few weeks later, some of my contacts within right-wing circles confirmed that local section leaders had received an email from their hierarchy discouraging them from participating. This email referred to me as a fake – possibly a journalist or opposition member pretending to be what I was not.

Building trust

Following this, I had to embark on several weeks of lobbying within right-wing circles. I met journalists and researchers sympathetic to Fidesz, as well as members of the KDNP, and managed to convince them I was trustworthy and my project had academic merit. Some accepted to vouch for me among those they knew within the party organisation. In this process, I discovered my Franco-Hungarian dual nationality and intermediate level Hungarian could play in my favour. While the story of my family was a topic of interest on both sides of the political spectrum, it seemed to give right-wing individuals reasons to believe they could win me over to their cause. Too foreign, I would have been perceived as necessarily supportive of the Left and critical of the Right. But if I had been a perfectly fluent, resident Hungarian, I could not have credibly claimed a non-partisan position. Politicised Hungarian citizens either violently reject the Fidesz government or are strongly supportive of it. Being neither fully Hungarian nor fully foreign meant my position was less predetermined in the eyes of my interlocutors, thus making me at least in principle winnable to their cause. When meeting new contacts on the Right, I increasingly tied my academic interest to my origins, made a point not to switch to English even when I struggled to find my words, and presented myself as eager to learn from my interlocutors.

These efforts ultimately paid off. Not only did group discussions start snowballing after a couple of weeks, but I ended up interviewing many of the Fidesz activists who had initially cancelled meetings when faced with the disapproval of their hierarchy. Given they would unlikely have gone against the advice of the organisation, it is plausible that someone higher up reversed their position and signalled that members could talk to me. Further evidence for this includes the participation of higher-ranked activists in some of the last group discussions. I even started being invited to Fidesz-organised events. My status seemed to have shifted away from that of potential political threat.

The way my research was perceived best explains differences between both fieldwork experiences. In France, my position as an impartial researcher went mostly uncontested. In this situation, taking part in the study was seen as an opportunity to contribute to the progress of knowledge. In Budapest, party members apprehended my work less as a scientific endeavour and more as a politically relevant activity: either an opportunity to push a certain agenda, or a potential threat to the party's image. This dichotomy is best understood in light of the extreme animosity which exists between both political camps in Hungary. In the current context, *one can only take sides*. Because I gave no signs of political support for either party, because activists had no guarantee that I was *with them*, I was easily suspected of being *against them*.

It was difficult to gain the trust of Hungarian activists, specifically on the Right, but the discussions themselves were evidence of success. Once we were together and the ice was broken, participants in both countries engaged in lively discussions which they seemed to enjoy. Many explicitly thanked me, with some sharing they otherwise lacked opportunities to reflect on their political engagement. As stressed by Alexis, an UMP activist 'there should be more debates like these, more introspection on our own thoughts, on how we feel about these things'. A number of participants in both countries, including from Fidesz, took pictures of the cards before we parted, and told me they planned to use a similar system for discussions with fellow activists in the future. These were all welcome signs that activists had taken ownership of their involvement in the study.

The Partisan View on Party Democracy

In the following section I home in further on how French and Hungarian activists understand the relationship between party politics and democracy within their own political system. In line with the secondary literature, two contrasted views of partisan politics emerge. In France, activists see partisan politics primarily as an appeased exchange of contrasting views essential to democratic life. In Hungary, participants describe partisan politics as a violent altercation between emotional positions, creating dynamics that destroy the very fabric of society. While the former regret at times excessive convergence between parties, the latter wish for more appeased interactions between opponents.

Shades of political disagreement

French party members see their political system as far less polarised than Hungarian activists do their own. In fact, many French activists, especially on the Left, highlight an excess of agreement between political parties, echoing the pitfalls of ideological convergence highlighted by the literature. This was apparent very early on in the discussions, as soon as participants started reacting to my initial instructions to classify prompt cards and associated policy issues according to their salience. Fourteen PS participants asked questions directed at the *criteria* according to which cards should be classified (instances coded QUESTIONING CRITERIA) and suggested two different logics of classification: one according to the ideals of political parties; the other according to what these do in practice. For instance, one young socialist, Sébastien, asked me whether the group should classify the cards 'according to what the PS actually believes, or [according to] the action of the [current] government?' In a similar vein, another participant, Samir, asked whether the classification should be 'UMP and PS, or Left and Right?'

For PS activists, mainstream parties might disagree ideologically, but they still largely adopt the same governmental practices. For a number of them, therefore, real-world party competition does not obey the logic dictated by the Left–Right dichotomy. This issue created lively debates within groups, as the following dialogue demonstrates:

> **Quentin:** But then the question is . . . is there a consensus . . . there is the practice, what we see from outside, but the degree of . . . Or is there a real consensus on the ideas? Because if that's the question . . .
>
> **Louis:** For me the question is, if we take the facts, the decisions taken, concretely, are different things being done.
>
> **Edgar:** But then, let's end the discussion now, the discussion is going to go real quick, because in that case we agree, there is agreement on every question actually, because . . . [. . .] We're not going to start a fiscal revolution! No sorry . . . on sexual minorities, maybe we can bring some change but . . . on environmental issues, we're going to do the same, on Law and Order, with Valls,[9] he's the Secretary of State for Home Affairs? We will do exactly the same!

Although less commonly, some UMP participants also emphasise how similarities between both parties complicated the card classification exercise for them. Some associate the issue not with a form of ideological

---

[9] Manuel Valls was PS minister of the interior between 2012 and 2014 and is known for having adopted a 'tough' position on crime and immigration. From 31 March 2014 to 6 December 2016, he held the position of prime minister under François Hollande's presidency.

convergence, but with the adoption by the Left of right-wing policies – as exemplified below:

> **Anaïs:** I find it quite difficult to do this classification because . . . we had the impression that the Left really wanted to differentiate itself, at least a few months ago. Now I find that on a lot of questions the government has tried to get closer to the position that we ourselves were defending. So I find it quite complicated to do this classification because a lot of this is blurry, and a lot of policies are ambiguous [. . .]

As for Hungarian participants, they struggle with the exact opposite issue: to find topics of agreement with their opponents. I coded for twenty-one instances of partisans saying they were unable to identify issues of low salience in their political system (instances coded NO CONSENSUAL CARDS). A young Hungarian socialist, Levente, sighed after considering the cards for a few minutes: 'In fact, I cannot find anything on which we would even remotely agree [with Fidesz]!' The very idea that parties might agree on some issues seemed unsettling to some Hungarian participants.

These differences are also apparent once we compare patterns of card classifications between French and Hungarian groups (see Table 4.1).[10] I attributed the code CONFLICTUAL when participants consider a

---

[10] Most tables in the following chapters follow the model of Table 4.1. The rows titled 'counts' reference the number of individual instances of partisan discourse with which I associated given codes. For Table 4.1, these include the numbers of assessments by French and Hungarian participants coded either 'CONSENSUAL', 'MIXED' or 'CONFLICTUAL'.

A code is applied to a portion of text (and therefore becomes an 'instance coded') when at least one participant puts forward a substantiated argument that supports the definition of the code (see Appendix 2 for a more detailed discussion of this point and the full code book). For instance, if a participant were to mention in passing that a given topic generates disagreement, without justifying their claim, this portion of discourse would not be associated with an independent code 'CONFLICTUAL'. If a second participant developed this argument and justified why the topic could be considered as one of disagreement, the code 'CONFLICTUAL' would be attributed to their claim. This portion of the transcript would then be counted as an 'instance coded' in Table 4.1 above.

The rows titled 'share of total' indicate the share of instances associated with a specific code within the total number of instances coded considered in the same table. In this case, each percentage indicates the share of any specific type of assessment by participants on the degree of disagreement between political parties within their total number of assessments. For instance, in 391 of their 542 total assessments, or in 72 per cent of all cases, Hungarian participants argued that the topics at hand generated disagreement between political parties. Given the small numbers involved and the fact my interest is in broad variations between partisan groups, percentages are expressed with no decimals.

given topic as one of disagreement between political parties and the code CONSENSUAL when participants agree that a given topic gathers relative consensus between political parties. Finally, I coded as MIXED instances where partisans issue a qualified judgement on the consensual or conflictual nature of a given topic, emphasising both similarities and differences in the positions of political parties on a given topic.

French participants are equally prone to consider the topics under discussions as gathering agreement or partial agreement between political parties as they are to consider them to fundamentally divide political parties (see Table 4.1). They can establish a hierarchy between the different cards and distinguish between topics according to their salience (see Table 4.2).

The larger share of MIXED assessments within French groups – where participants produce a qualified assessment of either the consensual or conflictual nature of a given topic – also reflects a more consensual view of the political world. In some of these instances, party members highlight how certain cleavages cut across dividing lines between Left and Right. Within French transcripts, I identified twenty-nine references to cross-cutting cleavages, approximately two references per group. This comes through in the following example, where a young PS activist insists that environmental politics does not strictly separate Left and Right:

> **Patrick:** When it comes to environmental issues, this is a card I set apart because [...] it's a transversal theme, that does not divide between the Left and the Right but divides the Left and Right internally. There are right-wing people against nuclear power as there are

Table 4.1: Assessments by French and Hungarian participants of the degree of partisan disagreement on the topics discussed (instances coded)

		FRANCE	HUNGARY
CONSENSUAL	Counts	115	87
	Share of total	22%	16%
MIXED	Counts	133	64
	Share of total	26%	12%
CONFLICTUAL	Counts	266	391
	Share of total	52%	72%
Total	Counts	514	542
	Share of total	100%	100%

left-wing people. There are right-wing people who are very concerned with everything that has to do with the renovation of buildings, social housing access [. . .] And on the Right and on the Centre Right there are some [people] – I'm thinking namely about Jean-Louis Borloo[11] – who will be much more concerned about these questions than many people on the Left [. . .]

In contrast, Hungarian participants judge the issues under discussion to be ones of agreement or partial agreement in only 28 per cent of the cases (see Table 4.1). In the majority of groups only one or two themes are classified as unquestionably consensual – the card 'Environment' generally among them (see Table 4.3). From here, participants most often declare that they can not find any more consensual themes and that all other cards were topics of dispute. As stated by Fidesz member Olivia: '(Consensual topics) in Hungary? Not really, this is not that kind of a country.' Most of the time, I have to ask repeatedly whether there are 'any more topics of agreement to be discussed, as they jump very quickly to what they see as more controversial issues.

Hungarian partisans then use several strategies to classify the cards. In some cases, participants distinguish between moderately and highly conflictual topics, but this distinction was not coded for specifically. In most instances, however, they do not establish a hierarchy among the cards, and proceed to explain why they consider each topic to be one of major disagreement. If we break down these assessments topic by topic, the result is that it is more difficult than in the French case to identify those cleavages that Hungarian participants consider as most salient (see Table 4.2 and Table 4.3). Indeed, seven out of twelve topics were classified as 'conflictual' over 70 per cent of the time, and eleven out of twelve over 60 per cent of the time.

The normative value of disagreement

Beyond these assessments of how polarised their political system is, what normative judgements do partisans cast on these states of play? Do they view political agreement, or its lack thereof, as a positive for democracy

---

[11] From 2012 to 2014, Jean-Louis Marie Borloo was president of the centrist *Union des démocrates et indépendants* (UDI), a party which has regularly allied with the UMP. He also was minister of environment, energy, sustainable development and the sea under President Nicolas Sarkozy from 2007 until 2010 and is known for his strong positioning on environmental issues.

Table 4.2: Classifications by French participants of the different topics under discussion (instances coded)

		CONSENSUAL	MIXED	CONFLICTUAL	Total
EU	Counts	25	16	3	44
	Share of total	57%	36%	7%	100%
PUBLIC FINANCE	Counts	15	17	7	39
	Share of total	38%	44%	18%	100%
ENVIRONMENT	Counts	15	14	9	38
	Share of total	39%	37%	24%	100%
PUBLIC MORALITY	Counts	19	9	9	37
	Share of total	52%	24%	24%	100%
PUBLIC SERVICES	Counts	10	8	18	36
	Share of total	28%	22%	50%	100%
INDUSTRIAL POLICY	Counts	3	6	10	19
	Share of total	16%	32%	53%	100%
MINORITIES	Counts	10	11	25	46
	Share of total	22%	24%	54%	100%
EMPLOYMENT	Counts	5	15	25	45
	Share of total	11%	33%	56%	100%
IMMIGRATION	Counts	5	16	31	52
	Share of total	10%	31%	60%	100%
GENDER	Counts	3	17	37	57
	Share of total	5%	30%	65%	100%
LAW AND ORDER	Counts	8	10	36	54
	Share of total	15%	19%	67%	100%
TAXATION	Counts	9	11	55	75
	Share of total	12%	15%	73%	100%

Table 4.3: Classifications by Hungarian participants of the different topics under discussion (instances coded)

		CONSENSUAL	MIXED	CONFLICTUAL	Total
ENVIRONMENT	Counts	16	1	5	22
	Share of total	73%	5%	23%	100%
LAW AND ORDER	Counts	5	12	30	47
	Share of total	11%	26%	64%	100%
MINORITIES	Counts	13	2	28	43
	Share of total	30%	5%	65%	100%
PUBLIC FINANCES	Counts	2	5	14	21
	Share of total	10%	24%	67%	100%

EMPLOYMENT	Counts	9	3	26	38
	Share of total	24%	8%	68%	100%
EU	Counts	5	10	37	52
	Share of total	10%	19%	71%	100%
INDUSTRIAL POLICY	Counts	7	8	40	55
	Share of total	13%	15%	73%	100%
PUBLIC MORALITY	Counts	9	4	37	50
	Share of total	18%	8%	74%	100%
NATION IN POLITICS	Counts	12	5	49	66
	Share of total	18%	8%	74%	100%
INSTITUTIONS	Counts	6	7	40	53
	Share of total	11%	13%	75%	100%
PUBLIC SERVICES	Counts	6	3	28	37
	Share of total	16%	8%	76%	100%
TAXATION	Counts	3	4	60	67
	Share of total	4%	6%	90%	100%

as a whole? Here I draw on the reflections of party members during the last part of the focus group, in which I asked partisans to weigh the democratic value of political agreement and disagreement, and to share personal experiences of inter-partisan dialogue (see the discussion guidelines in Chapter 3). In both cases, I coded for the positive and negative connotations that party members associated with political disagreement.

The French perspective: Disagreement as a democratic principle

As shown in Table 4.4, French participants are close to four times more likely to either point to the benefits of political disagreement or the pitfalls of political agreement than Hungarian participants were. Party

Table 4.4: Value associated by French and Hungarian participants to political disagreement and agreement (instances coded)

		FRANCE	HUNGARY
VALUE OF DISAGREEMENT	Counts	39	11
	Share of total	54%	18%
VALUE OF AGREEMENT	Counts	33	50
	Share of total	46%	82%
Total	Counts	72	61
	Share of total	100%	100%

members in France regularly express their belief that political disagreement is a necessary and positive feature of a democratic society – much in line with the literature on democratic partisanship (see Chapter 2). In the following example, UMP participants explicitly emphasise that democracy entails the confrontation of alternative programmes of government:

> **Nelson:** Actually, compromise cannot be found. I think that there are issues on which we will not be able to find a compromise.
>
> **Agnès:** And fortunately so. Because it's . . . it's the foundation of democracy, I mean, if we agreed on everything, it would be . . . I mean, I don't know. It leads to totalitarianism.
>
> **Jeanne:** Well, others speak of unity. . .
>
> **Nelson:** Well, I don't know, because we speak of conflict t— I would say we need more alternatives. See, because conflict is a bit . . . warlike, it's maybe just that when it comes to discourse we should actually have the possibility of comparing different discourses on every topic [. . .]

PS participants also value partisan disagreement for its own sake. In the following dialogue, Didier and René equate democracy with a continuous struggle in which each party tries to convince others of the validity of their views, yet each party is aware that their views cannot and should not fully triumph:

> **Didier:** That's it actually, I don't really see the point of consensus . . . For me, politics is a struggle, it's [about] creating cleavages. That being said, as we are in a democratic society I have no enemies, I don't have . . . I mean, if the person I'm faced with disagrees with me, I will talk with them, I will try to convince them, but I won't reach a consensus [. . .] I'm not engaged in politics to find a consensus actually.
>
> **René:** It may seem a bit paradoxical because we each promote . . . At first glance, one could think that people get engaged in politics to see their ideas triumph. So the more they triumph, the more we should be glad.
>
> **Didier:** But at the same time, the day when they triumph completely, and everyone agrees, it's the end of democracy because that would mean . . . We can't always think 100 per cent in the same way [. . .]

In fact, PS participants often lament *insufficient* disagreement between parties, and wish that their own organisation would do more to nourish a healthy confrontation of ideas. In the following statement, a young PS activist is talking about the topics they wish were more salient than they currently are:

> **Patrick:** All of them! All of them, to be plain. Because the Left should be much more feisty on [the question of] public morality, the Left should be much more feisty in its discourse and in its actions when it comes to immigration, on [the question of] secularism, on [the question of] protectionism [...] On European integration we need to go much further, and do things very differently, on environmental issues we need to be much more aggressive. On every card today there is not enough [of a] cleavage [...]

French partisans also see the value of inter-partisan dialogue in their day-to-day life. As shown in Table 4.5, over two-thirds of the experiences recounted by French participants are positive or described in neutral terms (65.5 per cent of instances coded in PS transcripts and 69.9 per cent of UMP transcripts). In many of these accounts, participants emphasise they benefit from these exchanges.

Some French party members describe discussions with political opponents as a necessary exercise for someone engaged in politics. In these cases, they insist on how such encounters allow them to refine their own views and arguments. The following statement from a young PS activist is a good example:

> **Edgard:** [...] I like to be confronted on these things, it forces you to refine your arguments as much as possible. To be not just capable of saying ... 'we should fight against unemployment because unemployment

Table 4.5: References by French and Hungarian participants to their positive or negative personal experiences of inter-partisan dialogue (instances coded)

		FRANCE	HUNGARY
NEGATIVE EXPERIENCE	Counts	17	25
	Share of total	33%	49%
POSITIVE EXPERIENCE	Counts	35	26
	Share of total	67%	51%
Total	Counts	52	51
	Share of total	100%	100%

is bad' and . . . Nowadays, I'm working for Élisabeth Guigou,[12] and these are [the type of] things one could say during a campaign period. So when I go to Seine-Saint-Denis[13] and say, 'What we want is to fight unemployment, because unemployment means no jobs.' Well, great, you will have huge support from the whole population who will applaud you, etc., it's really easy. But try to say the same thing in the 7th arrondissement,[14] to guys who tell you, 'Well, I'm not unemployed!'

The experiences of UMP participants are recounted in similar terms. In the following example, Lois emphasises not only that they enjoy talking with opponents, but that the challenge it represents also makes it particularly interesting:

> **Loïs:** [. . .] It's more enriching than to talk with the UMP section of my town, where we all agree on the same topics, so in the end we conclude ten topics in the space of five minutes. With people from the PS . . . it's really fascinating, because . . . we don't try to convince each other at all costs . . . [With statements like] 'He's in the wrong, etc.', so really there is mutual respect. Then, of course, there are people with whom you can't talk, for instance, on the Far Left, it's true that . . . not necessarily physically, but at least verbally they are quite violent. It's true that with them there is little dialogue. With people from the FN not really either, so . . . but with people from the Left, yes, yes, of course.

As transpires from the last example cited, participants' negative encounters are often not with partisans of the main opposition party, but with supporters of fringe political parties on either side of the political spectrum. When accounting for 'negative' experiences of inter-partisan dialogue, French participants more generally tend to blame the radicalism of their opponents, but not the actual experience of encountering divergent views altogether. In short, French party members see inter-partisan dialogue with members of their mainstream opposition as experiences they can *benefit* from, either politically or personally. Beyond a mere acceptance

---

[12] PS member of parliament for Seine-Saint-Denis and head of the Foreign Affairs Commission in the French Parliament.
[13] Seine-Saint-Denis is one of France's poorest departments, with one of the highest unemployment rates. This has traditionally been a left-wing bastion.
[14] The 7th arrondissement is one the wealthiest neighbourhoods in Paris, also called Saint-Germain-des-Près.

of the inevitability of political disagreement, the latter is seen to have a value in itself and to produce fundamentally positive outcomes. At the same time, many party members share a sense that, in practice, there is insufficient confrontation of opposing views in their party system.

The Hungarian perspective: Disagreement as a destructive force

In contrast, Hungarian activists view partisan disagreement in a primarily negative light, and only rarely recognise the benefits of partisan contestation. As shown in Table 4.4, participants in Hungary are five times more likely to emphasise the pitfalls of political disagreement or the merits of political consensus than they are to stress the positive value of political disagreement. They recognise a lack of ground for agreement between mainstream parties and regret this state of affairs. They long for a more united political community and for broader forms of agreement within society. Participants often emphasise that such minimal forms of agreement are necessary for parties to govern effectively. One Fidesz group gave me the following reasons for why they wish for more appeased dialogue between parties:

Tamás: It would be better if there was more consensus.

Olivia: It obviously would be better.

Tamás: Of course it would be better. The most important thing would be to have a national minimum. If we had that . . . in reality a very divided country cannot make progress. In fact, it leads to a lot of backsliding. And society also falls apart. In reality, it's much harder this way. It's harder to solve economic problems than if we were united. Of course, society will never be 100 per cent united, because we are human. But it would still be necessary to somehow find a common way of thinking.

MSzP-Együtt participants adopt very similar positions. In the following, Dávid takes Germany's consensus-based politics as an example to strive towards:

Dávid: [. . .] Like the fact that in Germany they will now have a grand coalition, that is possible because they have a very developed political culture. And, in fact, such big, huge differences do not exist between what the CDU and the SPD say. There they have that sort of consensus that you've talked about. Those agreements that last for several governments, that nobody will tamper with, because it works this way.

Well, we have none of these [agreements]. None. Past governments have been unable to agree on an educational policy that would be approved by all the parliamentary and extra-parliamentary parties, and that would be carried forward by the next government. If we begin anew every fourth year, then nothing can ever be achieved [. . .]

Beyond the negative consequences of partisan polarisation on good governance, activists also frequently point to its adverse effects on interpersonal relations and societal cohesion more generally. Hungarian participants describe a political context in which individuals of opposite political conviction either cannot talk about public affairs or are uninterested altogether. This comes through in the following dialogue between MSzP activists:

László: According to me the greatest problem in this whole thing is that public life, like everything else, has been made into some kind of a constant war [. . .] All this has come to a point where families fall apart, where circles of friends break down. And a Fidesz and an MSzP supporter simply can't sit down – I'm talking about party members – at the same table and talk normally.

Margit: For it to come to this, you don't even need to be a party member. It's enough to be a sympathiser.

László: It's true, sympathisers, too. Of course, among sympathisers there are also more normal people and we also have more dogmatic elements [in our ranks]. But people have been turned against each other. There is such a deep divide in society between partisans of the different parties. And then we have the third largest category, which is completely alienated from it all. And there is absolutely no way that they will . . . so it will be very difficult to get them interested again in public affairs, in politics [. . .]

In the following example, Fidesz participants similarly emphasise the pervasive and intense nature of partisan divisions. As they explain, if politics is so conflictual, it is because the 'partisan lens' is overwhelming in public life. Partisanship defines how citizens look at each other. As Olivia explains, these preferences tend to take precedence over affective ties as a basis for interpersonal relationships:

Olivia: Politics contaminates society. What [politicians] do, it does not stay within the walls of Parliament.

[. . .]

Tamás: Discussions in friendship circles, in the family. It's there, in the practice of our everyday life.

Olivia: It's very much there. So the fact that . . . people have internalised this to a point that you judge people immediately when you learn that a person is . . . you immediately identify the person with that party. For example, if they say 'I don't like Viktor [Orbán]', you immediately say, 'Aha, all right, I see.' And it's really built into people, they look at one another like that, like [through a] red and orange [lens].[15] And that's really not good. Because it becomes difficult to build human connections, you just can't forget it. Because it's so decisive in one's own life . . . at least where we live, in our own lives, that you just can't really let go of it when you meet somebody [. . .] If somebody says he is voting for the MSzP, then you know that you won't agree on much. Even though they possibly are a really good person. But you feel like, how is it that this person can stand for these things that are completely opposite to the ones that I stand for? I think that for us it is something that is very emotional.

Key Findings

This chapter has provided an overview of the specific political context within which French and Hungarian party members are socialised today. These cases represent two specific articulations of the contemporary relationship between parties and democracy. Ageing political parties in the established French regime seem less and less capable of mobilising citizens on the basis of distinct platforms. In Hungary, acute party polarisation has contributed to the undermining of still-young democratic institutions. My fieldwork experience and the views of partisans themselves largely resonate with the views of academics on these two situations. I found a particularly tense context in Hungary. The strong animosity between both camps means partisans expect observers to take sides. This made it more challenging for me to navigate my position as an impartial scholar. In France, on the other hand, I was faced with far less suspicion. Party members engaged with me on a basis of trust, despite not knowing my political orientation, accepting the risk that my views might be different from theirs. It is presumably because partisans from either side of

---

[15] Red is the colour associated with the MSzP and orange the colour associated with Fidesz.

the political spectrum share a community of practice with opponents – because they have governed together, alternated in power, and defended comparable programmes – that they also have less to fear from outsiders.

How partisans see the relationship between party politics and democracy in their own country is also remarkably consistent with normative accounts in the academic literature. In France, party cartelisation and ideological convergence might have had the positive side effect of lowering the stakes of political competition and allowing for more appeased inter-partisan dialogue. Disagreement between parties exists on selected topics but does not preclude large areas of consensus. As a result, party members do not see partisan conflict as needing elimination, but rather as a positive feature of democratic life. In fact, and as will become clearer in the following chapter, many PS members would welcome greater divisions within their political system, regretting the relative lack of assertiveness of their own party in power. Hungarian partisans also show strong awareness of the pathologies of their own party system. Partisan conflict does not discriminate across policy areas, and polarisation pervades social relationships to the point of making constructive exchanges across the divide difficult. Party members see political conflict as a destructive force which shatters the very fabric of Hungarian society. They know that they need more common ground with their opponents, and that current modes of political disagreement bring governmental deadlock and political apathy.

In the following two chapters, I shift from the views that partisans have of politics to the democratic nature of their political convictions. I explore how partisanship in both countries resonates with the two key dimensions of democratic partisanship: cohesiveness and pluralist respect.

5

The Cohesiveness of Partisan Identity

This chapter turns to the degree of ideological cohesiveness in French and Hungarian partisanship. The analysis relies on the indicators developed in Chapter 2, focusing on the ways in which partisans describe their own political identity, and the coherence with which they do so. This exercise entails paying attention to the value systems different partisans claim as their own (Attribute A), how members articulate these value systems with the policies their party defends (Attribute B), and whether they can clearly distinguish this political offer from those of rival platforms (Attribute C).[1]

The chapter finds strong variations in partisan cohesiveness both between and within countries. Counter-intuitively, intense polarisation in Hungary does not translate into cohesive platforms. As shown in the previous chapter, Hungarian party members struggled to identify any area of consensus with their opponents. However, the evidence below shows they also struggled to account for key differences between parties. Often, party members in Hungary could not explain which values their party stands for, which policies it advocates, and what sets their party apart from their political opposition. This lack of cohesiveness is particularly apparent on social and economic issues. Conversely, while French partisans were far more likely to highlight areas of agreement between opponents, they also identified far more easily what sets them apart. French party members deploy a more normatively grounded, policy-informed and comparative justification of their positions. To this extent, compromise among French parties does not preclude an understanding of difference. These general findings should not obscure key differences between left and right-wing partisanship within each polity, with left-wing partisans demonstrating relatively less cohesiveness. This takes the form of *ideological dissonance*

---

[1] For a summary of key indicators, see Table 2.1.

among PS members, whereby partisans can distinguish party platforms in ideal, theoretical terms but struggle to highlight how these abstract differences translate in different strategies of government. MSzP party members in turn display a more acute form of *ideological confusion*, whereby partisans mostly criticise their opponents' position without clear ideas about what their own party defends.

French partisans between substance and dissonance

The focus groups provide evidence for the normative, programmatic and differentiation attributes of French partisanship, but with some important limitations for young socialists. While these hold a relatively cohesive partisan identity, they perceive important gaps in the consistency of their party's stance, with a strong dissonance between their own values and the policies they see enacted in government.

Attribute A: A solid normative grounding

Cohesiveness implies first that partisans account for the objectives and problems that justify their party's exercise of political power (Indicator 1), and for the principles that underlie such an exercise (Indicator 2). This is linked to the idea that parties should stand for a distinct vision of the common good, rooted in rival interpretations of the meaning of fundamental principles, such as equality or freedom. By weaving individual concerns together in an overarching narrative, parties contribute to citizens making sense of their own grievances as issues of political relevance. The normative commitments of political parties thus contribute to locate particularistic appeals in a broader understanding of the political world.

The discourse of French party members resonates with this. They frequently refer to the objectives that their parties intend to further and to the principles and values that structure their identity (Indicators 1 and 2). Participants also recognise explicitly the importance of ideas and intellectual traditions for their movements.[2] This is apparent from the coding-based evidence. When discussing their card classification, participants offer an account of the dimensions of their party's platform that they consider either similar or dissimilar to those of their opponents. I coded specifically for instances where partisans insisted on differences or similarities in the

---

[2] There are key cultural reasons that help explain the importance of ideas in French partisanship, particularly on the Left of the political spectrum. Chapter 3 discusses my understanding of the role of political culture in democratic partisanship, while in Chapter 7 I analyse the cross-national and cross-party variations I uncover in light of this factor.

Table 5.1: Dimensions of partisan platforms emphasised by French participants to justify their card classification (instances coded)

		PS	UMP
IDEAS	Counts	107	129
	Share of total	46%	46%
PRACTICES	Counts	125	149
	Share of total	54%	54%
Total	Counts	232	278
	Share of total	100%	100%

ideas of parties (instances coded IDEAS). I also coded for instances where participants insisted on the different or similar types of political practices that parties defend or undertake (instances coded PRACTICES). As is apparent from Table 5.1, French partisans rely on ideals and practices in a rather balanced way to justify their agreements or disagreements with political opponents.

In left-wing groups especially, it was not uncommon for PS members to discuss the meaning and relevance of socialism as an intellectual tradition. The following dialogue is a good example of this. Didier has just emphasised that they would welcome institutional reforms encouraging greater citizen participation in political decision-making; René answers with the following:

> **René:** [. . .] What is easy to see is that you are quickly going to bump into economic problems. [. . .] Let's imagine, we establish the thirty-hour week. I push all economic questions aside. The worker will work five hours fewer every week – does that necessarily mean that he will become involved in local councils, etc.? So you get to a bunch of questions that have to do with culture, schooling, etc., and with the democratisation of knowledge. You also get to economic questions, what will be the relation of the worker to the factory, to his work tool, of the cashier in the supermarket, etc. And what you end up saying is that you want a more democratic society, and to reach this in fact you get to socialism, so in the end . . . honestly, these are the roots of [our] engagement.
>
> **Didier:** Fundamentally that is it, we agree. We completely agree. For me socialism is about deepening the democratic project, what Jaurès[3] used to say, democracy until the end, that is to say the capacity to deepen democracy until . . . its most extreme point [. . .]

[3] Jean Jaurès (1859–1914) is considered one of the founders of the French social-democratic movement in the early twentieth century.

The coding categories were further refined according to levels of abstraction following Schmidt's categorisation of political ideas (see p. 27, fn 11, and Schmidt, 2008). I associated the code WORLDVIEWS to examples where participants insist on the more abstract principles, values and normative commitments that structure their commitment. On the other hand, the code DIAGNOSTICS/OBJECTIVES was attached to the problems their party identifies as needing remedy through policy, or the objectives that their party wishes to achieve.

As shown in Table 5.2, a similar share of PS and UMP references to ideas focus on abstract principles as compared to policy objectives (60 per cent and 54 per cent of total assessments of ideas, respectively). From the qualitative evidence, however, both PS and UMP participants see the Left as more ideologically inclined than the Right. This fits with the characteristics associated with traditional Left–Right registers: the Left is generally understood as being more idealistic and the Right as more pragmatic in its approach to social reality (Bobbio, 1995; Lukes, 2003). In the following exchange among UMP party members, Gilles sees their own party as held together by charismatic personalities, rather than ideas. The rest of the group contrasts this tendency with the PS's attachment to socialist ideology:

> **Gilles:** We tend to gather more around someone that we consider to be the most pragmatic at a given moment, but we do not have an ideology. Well, actually this is a great problem at the moment, that we are incapable of redefining ourselves as the UMP. Sarkozy[4] is gone, *what else?*[5]

Table 5.2: Ideational dimensions of partisan platforms emphasised by French participants to justify their card classification (instances coded)

		PS	UMP
DIAGNOSTICS / OBJECTIVES	Counts	41	59
	Share of total	40%	46%
WORLDVIEWS	Counts	61	69
	Share of total	60%	54%
Total	Counts	102	128
	Share of total	100%	100%

[4] Nicolas Sarkozy was minister of the interior under Jacques Chirac's presidency (2002–4 and 2005–7) and then as president of the French Republic (2007–12). At the time of my interviews, he had stepped away from party politics, but returned at the end of 2014 as president of the UMP.

[5] English used in the original interview.

Agnès: But this is a key question, because in fact what is the UMP? With the UMP, the problem is that it is a blend that does not hold together, well, there are people that are too different within it . . .

Nelson: Well, you know, the PS also has very different people . . .

Agnès: Yes, I don't know . . . I think it is worse in our camp . . .

Gilles: Yes, but within the PS, you can tie yourself to great ideologies, well . . . you can also, you have certain authors . . .

Nelson: Karl Marx. . . (*laughter*)

Gilles: But yes, exactly! [. . .]

PS participants are aware of the common opposition between left-wing idealism and right-wing pragmatism. In the following discussion, a PS group discusses the respective weight of principled conviction in left- and right-wing partisan identities and point to the fact that parties attribute more or less importance to ideas depending on the issues at stake. While all agree that the PS may be more principled than the Right on economic questions, Jean suggests that the Left may be more pragmatic than the UMP on cultural and identity-related issues:

Léonard: Well, I consider . . . I think the Right gives precedence to efficiency . . . We sometimes hang on to principles, sometimes a bit foolishly . . .

Jean: Well, no, see the burqa,[6] the legalisation of cannabis . . .

Léonard: Well, I mean on economic questions [. . .] I think we are ready to cut back on economic growth in order to redistribute, to ensure principles of equality.

Sonia: Yes, [. . .] people that are left-wing are more conscious of being of the Left than people who are right-wing [are of being on the Right]. Because the Left insists more on values, on the fact that, at the end of

---

[6] An UMP parliamentary majority under President Nicolas Sarkozy made it illegal to wear a face-covering veil or other masks in public spaces on 11 October 2010. This legislation has come to be known as the 'Burqa law'. PS members imply here that this decision was more principled than pragmatic, as is the right-wing's opposition to the legalisation of cannabis.

the day, everything can be political... and that we have certain values on the Left, something which is less emphasised on the Right...

But UMP participants still consider ideas to matter to their own political identity. As is apparent from the exchange between Gilles, Agnes and Nelson above, right-wing activists oscillate between shunning the PS for holding on to what they perceive as outdated ideas and regretting the looseness of their own ideology. In the following example, the same group discusses the ideational foundations of their own party. While they disagree on which ideological tradition currently dominates their party, the fact they engage in this debate reveals that value systems still matter in their activism:

Nelson: Well, yes, I don't know... when you look at the different right-wing traditions, we basically have three of them.[7] We have the *Bonapartiste* Right, the *Legitimiste* Right, and the *Orléaniste* Right. *Bonapartisme* is a bit like *Gaullisme*,[8] it is in the same spirit. *Legitimisme* is more the Right in the style of De Villiers and the *Orléanistes* are the liberals. So, I think that we got... but yes, I don't know, we've tried so hard to signify that... for me on the Right it is *Gaullisme* that has won, completely.

Jeanne: No, no! Not in practice...

Agnès: I don't think either...

[...]

Jeanne: But no, it is the liberals who have won! Are you kidding me or what?

---

[7] Nelson refers here to the typology established by René Rémond in *Les Droites en France*, one of the seminal works in French history of political thought (Rémond, 1982). According to Rémond, the French Right is divided into three different ideological currents since France's century of revolutions: Legitimism, a reactionary brand inherited from post-1789 counterrevolutionary monarchists; Orleanism, the liberal Right that was in power for eighteen years following the 1830 revolution; and Bonapartism, the authoritarian Right that ruled over France from the 1848 revolution to the birth of the Third Republic, in 1870.

[8] Gaullism is the tradition of thought attached to the political leadership of Charles de Gaulle. He headed the French resistance against Nazi occupation during World War II and held a number of appointments from 1944, most notably as last president of the Council of Ministers under France's Fourth Republic, founder of the Fifth Republic in 1958 and France's first president elected by universal suffrage in 1965.

UMP party members disagree about which intellectual tradition is most central to their partisan identity. This strengthens the previous conclusion that the ideological basis of right-wing partisanship is looser than that of left-wing partisanship in France, but it also shows that it matters to UMP participants which values their party abides by. Overall, French partisans of both political orientations justify their engagement with reference to contrasting objectives (Indicator 1) and worldviews (Indicator 2), thereby providing evidence for the normative grounding (Attribute A) of partisan cohesiveness.

Attributes B and C: Programmatic substance and capacity for differentiation

Evidence across left- and right-wing partisanship

Cohesive parties provide citizens with the sense that normative goals can effectively be executed through the use of state power, an attribute of ideological cohesiveness I have called programmatic substance (Attribute B). Cohesive partisans link policy proposals to their understanding of the common good (Indicator 3) and recognise their own political agency in discourse (Indicator 4). Partisans also need to be able to differentiate their platforms from that of their opponents, to offer citizens distinct normative goals and policy proposals (Attribute C, Indicator 5). Cohesive partisans make clear their own commitments, mobilise citizens on their basis, and publicly justify their claim to exercise political power vis-à-vis their political opponents.

French partisanship resonates with both of these attributes. French participants are generally coherent and systematic in the ways they link political ideas to governmental practices (Indicator 3). The topics on which they are most likely to make such connections are also those which, according to them, generate the most disagreement between parties (see Table 4.2): taxation, law and order, and gender. These topics are also among those which French participants spend the most time discussing (see Table 5.3).

The fact that party members most frequently associate ideas to practices on the issue of taxation reflects the continued prevalence of the Left–Right economic cleavage in French politics. PS participants emphasise equality as a key principle, and the role of the state in correcting inequalities through heavier taxation and redistribution. UMP participants stress that the state should minimise economic interference for individuals to realise their full potential. These different understandings of the role of

Table 5.3: References to the topics under discussion by French participants (instances coded)

		PS	UMP
PUBLIC FINANCE	Counts	27	10
	Share of total	11%	3%
INDUSTRIAL POLICY	Counts	7	12
	Share of total	3%	4%
PUBLIC MORALITY	Counts	22	16
	Share of total	9%	5%
MINORITIES	Counts	26	19
	Share of total	10%	6%
ENVIRONMENT	Counts	19	20
	Share of total	8%	7%
EU	Counts	23	21
	Share of total	9%	7%
PUBLIC SERVICE	Counts	12	25
	Share of total	5%	8%
LAW AND ORDER	Counts	28	26
	Share of total	11%	9%
GENDER	Counts	29	27
	Share of total	12%	9%
EMPLOYMENT	Counts	17	30
	Share of total	7%	10%
IMMIGRATION	Counts	16	38
	Share of total	6%	13%
TAXATION	Counts	26	51
	Share of total	10%	17%
Total	Counts	252	295
	Share of total	100%	100%

taxation, and how ideas are given practical significance through policy, are evident in the following statement by UMP activist Pascal:

> **Pascal:** [. . .] There is a profoundly diverging understanding of what taxation is, what is its role. For the Right, historically, it is about contributing to the functioning of the state. There needs to be a state, it needs to function, that involves [having] means [to do so], so we pay taxes. On the Left there is a punitive, restrictive dimension to taxation. We see this with the 75 per cent tax,[9] taxes have the function of

---

[9] During the presidential campaign of 2012, François Hollande promised to introduce a 75 per cent tax on revenues superior to a million euros per year. While this tax was introduced in 2012, the French Constitutional Council declared it unconstitutional in

rectifying unfair inequalities. This dimension is basically nonexistent, or barely present on the Right. Yes, we agree that each should contribute according to what they earn, but there are limits. The Left gives the impression that they wouldn't mind taxing 99 per cent of earnings over 10 million euros. At the end of the day, they can pay, so they should [. . .] Concerning taxation, we really don't have the same ends, the same objective.

In the following example from another UMP group, participants talk not only about taxation, but also about the question of education and labour market regulation. Crucially, the traditional registers of the Left and Right allow these participants to tie different policy choices together, and make sense of them within a broader ideational divide:

Gilles: [. . .] The Left tends to want equality, which concretely means that any head above another gets cut off, and this [logic is applied] until the level of the lowest head. Then we redistribute and . . . well, in general it is more of a system of redistribution. Instead of equality, the Right is more likely to want real equity, which is the idea that everyone, individually, can realise their full potential. We see this clearly when it comes to education. When it comes to the schooling system it's really simple, the (left-wing) discourse is that we need to help the weakest, when in reality the discourse should be about allowing each and every one to go as far as possible. Some are really, really gifted, but are held back by the relatively slow general movement . . .

Nelson: I totally agree with you, but you said . . . you opposed equality and equity, and I would rather have opposed equality and freedom. I find that the Left constrains and prevents people from moving forward, I think there is a will to constrain. To forbid [people from] working more than thirty-five hours [a week], it is necessary to put economic barriers to prevent [them] from doing so.[10] On the other hand, I would rather be like, well honestly, if you want to work 45 hours (a week) that's your problem, not mine. So I think it's more . . . well, I would rather oppose equality and freedom, like, be free, do what you want, while the Left always tries to . . . set limits, to stifle.

December 2012. A revised version of this tax was then introduced in October 2013, but by October 2014 Prime Minister Manuel Valls announced that it would be suspended from early 2015 onwards.

[10] The PS government of Lionel Jospin voted two laws in 1998 and 2000 to reduce the legal working week in France from thirty-nine hours to thirty-five hours. This measure became compulsory for all firms from 1 January 2002.

Well-established, Left–Right registers also act as shortcuts for partisans to associate ideas and practices on the question of law and order. The Left stresses the role of structural factors in feeding criminality and therefore tends to favour public policies addressing the social roots of public disorder. The Right emphasises that individuals carry a responsibility to respect the law and they are thus in favour of repressive policies to address public disorder. The following example from a PS group reflects how different assessments of the causes of criminality result in divergent policy prescriptions:

> **Didier:** [. . .] For the Left, public order is not only about the police; it is also about prevention. This is because public disorder is also caused by reasons that are social and economic, and it is by addressing these social and economic reasons, it is first by addressing these social and economic questions, that we can contribute to public order [. . .] I think that this is where we find the cleavage between the Left ... fundamentally, between the Left and the Right. The Right will have a vision ... I will not say simplistic because that would be a bit ...
>
> **Philippe:** [. . .] of a caricature. But yes, I would say yes, at least for Sarkozy's right[-wing ideology].[11]
>
> **Samir:** It's a reactionary type of politics.
>
> **Didier:** It's true that the Right is mostly [dealing with this] through reaction and through the repression of offences.

Last, French activists are particularly prone to connect ideas and policies when discussing the card 'Sexual minorities and social change'. This card covers issues generally associated with the 'New Left', including questions surrounding equal pay, reproductive rights or LGBTQ+ rights. The PS's decision to introduce 'same-sex' marriage in the spring of 2013, at the time when I did my interviews, spurred a lively debate in Parliament and deeply polarised French society.[12] In the group discussions, value-based arguments

---

[11] Philippe refers here to 'la droite Sarkozyste' (the Sarkozyst Right). Nicolas Sarkozy is known to have initiated a repressive turn in law enforcement matters as minister of the interior under Jacques Chirac's presidency (2002–4 and 2005–7) and then as president of the Republic (2007–12).

[12] A law authorising same-sex marriage was first suggested by the French PS government on 7 November 2012, debated in the French Parliament from November 2012 to April 2013, and adopted on 23 April 2013. UMP participants generally refer to 'gay marriage', while PS participants tend to refer to 'same-sex marriage'.

are often used by either side to support or question the decision. Despite this being a newer topic of discussion, partisans use older Left–Right registers to defend their positions. As comes through in the following statement by a PS member, left-wing participants typically emphasise the necessity of equality between heterosexual and same-sex couples, while UMP participants are more likely to defend marriage as a traditionally heterosexual institution:

> **Justin:** The difference in terms of values is that the Right is more about . . . tradition, nature, well [a] fantasised [vision of] nature. On the Left instead, it is the idea of justice that takes precedence over everything, and inevitably when there is justice, there is equality, and . . . well, it is unjust that one person has the right to marry and another does not, although these people are exactly the same except for those they love. And so, it is compulsory to be in favour of [allowing] marriage for all when we have this ideal of justice in us. When you have instead this ideal of tradition, of the established order, and things like that, well, you see everything as a shake-up of society [. . .]

The examples above provide evidence that French partisanship can associate given value systems with state policy (Attribute B, Indicator 3). Crucially, in all of these examples, partisans also *compare* their own ideas to those of their opponents and ground their own identity in this opposition (Attribute C, Indicator 5). They show an ability to position their own identity and the identity of their opponents, to highlight what sets party platforms apart and what brings them closer. As shown in Table 5.4, French activists adopt a comparative perspective in over half of their accounts of partisan agreements and disagreements (instances coded COMPARISON). The established nature of the Left–Right dichotomy gives participants a

Table 5.4: Actors emphasised by French participants when justifying their card classification (instances coded)

		PS	UMP
OPPONENT-FOCUSED	Counts	24	93
	Share of total	9%	37%
SELF-FOCUSED	Counts	90	27
	Share of total	36%	11%
COMPARISON	Counts	139	131
	Share of total	55%	52%
Total	Counts	253	251
	Share of total	100%	100%

frame within which their own partisan identity is de facto defined in a relation of adversity with a partisan other.

Ideological dissonance among PS activists

A closer analysis of the interviews nevertheless reveals the relative frailty of left-wing partisan identities. PS participants link their ideals to specific types of policies in the abstract, but they do not always see these distinctions as characterising real-world politics. PS participants often point out how their party enacts policies that contradict left-wing ideals (Indicator 3) and their party's incapacity to distinguish itself from its main opponent (Indicator 5). They also bemoan their party's lack of political agency (Indicator 4). In other words, while their personal partisan identity displays programmatic substance and a capacity for differentiation, they judge and criticise their own political party for not upholding these standards. This disjuncture, between their lived-experience of partisanship and partisanship as enacted by their party leadership, creates a form of disillusion. At the extreme, this leads them to question the relevance of their own political engagement. While party members tend to be more radical than governing elites, the PS was the only one of the four political families I interviewed where this discourse prevailed.

PS participants perceive a growing convergence in the practices of mainstream political parties in government. This is also why they are more likely than UMP participants to emphasise agreement or partial agreement between political parties on the topics under discussion (see Table 5.5).

These activists attribute policy convergence to external pressures that constrain the actions of national governments. In this, they show weak fulfilment of Indicator 4 for partisan cohesiveness: they have little belief in the agency of their own political party. They stress how the process

Table 5.5: Assessments by French participants of the degree of partisan disagreement on the topics discussed (instances coded)

		PS	UMP
CONSENSUAL	Counts	66	49
	Share of total	26%	19%
MIXED	Counts	65	68
	Share of total	26%	26%
CONFLICTUAL	Counts	120	146
	Share of total	48%	56%
Total	Counts	251	263
	Share of total	100%	100%

THE COHESIVENESS OF PARTISAN IDENTITY   109

of European integration and the internationalisation of local economies, especially, limit the policy space within which mainstream parties can distinguish themselves. In the following example, a young PS member talks about the reasons that underlie mainstream policy convergence:

> **Laure:** I have the impression that this concerns all those issues that have an international dimension, be it the question of European integration, or the question of addressing public deficits. It's not just about addressing French deficits, because it is part of a more global economic policy. If we can't change things at the EU level, it's impossible to do anything differently on the question of public deficits, so these questions are linked. The environmental question is also linked [. . .] Maybe it is that everything that takes place a bit outside of France, I think that it ends up being consensual. There is this feeling that things are beyond our control, we are overwhelmed by events that we cannot deal with ourselves. The French State is not that powerful. And we get sent back to the Bourget speech, where François Hollande said that his first enemy was the financial sector.[13] Now we see that it's not that . . . it doesn't work like that.
>
> **Clotilde:** It's quite a disappointment too . . .

The consequence of this process is that parties enact very similar policies *despite* having divergent ideational foundations. When talking about a given topic, young socialists often make a qualified assessment (instances coded MIXED), stressing differences in the ideas of political parties despite similarities in their practices (a subcategory of MIXED coded as CONFLICTUAL IDEAS VS CONSENSUAL PRACTICE). As shown in Table 5.6, they are twice as likely to use this type of argument as compared to UMP participants.[14] The following statement by Benjamin is a good example of this:

> **Benjamin:** What I think is that, if you take the official positions of the PS and the UMP, then there is a cleavage. But then if you actually

---

[13] The speech referred to was given by François Hollande during the 2012 presidential campaign, in the town of Bourget on 22 January. The future president then stressed: 'In this battle that has just started, I will tell you who my adversary is [. . .] This adversary is the world of finance' (Hollande, 2012).

[14] As coded under the label CONSENSUAL OBJECTIVES VS CONFLICTUAL PRACTICES, UMP participants were in turn over three times more likely than PS participants to point to similarities in the broad objectives of political parties (e.g. reducing unemployment), while emphasising that parties employ different policy means to reach these objectives (e.g. state subsidies for the PS and market liberalisation measures for the UMP). This type of argument will be discussed at more length in the following chapter.

Table 5.6: Arguments used by French participants in their MIXED assessments of partisan disagreement (instances coded)

		PS	UMP
CONFLICTUAL IDEAS VS CONSENSUAL PRACTICE	Counts	34	16
	Share of total	52%	23%
CONSENSUAL OBJECTIVES VS CONFLICTUAL PRACTICE	Counts	14	43
	Share of total	22%	61%
CROSS-CUTTING DISAGREEMENT	Counts	17	12
	Share of total	26%	17%
Total	Counts	65	71
	Share of total	100%	100%

consider the facts, the cleavage isn't that strong. From what I see the UMP has a very clear policy when it comes to the question of employment. It's an intense form of flexibility, completely based on liberalism or neoliberalism. With the PS there is greater ambiguity when it comes to what is actually being done . . . [. . .] Hollande promised he would reduce the deficit, but he is also in favour of economic growth and maintaining public services. He tries to help employment, but only goes halfway because of the politics of austerity that are also currently being led. So I think that ideologically, there is a real cleavage, but when you consider the facts . . .

Many PS participants are anxious about this situation, fearing a deeper, irreversible transformation at the outset of which the PS would alienate itself from its own foundations. Overall, PS participants discuss their own party's positions three times more often than UMP participants (see Table 5.4), precisely because they are concerned about this identity crisis. In the following example, Didier speaks of their party's budgetary policies as a betrayal, and a sign that the ideology of the PS itself is fundamentally changing:

Didier: [. . .] There is also at the very heart of the PS, and even in its majority, an ideological alignment with the idea that public spending must be limited, and more than reason would dictate . . . When it comes to spending, there is this idea that we shouldn't spend too much, there is this tendency to think about the economy . . . well, anyway, it is very widespread within political parties, and within the PS, to use the image of the breadwinner,[15] who is pragmatic . . . The

---

[15] In French: *bon père de famille.*

economy is not at all thought of as an instrument that can serve a political programme, it's just thought of as something that needs to be managed in a pragmatic way [. . .] And we find ourselves today in this type of bookkeeping logic that is gathering consensus.

Other young socialists similarly voice concern over the structural, long-term nature of the changes at play. In the following example, Sophie describes how the PS has failed to defend religious and ethnic minorities in the last decade, and emphasises the disappointment this has been for both her and her parents:

Sophie: [. . .] I see people like my parents . . . well, they are left-wing sympathisers and it's a really important topic for them, I see that it's really . . . What I see is people who are disappointed, and I am too, because . . . [. . .] Well, I think that when it comes to religious minorities, the Left has involved itself in muddy debates with the Radical Right, or the Right, and has never really asserted its ideas. I think that in the last ten years it never knew how to deal with this, it never could decide on a strong political position. And on the Left, we had always defended this . . .

To conclude this section, in many regards French partisanship resonates with the normative, programmatic and differentiation attributes of cohesiveness. There are nevertheless key differences between the discourse of PS and UMP participants. While for UMP participants, the Left–Right dichotomy still very much structures day-to-day politics, PS participants perceive the weak programmatic substance and capacity for differentiation of their party – the second and third attributes of partisan cohesiveness. They see a strong disjuncture between their party's practice in government and the left-wing ideals that form the basis of their own identity (Indicator 3). They also have limited trust in the agency of their own political party (Indicator 4). Finally, while they can distinguish Left and Right from an ideational perspective, they have difficulties doing so for governmental policies (Indicator 5).

Hungarian Partisans in Search of Ideological Grounding

The focus groups provide limited evidence for the normative, programmatic and differentiation attributes of Hungarian partisanship. Fidesz party members show greater awareness of the key values and political objectives promoted by their party than MSzP counterparts. But partisans on either side of the political spectrum have difficulties linking value systems with specific policies, or distinguishing their party's platform from the programme of opponents.

Attribute A: *Asymmetrical normative grounding*

When investigating the extent to which Hungarian partisans anchor their engagement in a well-defined set of normative commitments, it is clear that political ideas surrounding the boundaries and nature of the political community take precedence over those focused on the role of the state in the economy. As made clear in Chapter 4, Hungarian participants consider most topics under discussion as generating partisan disagreement. The card 'The nation in politics' nevertheless stands out as a topic crystallising political opposition. Participants from both sides of the political spectrum point to this card as one of the most divisive (see Table 4.3) and generating the clearest normative commitments from partisans.

Fidesz participants, however, are noticeably more concerned with issues of culture and identity than their opponents, discussing the card 'The nation in politics' over twice as often as MSzP party members (Table 5.7). Fidesz participants not only see this topic as most divisive (Table 4.3), but they place it at the heart of their own normative commitments. In the following example, Eva and Virág are talking about the cards 'The nation in politics', 'Religious and/or national minorities' and 'EU politics':

> **Eva:** These are the three cards where, when I see them, I can say: yes, I am on this side, these are the reasons why I am here.
>
> **Virág:** This is why we are here, because of these three topics.

Fidesz participants consistently defend a nationalist idea of the political community (Indicator 2), and most often root this opposition in historical narratives. References to twentieth-century history form a core pillar of Fidesz rhetoric and were close to twice as present in these groups as compared to MSzP ones (41 versus 23 instances coded). Fidesz activists picture their opponents as carrying the legacy of an internationalist and secular communist regime, and in turn see their own party as defending a form of nationalism that was censored before 1989. This is articulated in the following dialogue between Fidesz members:

> **Olivia:** Well, I am also biased when it comes to this theme. I've always felt that Fidesz stands out. Hungarians are always . . . the nation always

Table 5.7: References to the topics under discussion by Hungarian participants (instances coded)

		MSZP-EGYÜTT	FIDESZ-KDNP
ENVIRONMENT	Counts	10	13
	Share of total	4%	5%
PUBLIC FINANCE	Counts	8	13
	Share of total	3%	5%
PUBLIC MORALITY	Counts	35	15
	Share of total	13%	5%
PUBLIC SERVICE	Counts	19	18
	Share of total	7%	6%
MINORITIES	Counts	25	19
	Share of total	9%	7%
EMPLOYMENT	Counts	16	19
	Share of total	6%	7%
LAW AND ORDER	Counts	27	21
	Share of total	10%	7%
INDUSTRIAL POLICY	Counts	28	26
	Share of total	10%	9%
INSTITUTIONS	Counts	28	26
	Share of total	10%	9%
EU	Counts	24	30
	Share of total	9%	10%
TAXATION	Counts	30	39
	Share of total	11%	14%
NATION IN POLITICS	Counts	22	47
	Share of total	8%	16%
Total	Counts	272	286
	Share of total	100%	100%

comes first. This is also because I've felt this way since my childhood. In general, this is also the way things are in my heart.

Author: But then, on the other side, what is there, if not the nation?

Gábor: Basically [opponents] can be traced back to another political system where people didn't really talk about the nation and religion. This was absolutely not a major theme. What was insisted upon was not the nation, but the people.

Tamás: The population.[16]

Gábor: The people, the population, and they based everything on this.

Tamás: I think this is a first a difference in value systems, and a historical one that pre-dates the change of regime [. . .] The concept of nation and the way of thinking about the nation. When after the change of system, Antall József said that he stands for 15 million Hungarians,[17] then all of those on the left-liberal side[18] made a big fuss about the fact that he was speaking about 15 million Hungarians. The argument that there will be another fascist system started appearing in the press. From this, one can see that there are different points of view. So I don't think it is possible to say this any other way; in short, that is the point. On this issue, there is a difference both historically and in terms of value systems.

Fidesz participants see the ways in which Hungarians interpret and position themselves with regard to the socialist period as one of the most divisive questions in Hungarian politics. Fidesz participants pride themselves in carrying the memory of the victims of communism. This outlook originates in personal histories, passed down within family circles. This is expressed by Imre in the following statement:

Imre: There were 800,000 members of the Communist Party before '89 and there were about 800,000 people who were actively . . . who actively suffered some kind of discrimination in the socialist times. So there are 800,000 on both sides, if you multiply it by three, by making a family, of course families tend to go together, you get 2.4 million people on either side, which is basically the number of steady voters that both

---

[16] In Hungarian, this is the distinction between *nemzet* (nation) and *nép* (people). Tamás also stresses the term *lakosság* (population).

[17] József Antall was prime minister of Hungary from May 1990 to December 1993. He was a member of the MDF, a conservative party that ceased to gather any substantial share of the vote from the 1998 Hungarian parliamentary elections onwards. Following his designation, he declared that he wanted to be the prime minister of 15 million Hungarians – a sentence that has remained the collective memory. This was a way of saying that the Hungarian nation does not only include the residents of Hungary, but also the Hungarian minorities that have lived in neighbouring countries since the 1920 Treaty of Trianon, when Hungary experienced a significant loss of territory.

[18] In Hungarian: *balliberális*. This expression is mostly used by the Hungarian Right in a pejorative sense. In their vocabulary, it implies the existence of a collusion between 'liberals' and 'left-wingers' in Hungary.

parties have. So it's a very . . . I think the most important cleavage in Hungarian society is this division or feeling towards the last regime.

On this basis, Fidesz participants describe their party's key normative objective as ridding Hungary of the traces of the communist past and ensuring the triumph of the Hungarian national interest in the same process (Indicator 1). Indeed, the main fault that Fidesz participants associate with the socialist period is that it was anti-national. By giving priority to national interests, Fidesz is thus simultaneously depicted as completing the post-communist transition. This is clearly stated in the following dialogue:

> **Olga:** We still have this political culture in Hungary where communism is still very alive. And in this regard, Fidesz . . . it is like it wants to create a different political culture. We've already started the transition towards this other [culture]. But this transition is still difficult. Because all you see is that there are big changes, and in general people don't really like changes. Even though the regime change happened twenty years ago, we still live in it. Because there have been no miracles in these twenty years. This upward progression is difficult. Getting out of that world . . .
>
> **Káldor:** I agree with what you are saying.
>
> **Olga:** This does not happen from one day to another. It's a whole society that we would need to replace, which . . . well . . .
>
> **Káldor:** This process only really started in 2010 . . .

This line of argument also accounts for the diverging objectives of parties in more specific policy areas (Attribute A, Indicator 1). Hungary's relations with the EU was a topic of choice, with Fidesz partisans establishing a parallel between resistance against communism pre-1989 and resistance against the EU today, both in the name of the national interest:

> **Mihály:** This is the defence of the national interest within the EU, in contrast to the socialists' position of opportunism and subservience.
>
> **Iván:** Servility, yes.
>
> **Mihály:** What they learned with Moscow for over forty years, they applied it to Brussels, it is the same servility, begging for charity . . . This is not the nation in politics, this is not the defence of the national interest . . .

Eva: But we don't need to say this to a French person.

Iván: We have this saying in Hungary, that Brussels is not Moscow.[19] We invented it.

The economic ideas of Fidesz participants tend to be less well defined. At first glance, their discourse highlights a *reversal* of the traditional Left–Right dichotomy on economic questions[20] – a trait of the Hungarian party system that right-wing participants flagged more often than their left-wing counterparts (13 versus 6 instances coded). As exemplified in the following, Fidesz activists minimally meet the normative attribute here by emphasising a statist outlook, and associating their opponents with pro-market positions (Indicator 2):

Kapolcs: [...] I think the Left... has been very... too eager to accept those kinds of liberal ideas... that are at the moment not in the best interest of Hungary. Uncontrolled privatisation, which went on after the regime change, these kinds of ideas... uncontrolled free market ideas, with the Western multinationals investing and of course making money and taking it out of the country, I think these are challenges that must be fought in Hungary [...] This is the most interesting thing in Hungary. It seems that in Hungary Left and Right on economic issues have reversed. Left-wing parties are capitalist and liberal, whereas right-wing parties are conservative and more socially... conscious or more statist anyways.

While Fidesz partisans do stress the importance of state intervention, a practice which tends to be associated with left-wing politics, they do not commit to the traditional *ideas* associated with left-wing economic policies: that structural factors condition individual trajectories, and that political, economic and social inequalities should therefore be rectified (Bobbio, 1995; Lukes, 2003). Fidesz's statism derives not from adherence to these principles, but instead from its nationalism and social conservatism. State

---

[19] This is a catchphrase regularly used by Viktor Orbán in his speeches. For instance, on 5 July 2013, following the discussion of the Tavares Report concerning Hungarian breaches of democratic principles, the prime minister declared on Hungarian Public Radio that 'Brussels is not Moscow and therefore it has no right to meddle in the lives of the member states. Hungary is a free country.'

[20] This will come as no surprise to students of European party politics: the thesis of an 'inversion' of the Left–Right economic cleavage in Central Europe is well established in the literature (Tavits and Letki, 2009).

action should favour Hungarian firms over foreign ones, and 'hard-working' Hungarians over benefit recipients. This is apparent in the following example from a Fidesz group:

> **Márton:** [. . .] With socialist governments, there was a statist way of thinking, say the A version of statism, which involved the state giving benefits. From this point of view, the strange thing in Hungary is that the right-wing party is also statist. But it says that the state should not distribute benefits, but rather it should distribute work.[21] Or that it should interfere with the market through, for example, buying companies that were previously private, or through cooperating with actors on the market, companies, to increase the employment rate. This is clearly not a classic capitalist method, but in the midst of the present global crisis, one cannot expect to use methods that were previously in use. So in this there is no agreement [between political parties] [. . .]

MSzP participants have less clarity on their normative commitments, including on socio-cultural issues. The MSzP emerged from the ruins of the former Hungarian Communist Party but built its identity on a break with its pre-1989 history (Grzymala-Busse, 2003). While Fidesz activists associate the MSzP with communism, MSzP activists themselves do not identify with this depiction. They do not defend the past socialist system nor bolster an alternative idea of nationhood. This results in a situation where, while French partisans share an understanding of the meaning behind left- and right-wing political identities, Hungarian activists have little common ground in their understanding of the political world. The MSzP's unwanted heritage is a particularly unreliable basis for defending political ideas in general, and left-wing ideas in particular. This is apparent from the coding, with Fidesz participants drawing more heavily on idea-related arguments than their MSzP counterparts and less heavily on practice-related arguments (see Table 5.8).

The discourse of MSzP participants is unstructured on socio-cultural issues, including on the topics 'The nation in politics', 'Institutional reform', or 'EU politics'. For instance, MSzP participants were vocal in

---

[21] The Fidesz government started its public labour programme on 1 August 2011. As of then, public work has become compulsory for the unemployed. The programme has sparked controversy, not only because jobseekers generally work part-time on less than minimum wage, but also because they can be made to move near their worksite and stay in live-in facilities. Work projects are being carried out by private companies commissioned by the government.

Table 5.8: Dimensions of partisan platforms emphasised by Hungarian participants to justify their card classification (instances coded)

		MSZP-EGYÜTT	FIDESZ-KDNP
IDEAS	Counts	97	136
	Share of total	33%	42%
PRACTICES	Counts	197	188
	Share of total	67%	58%
Total	Counts	294	324
	Share of total	100%	100%

depicting Fidesz's nationalistic focus as excessive but did not provide the terms of an alternative approach to the political community (Indicator 2). This is apparent in the following dialogue:

> **László:** The nation in politics. I've classified that at the very fringe [of topics of disagreement]. [This is] at least partly [the case], because of course for us too, the nation has an important place in politics. I mean this is why we do politics in the first place. But Fidesz's view [on this] is so, so radical, and given that they try to bring everything back to this national line, I classify [the topic] at the fringe. Because for us, this is an absolute no. I mean everything is 'national', national cigarettes,[22] national I don't know what, everything national . . .

Like László, MSzP participants often insist that it is only because Fidesz's stance is so aggressive on these questions that the topic breeds political conflict. In contrast to Fidesz activists, they do not perceive two, alternative understandings of the political community. As also shown in the example above, most left-wing activists are intent on reassuring their audience that they also care about the nation. A participant from a different group, Kálmán, similarly emphasised that 'on the Left we love our homeland just as much, and for us the nation and issues that have to do with the nation are just as important'.

On socio-economic issues, MSzP partisans picture the policies of Fidesz as statist and recognise that their own party implemented liberal policies in the past. As emphasised by a young left-wing activist:

---

[22] The Fidesz majority legislated on the retail sale of tobacco in Hungary in December 2011 and introduced a state monopoly in the industry. From 15 July 2013, only government-approved National Tobacco shops – granted concessions via public tender – have been authorised to operate.

Zsuzsa: In reality, what happens in Hungary is that when the right-wing is in power, then there are nationalisations, when it is the left-wing, then there are privatisations. So if there is a change of government every four years, this can generate problematic situations. So now we have nationalisations in various areas . . .

Crucially however, the left-wing activist I interviewed in Hungary did not actively *defend* ideas traditionally associated with economic liberalism, such as the responsibility of individuals for their social trajectory, or an ideal of the common good akin to meritocracy. To this extent, the party's free-market policies are not linked with specific objectives (Attribute A, Indicator 1) or value systems (Attribute A, Indicator 2). This resonates with how the party leadership framed free-market policies prior to 2004, as a means for reintegrating the West rather than as desirable for their own sake:

Csaba: [. . .] The general direction taken by the current government is to have strong Hungarian companies, with strong Hungarian entrepreneurs, and behind that a large strong national industry. And this is not based on free market values, but on the need for state subsidies.

Miklós: Well, yes. The other thing is that we are going back to the Rákosi regime. Because Orbán is gradually concluding that [. . .] we should be the country of iron and steel.[23]

Zsófi: All right, but to what extent is the Socialist Party a free-market party? [. . .] In truth, from what I know, very few people, I mean very few politicians, are favourable to the market in Hungary [. . .]

A minority of MSzP partisans do take pride in socialist ideas and pledge to protect the most vulnerable. MSzP's ageing electorate – a large part of which has remained faithful to the organisation after its reform in 1990 – pushes the party in this direction. In the following dialogue, for instance,

---

[23] Mátyás Rákosi was the leader of Hungary's Communist Party from 1945 to 1956. He was determined to speed up Hungarian industrialisation, and especially to transform Hungary into a 'land of iron and steel' (cited in Flett, 2007, p. 35). This was a particularly laborious process as Hungary had neither coal nor minerals. Rakosi has today become an emblem of the absurdity of economic planning under communism, and of misplaced state interventionism more generally.

MSzP participants emphasise the importance of considering social factors in their party's approach to fighting crime:

> **Kálmán:** [. . .] The Left thinks that . . . of course everyone's possessions should be secured, one's weekend plots of land, because property rights are sacred and inalienable.
>
> **Nándor:** But we think in a more social manner.
>
> **Kálmán:** What we think . . .
>
> **Levente:** . . . is that those in need should be helped.
>
> **Kálmán:** But, however, it is necessary to examine why somebody would steal in the countryside. [. . .] If they steal because their four children are famished, then they need to be given work. Benefits programmes need to be set up. If, despite all of this, they still go out and steal, then we can bring in the harsher laws [. . .]

In some, albeit rare cases, MSzP participants also cast the period of post-communist economic transition as a parenthesis and express hope that their party will start defending socialist principles more openly. Dávid, a young MSzP member, speaks of their party's evolution since the early 1990s in the following terms:

> **Dávid:** [. . .] For example, we had this MSzP gathering, and as the younger generations we sang partisan hymns.[24] And the elder ones just looked at us like this (*staring with wide eyes*). Of course, I know that during their childhood this is what they grew up with, and that they were part of all of this. But in 1989 they gave up on this system. Not only on the system, but on the whole concept. True, they are starting to say that the MSzP is turning left again. Because this whole bourgeois, fake Left was in place these last ten years. [. . .] But nevertheless we need to differentiate ourselves from liberalism, and from the bourgeois way of thinking. Let's be social democrats, let's be left-wing. We need to differentiate ourselves from the Right, Fidesz, and from the liberals too.

---

[24] In Hungarian: *mozgalmi dalokat*. Dávid is referring to songs that are part of the left-wing corpus, such as 'The International' or 'The Partisan Song'. These take on a particular connotation in the post-1989 Hungarian context, given that they were an integral part of the communist regime's propaganda, and sung especially during official mass gatherings.

What emerges from this analysis is a far more complex picture than a simple reversal of the traditional left and right economic registers. While Fidesz participants emphasise a strong role for the state in the economy, this is in the name of nationalism and social conservatism, not to reduce inequalities. Conversely, left-wing activists do not display attachment to the pro-market position of successive MSzP governments, nor do they justify these in the name of neoliberal principles. In parallel, participants are not entirely cut off from a traditionally left-wing rhetoric, mindful of socio-economic inequality. While the economic ideas of Fidesz participants retain a certain coherence and function within its nationalist outlook, the focus groups provide little evidence that MSzP activists have well-defined ideas about the values structuring their party's economic policies. The gap is even clearer on socio-cultural issues. The nationalism of Fidesz participants is coherent and clearly anchored in a well-defined historical narrative. MSzP participants, on the other hand, lack a clear value system defining their approach to the political community. Overall, Fidesz partisans fulfil the normative attribute for ideological cohesiveness (Indicators 1 and 2), MSzP party members less clearly so.

Attributes B and C: Lack of programmatic substance and differentiation

While Fidesz participants fare better on the normative attribute, both groups show low cohesiveness on the programmatic and differentiation dimensions. Hungarian party members have difficulties linking the value systems and political objectives of their organisations to concrete policy proposals. As a consequence, they struggle to distinguish these policies from those of opponents. These findings are all the more significant because I conducted my interviews six months ahead of the April 2014 general election, at a time when the Fidesz apparatus would have been preparing a defence of its achievements and the opposition devising an alternative government programme. I found different manifestations of these weaknesses, including partisans bolstering general principles with no policy examples, describing policies without attaching a rationale to them, admitting their own ignorance over the decisions of their party, and describing policy as a domain for experts rather than politicians.

Principles without policies, policies without principles

Fidesz members can define the promotion of the national interest as an objective of state action, but have very few examples of the ways in which their party's policies effectively furthers this objective. To this extent, their discourse lacks the second attribute of cohesiveness, programmatic substance (Indicator 3). In many cases, their references to these decisions are vague and reveal a certain indifference to detail. In the following example, Káldor insists that since 2010 Fidesz has put an end to 'postcommunism' and promoted the national interest, but does not specify *how* the party has accomplished this:

> **Káldor:** [. . .] After the regime change and until 2010, this two-thirds majority [for Fidesz], it did not exist because communists always had some hand in the whole thing, in the exercise of power [. . .] In 2010, for the first time since the regime change, this was not the case anymore. Now that there is a two-thirds majority, Fidesz can place whoever [it wants] anywhere, it can change whatever it wants. There are some things, small mistakes, yes. But we have never had such a thing. Now that . . . how can I say? . . . that there is right-wing . . . not right-wing, that would not be the appropriate term . . . simply . . . how can I say? . . . [the promotion of] the interest of Hungary [. . .] This never happened before 2010. Because there was always a left-wing government. In 1998, there was a Fidesz government, but even then [the left wing] was present in the person of the president.[25] There has never been anything like [what we have] now. *And because of this, now everything is changing. There are a lot of reforms, new constitution, local administrative system, new taxes. Now a lot of things can change. Until now there were not enough of us* . . . [my italics]

Olivia, below, expresses the underlying idea behind this discourse even more clearly: it does not matter that much what exactly Fidesz does in power, because the party necessarily furthers the national interest, whatever it chooses to do:

> **Olivia:** Fidesz gets attacked a lot because it pursues a political trajectory that is very much centred on the nation. So it is very much the Hungarians that they . . . so *whatever rule they create, they take into account the interests of the Hungarians, and the nation's interests*. Until now this wasn't really typical. It was there, but never in a clear-cut

---

[25] From 1990 to 2000, Hungary's president was Árpád Göncz, member of the liberal SzDSz, a coalition partner of the MSzP between 1994 and 1998. Between 2000 and 2005, this position was held by Ferenc Mádi and by László Sólyom between 2005 and 2010. Both were independent, non-party members. The presidential function in Hungary is not endowed with formal political powers.

manner. For this, Fidesz gets a lot of attacks at the EU level. Because they don't feel that this supports the EU's rules and its expectations. [my italics]

Conversely, Fidesz participants also regularly describe partisan policies or practices without identifying the objectives or values that underlie them. In the following, one activist asserts that Fidesz's social policies are better than the ones defended by opponents, but does not give reasons for this assessment:

Káldor: Concerning [the card] 'Social policy' [Taxation, social policy and redistribution of wealth] there is the issue of social policy support. That could be requested back then. I believe Fidesz created this policy in 1998. One could request benefits for housing, and ... young people especially could ask for help to acquire housing. The MSzP has abolished it; it probably gave different sorts of benefits. But now, thank God, the government has brought this measure back. Now you can request this to acquire a car, too. Social policy support. This is a good thing. Or, for example, take the question of benefits. The left-wing government gave benefits to the Gypsies [sic] for example. The current government doesn't do that; it instead created the public labour programme.[26]

In addition, Fidesz activists are often misinformed about the specific policies of their party in government. In the previous statement, Káldor, head of one of Fidesz's district youth sections in Budapest, starts by asserting that 'social policy support' (*Szoc.pol. támogatás* in Hungarian) – a one-time financial contribution given to first-time homeowners planning to start a family – was first put in place by Fidesz in 1998. However, this policy has been in place since the Kádár era – which ironically Fidesz has vowed to take a break from. Inaccuracies of this kind were quite common, with Fidesz participants regularly speaking of certain policies adopted by previous governments as their own. In other words, Fidesz activists are inclined to judge any decisions taken by their party as necessarily good, but also to consider any policy they view positively as coming from their own party. In the following dialogue Sándor corrects Eva when they wrongly associ-

---

[26] On Fidesz's public labour programme, see p. 117, fn. 21. Fidesz's public work programme is not officially targeted at the Roma people. Given the significantly higher unemployment rates within this minority in Hungary, Fidesz's opponents have nevertheless often accused the party of catering to anti-Roma sentiment with this measure.

ate a policy that made landownership conditional on residence to the first Fidesz government (1998–2002):

> **Virág:** And the last thing concerns land acquisitions. It's not as simple for foreigners to buy land in Hungary as compared to before. It's now subject to the condition of how long one has lived here. I think.
>
> **Eva:** But that always was a condition.
>
> **Virág:** Well, but not in the same way.
>
> **Sándor:** Not always. Before the land reform of 1994, mainly Austrians and Germans bought land and they could keep that land in a totally legal fashion. After that, yes.
>
> **Eva:** Then I would say, I think . . . this was decided under the first Fidesz government.
>
> **Sándor:** No, however unbelievable it seems, it was done by Horn's MSzP government.
>
> **Eva:** All I'm saying is that I always thought that we didn't figure this out just now.

The empty platform: opposition with no alternative

While Fidesz activists often misrepresent their own party's policies, left-wing participants rarely mention the MSzP's political decisions at all, even though their party spent twelve full years in power. They were also silent about the party's 2014 campaign proposals. MSzP participants mostly criticise Fidesz's decisions in government, without emphasising the alternative that their own party might defend in response. This is also apparent from the coding. As shown in Table 5.9, 62 per cent of MSzP participants' assessments are focused on their opponents, 33 per cent of these are comparative, and only 5 per cent focused exclusively on their own party. On the other hand, the larger share of Fidesz participants' assessments, 54 per cent, are comparative. They dedicate less than a third of their assessments to their own party, and only 18 per cent of these assessments focus exclusively on their opponents. While Fidesz participants represent by default their party's actions as fundamentally and necessarily good, MSzP participants display a mirror issue: an excessive focus on the faults of their opponents' policies with little justification offered for why these might be problematic. To this

Table 5.9: Actors emphasised by Hungarian participants when justifying their card classification (instances coded)

		MSZP-EGYÜTT	FIDESZ-KDNP
OPPONENT-FOCUSED	Counts	164	52
	Share of total	62%	18%
SELF-FOCUSED	Counts	12	79
	Share of total	5%	28%
COMPARISON	Counts	88	151
	Share of total	33%	54%
Total	Counts	264	282
	Share of total	100%	100%

extent, they show weak programmatic substance (Attribute B, Indicator 3) and capacity of differentiation (Attribute C, Indicator 5).

The group discussions include many examples of these weaknesses. In the following dialogue, MSzP participants assess labour policy as a topic of disagreement, but focus only on Fidesz's positioning:[27]

> **Adri:** Well, so public work is designed to bring the unemployed back into the labour market, except that there is no labour market which they could be brought back to.
>
> **Eszter:** Yes, there is nowhere to bring them back to. That is why in my opinion, when those poor devils are given the possibility to go clean up snow in the streets for 20,000 Ft,[28] I wouldn't call that fixed, secure work.
>
> **Adri:** People don't have any financial security.
>
> **Réka:** And [Fidesz] stresses this explicitly, that 49,000 Ft[29] is enough to ensure financial security. They should just try to live with 49.000 Ft. And, in most cases, people do not live alone either.
>
> **Eszter:** Of course, they need to support a family.
>
> **Réka:** So this is the second most divisive topic . . .

---

[27] On Fidesz's public labour programme, see p. 117, fn. 21.
[28] Approximately £48 at the time of my interviews.
[29] Approximately £119 at the time of my interviews.

As this happened regularly in MSzP groups, I followed up by prompting participants to talk about their party's own positions. Their responses expressed embarrassment, with activists either admitting that their party has no alternative on the topic, or that they did not know what their party's alternative is. The following statement follows a long monologue describing the pitfalls of Fidesz's land reform:[30]

> **Eszter:** [. . .] I don't really know either what we would do . . . for now it's enough, but I'm not even convinced that it is up to us to resolve these agricultural issues. But somehow this [the way Fidesz is doing things] is not right.

On the topic of 'Institutional reforms' especially, MSzP participants show strong awareness of the lack of alternatives offered by their party. Dávid, a young MSzP member, explicitly recognises this:

> **David:** In this matter, we still haven't figured out what we want. If we win the elections, then what it is that we want. Sure, Bajnai[31] did mention that a referendum would be needed to decide on a new constitution.

MSzP participants are also aware of the reasons why putting forth such an alternative is particularly difficult. Changing the 2011 Constitution would require that the opposition win a two-thirds majority, an unlikely event given the low level of popularity of the MSzP. The discussions of activists on this subject express fatalism, powerlessness and a lack of agency – thereby contravening another key dimension of programmatic substance (Attribute B, Indicator 4):

> **Adri:** [. . .] In the end, who wins has no importance, because to have a modification of the Constitution a two-thirds majority is required, for these bad things to be . . . so it may be better [to have a situation] now where Fidesz wins, and in which Fidesz eventually pays for these things. The only case in which that would not happen is if

---

[30] The Fidesz majority passed a land reform bill in June 2013 to auction out approximately 20 per cent of Hungarian state land to owners of small or medium-sized farms. The justification was that this would encourage family-run, Hungarian agriculture. The opposition argued that it would offer Fidesz a way of distributing benefits in kind to their supporters.

[31] Gordon Bajnai was Hungarian prime minister from 2009 to 2010 after the resignation of Ferenc Gyurcsàny. He established the coalition of left-wing parties, Együtt 2014, in October 2012, which became its own party in March 2013. In 2014, Együtt 2014 ran along with the MSzP and Gyurcsàny's newly founded DK under the common platform Összefogás 2014.

somebody would win a two-thirds majority or succeeds in forming a coalition that would have [such a majority], then they could change these things. But personally, I don't see much of a chance for that presently. So whatever happens in 2014, it won't be easy, this system is so secure by now. Just with the fact that everything is in the hands of the state, controlled by people close to Fidesz. So even if Fidesz loses the elections, they can do anything, even just stop the electric power from working in Hungary. Because they control everything, it's a totally absurd situation. They can do anything because in the last three years they have taken control of just everything, so what happens next year is just irrelevant.

Policy is a matter for experts, not partisans

Activists not only struggle to distinguish and compare the policy proposals of rival candidates, but they also do not seem to consider it is necessary for them to have such knowledge. Characteristically, party members often justify their ignorance by insisting they are not 'experts' on the topics under discussion. The following statement from a Fidesz participant is a good example of this tendency:

> **Tamás:** In reality, we only hear about the difference between a progressive imposition rate and a flat tax through the media. In reality, we are not aware of which advantages [the flat tax] has exactly. I think that many people don't know. But in these types of matters it is hard to give an opinion if you are not an expert.

This theme is also common among MSzP groups. Following the card distribution, some left-wing participants seem overwhelmed at the idea of having to discuss each theme in detail:

> **István:** Well, we have here these twelve themes. I'm not the kind to give short answers but these are very large themes, very large questions... I'm not sure that I can answer your question just like that.
>
> **Pál:** Yes, I mean for each of these themes you would need a different expert.

In reverse, it is not uncommon for partisans to emphasise their own expertise – for instance the fact they are completing, or have completed, a degree in a specific area – in order to legitimise their opinions. In the following example, a young MSzP member, Barnabas, stresses that they have written their MA thesis on fiscal regimes in Hungary:

> **Barnabas:** Yes, taxation is a crucial point, it's quite obvious. And for me it is linked to my studies, I've written my MA thesis about it, so this is why . . .
>
> **Csilla:** All right, no need to show off,
>
> **Barnabas:** So this is why I don't really want to go into it, because I would probably monopolise the discussion, and the point is not for me to start talking about this for a whole hour . . . [. . .]

Barnabas then voices their position while the others remain silent. The discussion on taxation ends with another participant, Lukács, concluding: 'This is very clear, I can't really add anything . . . Moreover, you're the one who wrote your thesis on this, so you understand [these things].' In this situation, again, matters of policy are seen to be a technical matter for experts, rather than a political question for partisans to make sense of.

Crucially, Hungarian partisans readily recognise that questions of public policy are not at the heart of Hungarian party politics, not only for them but within public debate more broadly. It was common for participants to recognise that the poor justification of policy proposals is a trait of Hungarian partisan discourse, and that partisan debates seldom involve *giving reasons* for particular political choices. In the following example, a Fidesz group recognises that lack of political justification characterises their political system as a whole. In the first statement, Olga describes what they would expect a high-quality political debate to be like, and how it is missing in Hungary:

> **Olga:** That you would be able to give an answer that you actually believe in, without involving feelings, without [saying something like], 'Well, if they said so, then I will oppose it.' Something that goes beyond giving arguments like 'They were crap, and I'll do better.' But that you say concretely, professionally, what steps are to be taken, in what order.
>
> **Káldor:** Fidesz doesn't do that either.
>
> **Olga:** So it would involve that they wouldn't answer, 'You are bad, I'm better than you.' It wouldn't be about that. Instead, they would show what makes another [solution] better. And it's not that [we say that] the MSzP was wrong for decreasing this or that, and therefore we will raise this and that. Now it's more or less that [parties] will do the

opposite of whatever has been done before. And they say, 'Before there were less job opportunities. With us there are more.' And that's what the discussions are made of [. . .]

When I ask this Fidesz group more specifically about how policy alternatives play into this, they give me the following answer:

> **Káldor:** No, that is not what the debate is about. The debate is not about something like, now let's sit down and look at the economy, and what solutions we have. What solutions have been applied abroad, etc. There are ideological debates on a number of issues . . . But there are no policy debates in my opinion. Right?
>
> **Nándor:** And emotional debates, yes.
>
> **Káldor:** Yes, emotional debates. Unfortunately, there is nothing like . . .
>
> **Olga:** Insults, acts of revenge, and the like.

This empty form of animosity between political parties, in which debates about policy have limited space, is also noticed by the Left. In the following, a young Együtt member emphasises the absence of what they call 'professional discussions' in the Hungarian public space, replaced instead by conflict over morality. The interdependence between ideological vacuity and lack of respect for opponents becomes apparent here – a central theme further discussed in Chapter 7:

> **Csaba:** The most important problem is the question of morality, that the whole communication is aimed at implying that the other is a criminal, and the response to any political move (from the opposition) is an accusation or a trial. So there isn't really a political discourse, no professional discussion in any field, the only goal is to make the other a criminal. And that has consequences on all the rest, because it strengthens the stereotype that politics equals crime, and that politicians are bad. That they steal and lie.

Key Findings

The evidence in this chapter shows strong variations in the cohesiveness of different partisan identities, both across and within countries. Overall, I find that French partisans are more cohesive in their discourse than Hungarian party members. They display a stronger capacity to connect the ideational and practice-related dimensions of their partisan identity, and they could also identify how these differ from those of opponents. Crucially, all three attributes of cohesiveness work together here. Partisan strength on the programmatic and differentiation attributes can be traced to the fact that values and principles are core to the self-definition of French partisans, and therefore to the strong normative grounding of French partisanship. Policies and practices are, to this extent, derivative of pre-existing, divergent value systems, transient means to reach more timeless political objectives. The interdependence of all three attributes of cohesiveness is explained concisely in the following statement by a young UMP participant:

> **Étienne:** I think it has to do with values, it simply has to do with values. Even when it comes to questions of economics, it's either liberal values that are going to guide policies, and therefore the means put into place, etc., or more interventionist values. On [our] goals there is some consensus, we want less unemployment, we want things to go better. But *at the start our values are different and this implies that the means put into place to reach these objectives will be different.* [my italics]

In Hungary, on the other hand, while partisans tend to emphasise greater disagreement between political parties than in France, they are also less able to account for these disagreements in terms of the respective values and policies of parties. They are often unclear as to which ideas ground their own commitments, and have difficulties linking such ideas to a coherent set of policies. Neither group of partisans can consistently point to what differentiates their platforms from those of their opponents, especially on socio-economic questions. If partisans do 'reverse' the traditional registers of Left and Right, they also, sporadically, adopt these traditional registers. To this extent, there is incoherence within the set of ideas and policies that parties on either side of the political spectrum stand for. It is not that Left and Right, conservative and liberal, simply take on a different significance in the Hungarian context. It is that this dichotomy is floating, vaguely defined, not profoundly characteristic of one or the other party's platform. In the absence of coherent value systems, party politics also lack constructive policy debates. This is succinctly put by a Fidesz partisan, who emphasises that political ideologies in Hungary are 'confused' at best, at worst non-existent:

> **Krisztoff:** How can I . . . How can I say this? So in Hungary there is some ideological . . . *ideological confusion.*[32] With this I'm trying to say

---

[32] English used in the original interview.

that it is not that we have a conservative party, a liberal party, a social-democratic party, or a green party that are in competition with each other. In important ways, the lines of division are different, this turned out differently . . . I think there aren't any ideologies, I think we can forget about that. [. . .]

Partisans on the Right in both countries nevertheless show more cohesiveness in their discourse than their left-wing counterparts. In France, there is a form of *ideological dissonance* between the identity of PS partisans and the way they perceive their party's identity. They know the ideas that ground their own commitments and the types of policies that they would want implemented. Compared to UMP members, however, they are less likely to point out how their party implements these ideas when in power. PS participants highlight how globalisation and EU influence create a gap between the discourse and actions of their own party, and lead to a situation where little differentiates how mainstream parties practice political power.

In Hungary, right-wing partisanship is also relatively more cohesive, especially in terms of normative grounding. The nationalism of Fidesz is anchored in a favourable historical narrative which pre-dates the era of democratic competition: the party is seen as carrying the legacy of the victims of communism, and the government's mission is to rid the country of communist influence. Hungarian left-wing activists, on the other hand, display few guiding principles and very little knowledge of their party's policy programme. While right-wing activists can anchor their identity in a relatively preserved tradition of nationalism, the reputation of socialism largely fell from grace in the 1990s. The Socialist Party also orchestrated the transition to liberal capitalism between 1994 and 1998 under important pressure from the EU and other international organisations. A constrained economic environment may also have therefore deprived the MSzP of the opportunity to salvage some aspects of its left-wing heritage. Of all four parties, the MSzP is therefore the least cohesive, partisans displaying a particularly strong form of *ideological confusion*.

Chapter 7 will return in detail to the core factors that help explain both inter- and intra-country variations in partisan cohesiveness. Ahead of this, the following empirical chapter turns to the second core pillar of democratic partisanship.

6

Partisan Respect for Pluralism

Respect for pluralism entails that activists place their opponents' right to disagree above conviction in the superiority of their own claims.[1] The analysis below relies on the indicators developed in Chapter 2, focusing on the ways in which partisans describe their political opponents, and the respect with which they do so. I pay attention to whether partisans focus on the practice of opponents or their intentions (Attribute D), the extent to which they acknowledge that their opponents hold principles (Attribute E), and whether they recognise the existence of a supra-partisan political community (Attribute F).[2]

Here also I find important variations between and within each country. Partisan discourse in France is more pluralist than in Hungary, but there are significant differences between Left and Right within each case. Right-wing activists show less respect for their political opponents, although to different degrees. In France, UMP members display a form of *benevolent holism*: they dream of a future where opponents align with their views, and they tolerate rather than celebrate party pluralism. The discourse of right-wing activists in Hungary embodies a more extreme brand of *intolerant holism*, whereby the moral deficiencies of opponents implicitly justify their exclusion from public life.

Exemplary Pluralism in France, and its limits

French partisans on both sides of the political spectrum display pluralism in their discourse, sometimes to an exemplary degree. While such

---

[1] Part of the data for this chapter was published in the *British Journal of Politics and International Relations* under the following reference: Herman, L. E. (2020). Can partisans be pluralist? A comparative study of party member discourse in France and Hungary. *The British Journal of Politics and International Relations*, 23(1), 22–42.

[2] For a summary of the different indicators attached to each attribute, see Table 2.1.

instances are not uncommon on either side of the political spectrum, the discourse of UMP activists can border on *benevolent holism*. In such instances, opponents are described as fundamentally mistaken in their understanding of the common good, and are therefore grudgingly tolerated rather than actively respected.

Attribute D: The dominance of practice-focused criticism

Focusing first on how French party members criticise their opponents, two indicators are relevant. First, pluralist partisans refrain from engaging in 'motive-cynicism' when they criticise political opponents (Indicator 6). Second, pluralist partisans will criticise their opponents' positions and practices by highlighting their limitations in advancing the common good (Indicator 7).

My first step was to evaluate the relative share of partisan discourse dedicated to the criticism of opponents and to criticism of their own party. As shown in Table 6.1, UMP participants are over three times more likely to criticise their opponents as compared to PS activists, while PS activists were almost three times more likely to be self-critical as compared to UMP participants. This is coherent with earlier findings on the relative cohesiveness of PS partisanship: left-wing participants criticise their own party for being insufficiently in line with traditional left-wing ideals. The fact that the UMP was in opposition at the time of my interviews also helps explain these differences: PS participants will have had less to say about their opponents at a time when the UMP had little policymaking power. These results are consistent in both countries: in Hungary as well,

Table 6.1: Praise and criticism by French participants of their own party and their opponents (instances coded)

		PS	UMP
CRITICISM OF OPPONENTS	Counts	37	136
	Share of total	30%	76%
SELF-CRITICISM	Counts	68	25
	Share of total	56%	14%
SELF-PRAISE	Counts	16	14
	Share of total	13%	8%
PRAISE OF OPPONENTS	Counts	1	3
	Share of total	1%	2%
Total	Counts	122	178
	Share of total	100%	100%

opposition partisans are more focused on governmental action, and partisans of governing parties have more to say about themselves (see Table 5.4 and Table 5.9).

The fact that partisans are critical of their opponents does not evidence their lack of respect for political pluralism. Conversely, self-criticism should not necessarily be interpreted as a pluralist form of restraint – indeed, we know that PS members have other reasons for questioning their own party. What matters are the *types* of criticism that partisans level against opponents, and whether they focus on the practices of opponents rather than their intentions (Indicators 6 and 7). I used the code ILL INTENTIONS when partisans engaged in 'motive-cynicism', raising doubts on the integrity of the reasons opponents have to say or do something (Gutmann and Thompson, 2010, p. 1133). When partisans deconstructed the practices of opponents, highlighting their limitations in achieving given political objectives or furthering key values, I coded such instances as FLAWED PRACTICES.

As shown in Table 6.2, PS participants focus equally on opponents' intentions and practices (50 per cent respectively of all instances of criticisms coded), while UMP participants tend to criticise their opponents on their intentions less than their practices (27 per cent and 73 per cent of total criticisms respectively). UMP participants still criticise the intentions of their opponents over twice as often as their PS counterparts (37 and 16 instances coded respectively), given their more critical stance overall.

A common focus on the political interests of opponents

Further exploring whether French partisans met Indicator 6, I divided instances in which participants criticise their opponents' *intentions* into

Table 6.2: Criticisms by French participants of their opponents' intentions and practices (instances coded)

		PS	UMP
ILL-INTENTIONS	Counts	16	37
	Share of total	50%	27%
FLAWED PRACTICES	Counts	16	99
	Share of total	50%	73%
Total	Counts	32	136
	Share of total	100%	100%

two categories. First, cases where participants criticise their opponents for being motivated by the political interest of their party rather than the public interest – specifically pandering to specific constituencies for electoral advantage only (coded POLITICAL INTERESTS). Second, I considered cases where participants accuse their opponents of acting out of concern for more personal interests, such as material gain, securing the personal power of their members or supporters, or being under the influence of certain sectoral interests (PERSONAL INTERESTS). While accusations of demagoguery, populism or vote-seeking behaviour fall under the first category, more serious accusations of corruption, clientelism and nepotism fall under the second.

As is apparent from Table 6.3, the majority of intentions-related criticisms among French participants are targeted at the political rather than personal motives of opponents. As shown in the following example, UMP activists depict the socio-cultural positions of opponents as an electoral strategy – the PS grooming individual communities for votes with targeted policies. In the following example, the way in which Édouard questions the intentions of their opponents implicitly amounts to denying their principled nature:

> **Édouard:** Here we mainly see that on societal issues... because societal issues don't just include gay marriage[3]... there is also the example of public drug consumption rooms,[4] the right to vote for foreigners,[5]

Table 6.3: Types of criticism by French participants of their opponents' intentions (instances coded)

		PS	UMP
PERSONAL INTERESTS	Counts	6	7
	Share of total	38%	21%
POLITICAL INTERESTS	Counts	10	27
	Share of total	62%	79%
Total	Counts	16	34
	Share of total	100%	100%

[3] On the PS legalising same-sex marriage, see p. 106, fn. 12.
[4] In the spring of 2013, the PS government authorised on an experimental basis the opening of a limited number of public drug consumption rooms, places where users can have access to clean utensils to inject drugs, as well as medical help and information.
[5] The PS has been advocating that non-EU foreigners be granted the right to vote in local elections since 1981, but in practice this right has never been granted. This was one of François Hollande's unfulfilled 2012 campaign promises.

all of these questions ... It's a form of demagoguery because in the end ... they operate, we see that the PS operates community by community. So when they suggest public drug consumption rooms it's for left-wing 'bobos',[6] when they suggest gay marriage it is for the gay community, when they suggest the right to vote for foreigners, it's the same... So, in the end, it's only for electoral ends, they don't necessarily think about changes in society, about the consequences it can have for society ...

Conversely, some PS participants accuse their opponents of catering to the far-right, *Front national* electorate. In the following example, they target the UMP's position on immigration and minority rights:[7]

René: The position of the Left is compromised because... because the question of secularism has essentially been raised around Islam these last years, and this creates a double problem on the Left ... So we have a problem of manipulation by the Right, because beneath the secularism of Sarkozy there was hostility to Islam itself. [This hostility is] more or less deep, more or less used as a political instrument. They played on the fear of Muslims, they played on the idea of getting back a share of the *Front national*'s votes on these cultural themes, etc.

Didier: While jumbling up Muslims, foreigners, immigrants ... well, there was a whole package.

More serious accusations of opponents being motivated by the desire to further personal, rather than political, interests are rare in French groups – fewer than ten instances on either side of the political spectrum (see Table 6.3). In none of these instances do partisans accuse their opponents of acting out of a desire to increase their personal wealth. Criticisms that come closest to this focus on specific instances of corruption affecting the opposition party. Within PS groups, for instance, only one participant refers to the Bettencourt scandal that affected Nicolas Sarkozy's 2007 campaign – despite the fact Sarkozy himself was

---

[6] *Bobo* in French is the contraction of the expression 'bourgeois-bohême'. It is a pejorative term targeting members of the upper middle class who adopt left-leaning political positions as a lifestyle statement, rather than out of genuine conviction or lived experience.

[7] As discussed in Chapter 3, there is considerable empirical evidence that the UMP has experienced a strong right-wing turn in the mid-2000s (Godin, 2013; Haegel, 2012).

under investigation in this affair at the time of the interviews.[8] As for the discourse of UMP participants, instances coded under PERSONAL INTERESTS mostly relate to accusations of nepotism. In the following example, Adrien emphasises the PS's illegitimate use of state resource in order to further the interests of fellow members:

> **Adrien:** [...] In parallel, the Left uses very powerful means ... we talked about the power of François Hollande, I would like to recall the fact that François Hollande created SOS *racisme* under Mitterrand, with M. Harlem Désir, and M. Dray ... So SOS *racisme* is absolutely not an organisation of nice guys who are trying to fight against racism, no, it was created politically, for a political use, to influence the media, public opinion, with public funds, and today they only live from public funds [...] Not to speak of the trials of Harlem Désir. Harlem Désir is today the president of the Socialist Party, and an investigation procedure was started against him last week with a number of others from the executive head of SOS *racisme*.[9] But this is all to say that the Left lives from public funds, it lives from politics. In its great majority, the Left does not do politics to solve problems.

Practice-oriented criticisms in right-wing discourse

French partisans nevertheless direct the vast majority of their criticisms towards the practices of their opponents, not their intentions (see Table 6.2). UMP participants, who are generally more critical of their opponents than PS activists, are particularly inclined to voice these types of judgements, with a specific focus on the inefficiency and irresponsibility of PS policies (see Table 6.4).

---

[8] Nicolas Sarkozy was suspected of having obtained illegal financing from Liliane Bettencourt, head of L'Oréal, for his 2007 campaign. Eric Woerth, Sarkozy's minister of budget and work between 2007 and 2010, as well as Sarkozy himself were put under investigation on 8 February 2012 and 21 March 2013, respectively. They were both released of all charges on 28 June 2013.

[9] SOS *racisme* – an NGO raising awareness on racial and religious discriminations in France – was founded in 1984, under the PS presidency of François Mitterrand, by personalities on the left-wing fringe of the PS such as Harlem Désir and Julien Dray. In December 1998, Harlem Désir was sentenced to a 30,000 franc fine for having benefited from a fictitious state salary between November 1986 and October 1987. No particular procedure was started against him in early 2013, however. François Hollande, French president from 2012 to 2017, also did not co-found this organisation.

Table 6.4: Types of criticisms by French participants of their opponents' practices (instances coded)

		PS	UMP
INCOHERENCE	Counts	5	15
	Share of total	33%	14%
INEFFICIENCY	Counts	5	52
	Share of total	33%	49%
LACK OF WILL	Counts	2	8
	Share of total	13%	7%
IRRESPONSABILITY	Counts	3	32
	Share of total	20%	30%
Total	Counts	15	107
	Share of total	100%	100%

UMP activists argue that the PS adopts counterproductive measures to reach widely accepted societal objectives. They criticise their opponents especially for their idealism and lack of realism, which result in the mismanagement of crucial issues. Right-wing participants are especially likely to voice these concerns over economic issues, as shown in the following example:

> **Charles:** There is an objective, which is more social justice. The Right would also like more social justice! But it is not by taking from the rich and giving to the poor that we will succeed. Nothing is created in this way. The only way for the poor to have a better living standard is to create wealth, that is the only way.

With this type of argument, UMP members often imply that the PS is out of touch with reality and misunderstands the basic mechanisms of both micro- and macro-economics. Here disagreement is rooted in error, rather than legitimate differences in outlook. In the following example, a young UMP activist explains how business owners perceive measures by the PS government:

> **Laura:** [...] What the Left fails to understand is that it is not in sync with how firms function. What I mean is that when firms read the report issued in September, on business taxes, they really felt like politics, and the government, were completely out of touch with what they were experiencing. We are in a crisis situation, and they increased taxes, they created new taxes, they modified previous taxes ... And [businesses] had the impression that the rug was being pulled from under their feet [...]

These types of arguments are also adopted on socio-cultural issues. UMP participants similarly criticise the PS for making flawed decisions on the basis of its skewed vision of reality. In the following dialogue, UMP activists are talking about Christiane Taubira, the PS government minister of justice at the time:

Pierre: The question of 'Law and order'. I think we will all agree . . . how can I explain this, how can I explain when we have our dear minister, Christiane Taubira . . . I'm having difficulties describing this person, she seems to me so bizarre and out of touch with the reality on the ground. I wonder when it is that she last set foot in a working-class neighbourhood . . .[10]

Charles: Well, you know, she comes from far away. . . (*Laughs*.)

Pierre: Yes, she comes from very far away . . . She doesn't know the country.[11] When she speaks of releasing prisoners sentenced to less than two years in prison, it encourages repeat offences permanently.[12] We see it clearly in this neighbourhood, with small dealers that got caught several times, who were sentenced, and then were set free again regardless of what they were guilty of.

Accusations of inefficiency or irresponsibility are specific to UMP activists (see Table 6.4) and can be understood in light of their position on the right side of the political spectrum. Traditionally, the Right has seen the role of the state as guaranteeing the triumph of a self-evident and pre-existing

---

[10] Pierre uses here the expression *quartiers populaires*, which literally means 'neighbourhoods of the people'.

[11] Christiane Taubira was French minister of justice from May 2012 to January 2016. She was born in French Guyana and most of her political career took place there until she was nominated for office under François Hollande's presidency. Taubira was the target of particularly violent racist content from extreme-right circles during her time as minister and beyond, including from a *Front national* candidate who compared her to a monkey on social media (Stille, 2013). With this sentence and subsequent laughter, UMP activists seem to imply that, given her origin and perhaps her BME identity, Taubira is not 'really French'.

[12] Christiane Taubira's major reform, promulgated on 15 August 2014, encourages judges to privilege alternative forms of punishment to prison in the case of petty crimes – for instance contributing to public work, reporting to the police regularly, having an obligation to be medically assisted, etc. The law also encourages judges to review sentences at two-thirds of their completion, and to commute prison sentences when and where appropriate.

order (Lukes, 2003). When the Left intervenes in the functioning of the market, encourages immigration or releases prisoners, UMP activists see this as an undue interference with the order guaranteed by the free market, a homogeneous community and a punitive legal system. To this extent, partisans on the Right in France criticise the actions of opponents based on their own value system (Indicator 7). However, PS participants do not develop an alternative line of criticism, anchored in a diagnosis of the injustices that the Right perpetuates by aiming to preserve these forms of order. As shown thus far, left-wing partisans are more focused on criticising the actions of their own government than the positions of their opponents. It is perhaps because they have doubts on whether their own party is still committed to questioning the established order that they find themselves in a weaker position to challenge their opponents on a similar basis.

Attribute E: An acknowledgement of the principled nature of opposition

French partisans recognise the principled nature of their opponents and frequently allude to the ideas that motivate the practices of their opposition (Indicator 8). As shown in Table 6.5 and Table 6.6, in close to half of the instances where PS and UMP participants spoke about their opponents, they also mention the ideas that motivate them (46 per cent and 47 per cent of cases, respectively). In fact, French participants tend to speak more frequently of their opponents' ideas than their own: PS activists only evoked their own ideas in 28 per cent of the instances when they speak about their party, and UMP activists in 44 per cent of these cases.

Table 6.5: References by French participants to the ideas of their opponents (instances coded)

		PS	UMP
IDEAS AND OPPONENT-FOCUSED	Counts	11	44
	Share of total	46%	47%
OPPONENT-FOCUSED ONLY	Counts	13	49
	Share of total	54%	53%
Total	Counts	24	93
	Share of total	100%	100%

Table 6.6: References by French participants to the ideas of their own party (instances coded)

		PS	UMP
IDEAS AND SELF-FOCUSED	Counts	25	12
	Share of total	28%	44%
SELF-FOCUSED ONLY	Counts	65	15
	Share of total	72%	66%
Total	Counts	90	27
	Share of total	100%	100%

The principles of opponents as a marker of legitimacy

When PS participants comment about their opponents' principles, it is most often to express an implicit form of respect for them. By acknowledging the principles that underlie their opponents' actions, partisans also recognise that there exists a plurality of legitimate worldviews. As shown in the following dialogue between PS activists about the role of taxation, they do not dismiss the positions of opponents as illegitimate just because they disagree with them:

> **Louis:** This is what I was saying in the beginning, that is . . . for me, this is one of the fundamental cleavages between the Right and the Left. People on the Right will tell you: 'This is a great example of individual success, and it will give others the desire to succeed in the same way, therefore it is better that he keeps his money.' This is a bit like the American Dream, where each and every one can succeed and everything . . . And in return you want to say, yes, he earned a lot [of money], but it is also because society gave him a chance, it is because he was lucky, so it is normal that he contributes, that he helps others to get . . . to enjoy . . .
>
> **Quentin:** Well and [that person] also determined his own salary so that helps . . . but yes, the justification . . . There are a lot of questions like this one, when you listen to the Right and the Left, the arguments are not that bad, I mean when you listen . . . I'm left-wing and listening to the arguments of people on the Right, I tell myself, 'Yes, that is an interesting argument.' But there is a basic idea, at the very foundation of the understanding they have that is completely . . . *We cannot say it is wrong, because that would be to say that what we think is completely true*, but there are still things . . . [my italics]

This last sentence is a particularly good example of a partisan exercising their 'negative capacity] (Muirhead, 2014, p. 106): Quentin refrains from asserting that they are fundamentally right and their opponents fundamentally wrong. By recognising the principles of opponents, partisans also recognise the pluralist nature of the political realm. They do not consider it as socially acceptable to claim that they hold the sole truth on what constitutes the common good. To recognise that opponents have values is also to recognise that political disagreement cannot be eliminated in a democratic society. This comes through in the following statement by another young PS member:

> **Marcel:** [. . .] If you followed the recent debates on same-sex marriage, I often say that this debate did not get the opposition it deserved. It means that . . . I mean that there are people who are deeply opposed [to the law], it's not my position, but I can understand where things get stuck. I'm not saying that I am supportive of this, I'm saying that I can understand, because there is a point where we are touching intimacy, people's deep convictions. And so, if you want, there are two visions of society, and if they are opposed, it is called a healthy opposition. This means that on certain topics we can say that we don't see things politically in the same way, very plainly because we don't see life in the same way. Because, for me, the objective of life is not the same as for a guy who would be a member of the UMP, rather on the right of the UMP, with a much more economic vision of society [. . .] With these guys, the gap is deep, it's really that we don't have at all the same vision, not only of society, but of life in general. And so there is an opposition, and the fact that there is no consensus on some topics, I would say that it's not a problem [. . .]

Importantly, recognising that opponents are principled is also a form of resistance to questioning their intentions. If having conviction is a fundamentally positive trait, then pointing towards the conviction of opponents also amounts to ascribing a positive value to their actions. This is apparent in the following dialogue between UMP activists, where Félix opposes the motive-cynicism of Pascal, and emphasises instead the 'noble' principles that motivate the Left to defend the right to vote for foreigners:

> **Pascal:** I've thought about [why they intend to grant foreigners the right to vote], I have a bit of an answer, my impression is that it is out of pure electoral cynicism . . .

Félix: No, it is out of [a commitment to] universalism, a universalism that is in my opinion distorted.

Pascal: Universalism is a convenient justification . . .[13]

Félix: Universalism has always been a convenient justification [. . .] but there is a difference. In this case, it is the return of . . . and if we can say that the Left is noble for something, it is because of this, it is because of this internationalism. It's a position that can be defended, that I do not share, but that can be quite noble. It also highlights the cleavage between those that defend the indivisible character of the nation, and the others [. . .]

UMP participants equating ideology with blind-sightedness

While, in the discourse of PS activists, references to the values of opponents serve to emphasise their legitimacy, such examples remain rare in UMP group discussions. Right-wing activists regularly discuss their opponents' ideas (see Table 6.5 and Table 6.6), but this is most often as part of a critical argument rather than a recognition of merit. Right-wing participants picture their opponents as blinded by ideological considerations. Instead of doing what is dictated by economic and social reality, the PS is accused of the inefficient and irresponsible measures that its left-wing identity commands. In most cases, the ideas of PS partisans are thus presented not as something worthy of respect, but as the source of the party's counterproductive policies. By hinting at the fact that there is only one proper means to address widely shared societal objectives, UMP activists engage in holist appeals (thereby breaching Indicator 9). This line of argument is well illustrated by the following UMP dialogue on budgetary deficits:

Eloïse: [. . .] It's really a typical example of . . . a topic where we all know what is needed to address the deficit, and we all know what reforms are necessary for that to happen . . .

Claire: Then the means are not the same on the Left and on the Right . . .

---

[13] Pascal uses a French expression 'ça a bon teint, l'universalisme', which literally means 'universalism has a good complexion'.

> **Eloïse:** It's not even that; I think at some point they will have to adopt the same means that we put into place, it's simply because it's not . . . Well, it's not in the history of the Left to adopt austerity measures and to be more rigorous. It's a painful nod, that is why they can't admit what really needs to be done.

In contrast, UMP activists cast their own party as essentially pragmatic, devoid of ideology and oriented towards problem solving – as in the following dialogue where the absence of ideology becomes a badge of honour:

> **Thomas:** Everything that has to do with immigration, even if you . . . I think that on the Left, and I hear a lot of people on the Left who say things like . . . and especially young people, [who argue that] it is necessary to give [identity] papers to everyone . . . It's very nice and all, it's . . . but there is no meaning behind it . . . I mean from my perspective, from their point of view there is meaning, it's . . . 'Freedom for all', it's. . .
>
> **Eloïse:** It's again a lack of pragmatism.
>
> **Thomas:** Exactly, we consider on the Right that we need to be pragmatic; they consider that it is necessary to be . . . That it is always necessary to be, even worse: utopian, in my understanding. And on this point, we can't change people; if they want to be utopian, I find it very nice and all but . . . I try to do politics by being pragmatic, exactly because I consider that [meeting] the needs of my country requires a form of pragmatism, or else . . . Or else we end up doing nonsense.

This line of argument can slip into negating the sincerity of the beliefs of opponents, where UMP activists associate their opponents' 'utopian thinking' with cynical political intentions rather than genuine conviction (thus breaching Indicator 6). In this scenario, the PS instead harms the interests of the country in order to get re-elected while pretending to act out of principle. This comes through in the following example, where Thomas is talking about PS measures to subsidise employment:

> **Thomas:** Well, yes, if we talk about state-subsidised jobs for instance, on the Right as on the Left. . . We are against it because we see that it does not work, but it's not a question of ideology, that is what I mean, it's just that . . . they do that out of demagoguery, it is just to show that they have found something when [in fact] they have found nothing at all. It's just to try to fake a direction. But it's not at all ideological, it's not [. . .]

Attribute F: *The recognition of a good in common*

Party members should see their opponents as guided by concern for the common good, even though they may disagree on what this means both in theory and practice. This last section looks at instances where party members explicitly deny or recognise the morality of opposition, and their orientation towards the common good.

The depoliticisation of morality

One indicator for pluralist partisanship is that partisans refrain from picturing opponents as immoral and morality as a dividing line of politics (Indicator 10). There are very few cases in which the discourse of French partisans can be interpreted as questioning directly the morality of opponents and thus explicitly stating that they are somehow morally deficient (coded MORAL DEFICIENCY). There were exceptions, such as PS activist Samantha insisting that UMP president Jean-Francois Copé 'would sell his father and mother if that would allow him to win'.

French participants nevertheless had more indirect ways of challenging the commitment of opponents to the common good. In eight instances within PS groups and three in UMP groups, partisans accused opponents of knowingly threatening the broad objectives understood to form part of the general interest, the fundamental principles at the basis of the political community, or the functioning of the democratic regime itself (coded THREAT COMMON GOOD). Partisans accused opponents of not being committed to defending the country's fundamental interests, or knowingly endangering them. Accusations of opponents being fundamentally intolerant, fascists, segregationists, totalitarian, dictatorial and so on would also fall under this category.[14] In rare instances, PS activists would oppose their own party, standing for the Republican values of equality and tolerance, to an UMP that defies these fundamental values:

> **Bertrand:** We said it with same-sex marriage, that the main value of the Republic, equality, stands for everyone, and we think that the Right does not respect the values of the Republic. Liberty, Equality, Fraternity. Here we have concrete proof with same-sex marriage: the Right is against equality, and we are in favour [...]

---

[14] This last style of rhetoric is often used against far-right parties, in an attempt to exclude them from the sphere of common political morality (W. M. Downs, 2002; Mouffe, 2005a).

In rare cases, UMP participants accused the PS of being fundamentally unwilling to defend the common good. This comes through in the following example. Here Adrien displays an interpretation of the common good that includes pride in one's history and cultural identity, and the use of the French flag on election day. While the pluralist position would consist in seeing this position as a particular one that opponents may not share, Adrien interprets the PS's lesser regard for national symbols as failing the political community as a whole, and thus as a challenge to the common good itself:

> **Adrien:** [. . .] We believe that we have the right to have a French identity, that we have the right to have a history, a culture, arts, etc., and we have a huge problem with the Left [on this question]. It's true that if you look at the American elections, be it the conservatives, I mean the Republicans or the Democrats, on the night of the election they all had the American flag. In France, on the night of the Bastille,[15] there were very few French flags, there were a lot of foreign flags, but on the Right, there were [French flags] [. . .] François Hollande in his discourse, and even ministers of state like Benoît Hamont or others, say clearly that they are here . . . that they have been elected by and for the people of the Left.[16] It's a shame because they should rather remind themselves that they have been elected by the whole of France. And I think that this is a sectarianism that we do not have on the Right.

While these can be considered as relatively isolated instances within French groups, counter examples of partisans explicitly resisting the moralisation of opponents or recognising their moral agency were more frequent. This was apparent in the refusal of many participants to politicise the card 'Public morality' and oppose their own, virtuous party to an unscrupulous opposition. As shown in Table 4.2, French participants classified this card as consensual in half of the cases, against a 22 per cent average of consensual card classification overall. This is also one of the topics they were least likely to classify as conflictual: they did so in only 24 per cent of their classifications of this card, against a 52 per cent average of conflictual card classifications. The following statement by a PS participant illustrates this:

---

[15] Celebration of the election of Hollande, organised at the place de la Bastille on 6 May 2012.
[16] In French: *peuple de gauche*.

Louis: Let's say that this is not a topic that causes debate, each will fight over . . . Each party has its lame ducks that are thrown back at them, everyone tries more or less to get rid of them . . . And we see actually that on questions like . . . the ban on holding concurrently several mandates, or on . . . transparency concerning [public officials'] wages, the cleavage is not between the Right and the Left, it's rather between those who want to be clean . . . well, those who want to make an effort on these questions and the others who feel like . . . without [necessarily] scheming,[17] but [who feel like] taking liberties, doing more or less what they want without being held to account.

Other, more isolated instances testify to their refusal to use morality as a political argument. The following dialogue between PS participants is perhaps one of the clearest examples of this, in which René regrets what they see as the tendency of their own camp to moralise their opponents, while recognising that you can be on the Right and still be a 'good person':

René: Because there is a bad tendency on the Left, and I think that on this the Right. . . if there is one thing that I hate on the Left, it is that tendency of always moralising politics. There are a lot of people on the Left, and namely when they are young, who think that, basically, left[-wingers] are in the camp of the good, that [the Left] is the good, [in the camp] of progress, that they hold each other's hand and march, etc. And if you are on the Right, in the end, you're not allowed [in this camp], because either you are very, very stupid, or you are an arsehole. So I think you can be right-wing for good reasons. I'm not at all a right-winger, I have no doubts about my convictions, but I think that political debates are very complicated, that these things are not clear-cut. And I think you can be from the Right and be at the same time an intelligent person, a good person. I think it does not affect one's personal morality.

French partisans also regularly express that they feel part of a suprapartisan political community, built on a shared commitment to the common good. French partisans see that what they share with opponents, a desire to serve the common good, supersedes their particular convictions on what this means exactly. This however took different forms in PS and UMP discourse.

---

[17] In French: *magouiller* (slang).

The socialist view: A supra-partisan community built on shared principles

Socialist activists go further than the criteria established in Chapter 2: not only do they refrain from picturing opponents as immoral or opposed to the common good (Indicator 9), they also explicitly recognise that they share with opponents certain fundamental principles and institutions. This is clear in the following example:

> **Edgard:** The consensus here has to do with . . . a way of seeing the separation of powers that is valid for everyone, the same way as [on both sides] introducing morality in public life is done on the basis of . . . not necessarily on questions like the holding of multiple public functions, but on a number of values, a number of engagements too, of respect for one's engagements and this starts with . . . At bottom there is this idea that elected representatives should have a form of respect for certain things, for their own work with regard to citizens. And that there should be respect for pre-existing institutions. An example of this is when the Right tried to call on the CESE, the Economic, Social and Environmental Council, as a public institution, for advice on gay marriage . . .[18] Well, there is a certain idea of respect, we don't agree on everything, but this idea of respect [. . .]

A similar stance from PS activists features in the last part of each group discussion, focused on the value of agreement and disagreement in a democratic society. The following dialogue is particularly striking on a number of levels. Two PS activists focus on a period of France's history where supra-partisan agreements did not exist, and then point to the emergence of a consensus on the Republic or 'public matter'. As René points out, it is *because* all parties value certain fundamental principles that an appeased contestation is possible around their interpretation:

> **René:** This being said, I don't regret that a consensus has emerged on . . . I think the society of the 1970s, the society of the 1960s and 1970s, was excessively conflictual . . . I wouldn't trade . . .
>
> **Didier:** But that's necessary, that is what the Republic is, it's a consensus. That is what the *Res Publica* is.[19] A consensus that exists today is the Republic. I mean that the Right and the Left are Republican . . .

---

[18] In February 2013, 700,000 French citizens signed a petition against the bill and addressed it to the CESE. The request was considered as invalid given the law had not yet passed at the time.

[19] Latin, translating literally to 'the public matter'.

René: In this sense... Yes, you see, I don't regret the 1900s... [...] we don't regret the Dreyfus affair, we don't regret the 1930s, to get closer [to the present day]. A real gathering of French society has occurred around the Republic, and around some fundamental values. These can be instrumentalised, but nevertheless I think that [the principle of] secularism[20] remains something... This is also actually why it can be used as a political instrument, we use it as a political instrument precisely because we know that at the end of the day it has a positive value for everyone.

Didier: Let's say there is a consensus on the organisation... at least on the rules of public debate. Generally speaking, these include the Republic, democracy, etc. [...]

The conservative view: A common good built on shared objectives

UMP partisans also explicitly recognise a good in common with opponents. However, rather than focusing on mutual principles, UMP activists stress that both parties aim to serve the political community and the common good more broadly. This is evidenced in the following statement by UMP activist Simon:

Simon: I don't think politics are like a civil war, on this point... I mean, it's possible to say things... it is possible to disagree on a number of solutions, it's possible to spell these out clearly, but it's not a civil war. I mean... we are here to work things out, in all logic we all have, on the Left and on the Right... I mean, *at the end of the day our preoccupation is to better the everyday lives of our fellow citizens*, to be very honest... [...] this is the aspiration we all have. [my italics]

Similarly, UMP activists see that their opponents have *in theory* the capacity to further the common good. For instance, in the following example, they emphasise their readiness to acknowledge the positive achievements of François Hollande by the end of his mandate:

Martine: I think that ... if the Right and the Left find common ground on certain topics it is better, because what is the objective? It is for the country to do better, for France to get back on its feet. So be it the Left or the Right that brings this forward, if it's a good reform, the right way for things to improve, then all the better [...] So if in five

---

[20] In French: *laïcité*.

years the mandate of François Hollande yields positive and beneficial results for France, it will hurt but I will be the first to recognise that, yes, there are things that worked. I don't think so, I don't think it will be the case [. . .] but I would recognise it.

UMP activists understand that their opponents are capable of doing good. However, they do not necessarily recognise that there are different legitimate ways of understanding what the common good is. In the last part of each interview, for instance, they were far more likely to stress the value of agreement than that of disagreement, as compared to PS activists (see Table 6.7). More specifically, they regularly stressed that greater agreement between parties would necessarily lead to better outcomes. This comes through in the following example:

Antoine: And today sincerely, what I would like would be to put these cards (*showing the cards they classified as 'conflictual'*), now that François Hollande is in power for five years, for the future of France, I would wish for these cards to be on the other side (*showing the 'consensual' part of their classification*), but I can't. Because today, after all, there is a difference between the Left and the Right, I would like for us to have the same objectives during these five years, for the country to be better governed, but I cannot . . .

Charles: I think that is the aim, in the end, to find solutions, so the consensual topics should be more numerous, that's what we all wish for, clearly . . . After all, we all wish for François Hollande to succeed, we don't believe in it, but we hope for it . . .

This stance is ambivalent, as it can also form the starting point of holist positions. UMP partisans often hint at the fact that there is only one way of defining the common good: their own (thereby contradicting

Table 6.7: Value associated by French participants to political disagreement and agreement (instances coded)

		PS	UMP
VALUE OF DISAGREEMENT	Counts	29	10
	Share of total	64%	37%
VALUE OF AGREEMENT	Counts	16	17
	Share of total	36%	63%
Total	Counts	45	27
	Share of total	100%	100%

Indicator 9). As expressed in the following statement, if a given path is self-evidently better and the PS suggests a different one, then it is logical to question the reasons why opponents deny such truths:

> **Thomas:** To tell the truth, those who look for disagreement in all circumstances are just trying to grab attention . . . So yes, we have to tell the truth. If we are really here to build something strong in France and to get our country to grow, there is nothing better than consensus, so we shouldn't be . . . we shouldn't be naive. I mean if someone is always looking for conflict, it means there is a reason behind it . . . I mean that at the core there is often a willingness to further personal interests, interests that are personal.

Some UMP participants even more explicitly present their own camp as holding a political truth that all parties should converge towards. In the following example, it becomes clear that UMP party members do not see compromise as something their own camp should also engage in:

> **Jean-Louis:** We would like less [disagreement] but . . . on our side I mean . . . in favour of what we believe in . . .
>
> **Simon:** Yes, I mean, once again, I believe in the virtues of consensus, but on all of these topics, we really need our left-wing friends to go through a cultural revolution, at least in their behaviours. On the question of immigration, etc., it will be necessary that they be hit by reality at some point, that they look at the world as it is and not as they would want it to be . . . as they always wanted it to be and as it never was, in the end. Because it is clear that their solutions have failed. So we can hope for a consensus, but on these issues I believe . . . I mean . . . if we take into account the fact that responsibility and rigour are on our side, it will be for our left-wing friends to come in our direction, and I don't think that will happen soon on these issues. They would need to abandon part of their very ideological vision on these issues, because in my opinion it has remained very deeply rooted in them, and for a long time! [. . .]

To conclude this section, many of the French participants I interviewed displayed respect for political pluralism, albeit more clearly so on the Left than on the Right. Left-wing participants explicitly state that opponents are principled and that their views are legitimate; they also perceive morality as a non-partisan issue. UMP activists recognise that their opponents are motivated by ideological considerations, more so than their own party, and recognise a shared pursuit of the common good. However, they describe socialist ideology as blinding opponents to an incontestable political 'truth'. To this extent, they do express a form of holism, albeit of a benevolent form. The common good is self-evident and best approached pragmatically: there is only one valid interpretation of what partisans should aim for, and only one valid set of means to realise these shared goals. Nevertheless, opponents are not to be eliminated: they may be wrong but they are not evil, and to this extent could still be convinced through discussion and debate.

The Threat of Intolerant Holism in Hungary

Hungarian partisanship is misaligned with respect for political pluralism on all three attributes considered in Chapter 2. Party members in Hungary tend to focus on the intentions of their opponents, picture them as void of principles and regularly challenge their intrinsic morality. The key difference between MSzP and Fidesz participants is that, while the former disparage opponents in the name of democratic principles, the latter do so in the name of a nationalist ideology.

Attribute D: The prevalence of intention-related criticisms

MSzP-Együtt activists criticise their opponents more often than Fidesz partisans, while Fidesz activists are far more likely to engage in self-praise (see Table 6.8). The more critical stance of the opposition party is consistent with my French findings, where UMP activists were also more likely than PS members to condemn their opponents. Government parties, in turn, appear more focused on the actions of their own organisations (see Table 5.4 for France and Table 5.9 for Hungary) – although this takes the form of self-criticism for the French PS (see Table 6.1) and self-praise for the Hungarian Fidesz (see Table 6.8).

Pluralist partisanship entails that partisans refrain from targeting the intentions of opponents and focus instead on their practices (Indicators 6 and 7). The types of criticism that Hungarian partisans level against their opponents are equally shared between attacks on the intentions and practices of opponents (see Table 6.9). As a point of comparison, in French groups less than a third of critical judgements on average are focused on the intentions of opponents (see Table 6.2).

Table 6.8: Praise and criticism by Hungarian participants of their own party and their opponents (instances coded)

		MSZP-EGYÜTT	FIDESZ-KDNP
CRITICISM OF OPPONENTS	Counts	171	99
	Share of total	84%	58%
SELF-CRITICISM	Counts	17	19
	Share of total	8%	11%
SELF-PRAISE	Counts	9	51
	Share of total	4%	30%
PRAISE OF OPPONENTS	Counts	6	1
	Share of total	3%	>1%
Total	Counts	203	170
	Share of total	100%	100%

Table 6.9: Criticisms by Hungarian participants of their opponents' intentions and practices (instances coded)

		MSZP-EGYÜTT	FIDESZ-KDNP
ILL-INTENTIONS	Counts	72	37
	Share of total	52%	49%
FLAWED PRACTICES	Counts	67	39
	Share of total	48%	51%
Total	Counts	139	76
	Share of total	100%	100%

The flawed practices of opponents

When criticising the practices of opponents, Fidesz participants are most likely to target the irresponsibility of their opponents' actions (see Table 6.10 below). This is especially the case when they evoke the MSzP's management of the economy from 2002 to 2010. The following dialogue is typical of this type of criticism:

> **Iván:** There is no consensus. I was struck by what Virág said, that the socialists took one loan after another instead of putting [the economy] in order. . .
>
> **Eva:** Yes, they did the same before 1990.
>
> **Virág:** It was the same in the Kádár period.

Iván: They acted with the idea that it doesn't matter what will happen later, it doesn't matter. To take the environment as an example, [it doesn't matter] what will happen with our grandchildren's Hungary, let's win the elections today. Let's build the Megyeri Bridge, it doesn't matter that it will be paid for with a loan. Let's have the bridge, it doesn't matter, the next government will pay back the loan. On the other hand, Fidesz . . . I think inflation has not been this low for forty years. And we have no debts towards the IMF [anymore].[21]

When left-wing participants criticise their opponents' practices, they mostly target the incoherence and inefficiency of Viktor Orbán's government (see Table 6.10). The decisions of the Fidesz government are depicted as ill-adapted to the objectives they intend to achieve, and as producing suboptimal outcomes. In the following dialogue between Együtt participants, Zsofi highlights what she perceives as the absurdity of Fidesz's public work programme, comparing it with employment policies under communism:

Brúnó: [. . .] In itself the public work programme is not diabolical, [the problem is] rather its execution. It is the 47,000 Ft [salary],[22] [it is the fact]

Table 6.10: Types of criticisms by Hungarian participants of their opponents' practices (instances coded)

		MSZP-EGYÜTT	FIDESZ-KDNP
INCOHERENCE	Counts	28	8
	Share of total	38%	18%
INEFFICIENCY	Counts	38	6
	Share of total	51%	14%
LACK OF WILL	Counts	2	9
	Share of total	3%	20%
IRRESPONSABILITY	Counts	6	21
	Share of total	8%	48%
Total	Counts	74	44
	Share of total	100%	100%

[21] On 12 August 2013, Hungary repaid all of its outstanding debt (2.15 billion euros) to the International Monetary Fund. This debt originated from a 2008 emergency loan programme contracted by an MSzP government, following the 2007 economic crisis.

[22] Approximately £112 at the time of my interview.

that they keep people in this programme and [that] they then replace the school cleaning lady with a public worker paid half the amount . . . So here it is rather the execution on which we can obviously not agree, but then the principle itself, that is not necessarily bad.

Zsofi: Yes, in my opinion there are strong similarities here in that the growth of employment is logically a central theme for both sides. But Fidesz has addressed this differently from previous governments, in that it has created useless jobs, which are not good [for the workers], from which you can't even live, but at least [these people] are not unemployed. This is a bit like in the Soviet era, with one person screwing the light bulb in, and two others holding the ladder. And in the meantime, all three were 'working' (*miming quotation marks*).

MSzP participants also emphasise that it is because the Hungarian government is subject to the whims and fancies of Viktor Orbán himself that it makes incoherent and wasteful decisions. In the following example, Péter describes how the prime minister's obsession with football is converted into absurd policies:

Péter: [. . .] It would be possible to use this money in other ways, but concretely they use the money [to build football stadiums] because Viktor Orbán has a weakness for football. And that's it. But it's likely that he really believes that football will offer young people a chance to break through, like in South America. Let's be strong at football, from this we will get money, and perhaps even the nation[al economy] can recovers because of it. So this is a completely, absolutely crazy thing. But anyway, this is the disadvantage of one-man leadership. For instance, Viktor Orbán got it into his head that Hungary could enrich itself through dental tourism, so he set aside a billion forints for dentists to advertise dental tourism in Hungary. So this is what you get with this leadership style, when you have just one man . . .

István: [Everything is done] haphazardly.[23]

Motive-cynicism in Hungarian groups

Hungarian partisans dedicate over half of their criticisms to the intentions of opponents (Table 6.9). Within this category of criticisms, both groups of

---

[23] István uses the expression *kézi vezerlés*, which literally means 'manual driving'. The expression is used to describe a situation where decisions are not made according to a well-established plan, but rather on an improvised, case-by-case basis.

Table 6.11: Types of criticisms by Hungarian participants of their opponents' intentions (instances coded)

		MSZP-EGYÜTT	FIDESZ-KDNP
PERSONAL INTERESTS	Counts	51	21
	Share of total	72%	57%
POLITICAL INTERESTS	Counts	20	16
	Share of total	28%	43%
Total	Counts	71	37
	Share of total	100%	100%

partisans tend to focus more heavily on the personal rather than the political motivations of their opponents (see Table 6.11). This is even more clearly the case for MSzP participants: 72 per cent of their criticisms of Fidesz's intentions target the personal interests of opponents, compared to 57 per cent of all corresponding criticism by Fidesz activists. In comparison, when French participants target the intentions of their opponents, they focus on their personal interests in only 26 per cent of cases on average (see Table 6.3).

In most cases, Hungarian party members frame their opponents as motivated by material gain or the personal exercise of political power. Accusations of nepotism, clientelism and corruption were rife. Importantly, participants do not only refer to specific and recent scandals or allude to isolated practices, but instead coined corruption as a characteristic trait of their opponents. MSzP participants, for instance, interpret the policies and institutional reforms of Fidesz solely as a tool to redistribute assets to its own network of politicians and supporters. This is clear from the following example, where a young MSzP member speaks about Fidesz's decision to reduce the number of seats in parliament:[24]

> **Miklós:** In the new institutional system, the only important thing is that their people fill all positions. If for a given institution they do not find the right person, then they'd rather abolish the institution itself. Now they have changed the ... we'll have fewer MPs, right? Also, there will be fewer seats in the local governments. They don't have enough people to fill all these institutions, so they have simplified [them], so that they can have a friend everywhere. And to avoid having somebody there who wouldn't be on their side. When we were governing, it wasn't such a problem if we did not have a person from

---

[24] A new Elections Act was passed as a cardinal law on 23 December 2011 and came into force on 1 January 2012. The number of Hungarian members of parliament diminished from 386 to 199 (Venice Commission and OSCE/ODIHR, 2012, p. 7).

our side to send in an institution, we were willing to accept somebody from Fidesz or Jobbik to lead the institution. We could work with them. We were aware that they were not on our side, but we could work with them.

MSzP partisans also interpret specific policies, such as Fidesz's land reforms and new regulations on tobacco shops,[25] in light of their opponents' corruption:

> **Eszter:** It is completely unfair, similarly to the tobacco shop business, that only [those close Fidesz] get [parcels of land], only they manage to compete successfully . . . they decide on the terms of competition in a way that only those who sympathise with them, those who are with them, who are family, relatives, cousins, friends, will be able to reach these conditions [. . .]

Finally, when MSzP-Együtt supporters focus on specific scandals involving their opponents, this is to make a more general claim on their corrupt nature. In the following example, an Együtt activist contrasts the general attitude of the MSzP in power when faced with corruption scandals, as compared to Fidesz's practices:

> **Tamás:** And yes, if we take these corruption affairs . . . I mean, the question of public morality is not only, not only. . . according to me it has a lot to do with . . . [one's] relation to power. The question of what those in power [allow themselves to] do. So, for example, it's true that the socialists were also stealing when they were in government. But if it was uncovered and the person was really indefensible, then they would exclude him from the party, marginalise him, and they tried . . . they were sorry, and tried to hide the whole thing . . . Now the situation is that when someone is implicated, let's say, in a moral scandal, like Papcsák today . . .[26] [. . .] he is not going to disappear from politics. . . [. . .] And then you have that Fidesz representative who was found to have beaten his wife, and he nevertheless remains an MP.[27]

---

[25] On Fidesz's regulation of tobacco retail shops, see p. 118, fn. 22.
[26] Tamás is referring to a scandal involving Papcsák Ferenc, Fidesz mayor of Zuglo, a district of Budapest. A recording made public in autumn 2013 revealed that the company HBF Építőipari Kft. was granted a contract for the renovation of public infrastructure in Zuglo under illegal terms: 20 per cent of the tender was to be given back under the table to the Zuglo municipality.
[27] Tamás here refers to Jozsef Balogh, a Fidesz MP and mayor of a small village who was found guilty by a court in October 2013 of beating his wife. Balogh lost neither his parliamentary seat nor his position as mayor, although he was expelled from Fidesz.

Fidesz participants similarly talk about corruption as a defining feature of their opponents and present their own party as fundamentally less corrupt than the MSzP. A young Fidesz member expresses this idea in the following statement:

> **Tamás:** In my opinion corruption scandals played a significant part in the fall of the previous government . . . It's true, there were so many of them. So many . . . *Now, such things do not happen anymore.* [my italics]

Or, further in the same group:

> **Olivia:** [. . .] Look for example at the speech in Öszöd,[28] it was completely the case that the whole government was in it together, until the end they . . . fooled the population. And I think that was more generally true then than it is now.

In certain cases, as exemplified below, Fidesz participants also more explicitly assert that their opponents are solely concerned with their private interests:

> **Virág:** That's how I feel about them. That for them nothing counts, except to have money. Really, their interest is to get rich; if I get rich, that's good for me. I'm not interested in what will become of all these poor people in five years. That I've sold buildings for less than their real value. I made a good business for myself, the rest is none of my concern. The socialists are totally egoistic, focusing only on their own interests.

Attribute E: *The unprincipled nature of opponents*

The principles of opponents as a target of criticism

The Hungarian participants do not systematically allude to the ideas that motivate the practices of their opponents. As shown in Table 6.12 and Table 6.13, in only one third of the instances where they focus solely on the position of their opponents do they also describe the ideas that motivate this position (31 per cent of cases for both Hungarian parties, against close to half of opponent-focused arguments in the French groups).

---

[28] Olivia is referring to a speech given by the former prime minister Ferenc Gyurcsány in May 2006 to his party congress. Sound bites in which Gyurcsány admitted to have lied during the previous electoral campaign were leaked by Magyar Rádió on 17 September 2006 and sparked public unrest.

Table 6.12: References by Hungarian participants to the ideas of their opponents (instances coded

		MSZP-EGYÜTT	FIDESZ-KDNP
IDEAS AND OPPONENT-FOCUSED	Counts	51	16
	Share of total	31%	31%
OPPONENT-FOCUSED ONLY	Counts	113	36
	Share of total	69%	69%
Total	Counts	164	52
	Share of total	100%	100%

Table 6.13: References by Hungarian participants to the ideas of their own party (instances coded)

		MSZP-EGYÜTT	FIDESZ-KDNP
IDEAS AND SELF-FOCUSED	Counts	5	43
	Share of total	42%	54%
SELF-FOCUSED ONLY	Counts	7	36
	Share of total	58%	46%
Total	Counts	12	79
	Share of total	100%	100%

While in a fair number of cases French partisans account for the values of their opponents in neutral ways, or even alongside explicit expressions of respect, there are virtually no such examples in the Hungarian transcripts. Where Hungarian participants did refer to their opponents' 'beliefs' or 'principles' or what their opponents 'thought', it was to criticise these values in themselves as misguided or irresponsible. In the following dialogue between Fidesz participants, references to how their opponents 'feel' and their 'liberal principles' mostly serve to point to the MSzP's irresponsible attitude towards the economy:

Náomi: [. . .] In my opinion, disagreement exists on how we understand . . . whether the state is a good manager, or a bad manager. The state, the current government feels it has this responsibility, because it takes more responsibility and wants to do things in a responsible way. The previous governments felt like this was of no interest to them, let's privatise, then we don't have to bother with it, and we may even get money out of it.

Bálint: And that the market will solve everything. This squares more with liberal principles. They were the party of small government [. . .]

In the MSzP groups, participants tend to recognise more explicitly their opponents' attachment to a nationalist ideology, but they present these ideas as excessive, fanciful and harmful, rather than legitimate:

> **Dávid:** [. . .] I don't know where this expression comes from, but I think it's very true that 'one shouldn't place the nation above the people'. Fidesz has done that, now also at the level of our vocabulary. I don't know whom they consider as part of the nation. But it's likely that poor people are not part of it. They have a picture of the nation, people sitting, posing for the picture in traditional Hungarian outfits and costumes with pheasant-feather hats on their heads . . . and so we are looking at a very nice picture, [where people are making] a pose . . . Or [they have an idea of the nation as people] sitting in the parliament and applauding them. But I don't know what they understand more generally as the nation. They talk about Hungarians in the world, 15 million people. But of those 15 million, there are progressively only 12 million who can speak Hungarian correctly.

Negating the principled nature of opponents

In parallel, it is not uncommon for Hungarian partisans to explicitly deny that their opponents hold any values whatsoever – thereby running against Attribute E, Indicator 8 for pluralist partisanship. Fidesz activists, for instance, frequently framed the Left as lacking any sort of ideological commitment. Paradoxically, Fidesz participants associated their attacks on the Left as non-ideological to a critique of their opponents' 'participation' in the past communist regime. For Fidesz partisans, the fact that so-called 'communists' were in the 1990s able to redefine themselves as democrats is the ultimate proof that their opponents have no ideals. This comes through in the following dialogue between two Fidesz members, Káldor and Nándor. They define as 'left-wing' those that are able to claim they are communist or social democrats in order to serve their own interests:

> **Káldor:** In 1989, they said that they did not need the reputation of the MSzMP,[29] but that they did need its money. What was in the party's cash desk they needed. They needed the people. 'We are not communists anymore, we are socialists.' The Hungarian Socialist Workers'

---

[29] Acronym for the *Magyar Szocialista Munkás Párt* (Hungarian Socialist Workers' Party), in power before 1989. It reformed as the *Magyar Szocialista Párt*, or MSzP (Hungarian Socialist Party), thus 'dropping the workers' in October 1989.

Party abandoned the 'workers' part of its denomination.[30] Sure, now they aren't like this, ideologically . . .

Nándor: I'm sorry but the people are the same.

Káldor: Well, the people are the same, but you don't actually think that they are communists.

Nándor: Absolutely not. But the people are the same, devoid of principles . . . who were content with Kádár, the same way as they would have been content with Rákosi . . .

Káldor: Power . . . but that is also a trait of Fidesz.

Nándor: Yes, but no . . . Among us no one was a censor. You understand what I mean. We didn't have party-state censors, executioners, and people like this. That's the difference. Regardless of that, I can accept the politician's attitude. But this is just unacceptable to the present day. That this post-communist . . . [that] the Hungarian Communist Party has simply changed its name, into democratic at present. *Believe me, if communism came back, they would immediately be the most fervent communists.* This is certain. [my italics]

For Fidesz participants, the 'reversal' of Left and Right registers discussed in Chapter 4 is additional proof of their opponents' lack of principled commitments. Drawing especially on the MSzP's record during the transition to capitalism in the 1990s and before EU accession in the early 2000s, Fidesz participants regularly accuse their opponents of not upholding the left-wing ideals that they claim to stand for. In the following example, a Fidesz activist is talking in these terms about the MSzP–SzDSz coalition between 2002 and 2006:

Zsolt: [. . .] And that's why we had all those criticisms and resignations during the Medgyessy government, because the SzDSz had at that time all those corruption scandals . . . By then it was crystal clear that [the government] was not leading the country to where it should have base on left-wing ideology but was rather delivering it to big business.

Relatedly, Fidesz activists show unease when using the terms 'Left' and 'Right', mimicking quotation marks with their hands, preceding

---

[30] See p. 160, fn. 29.

the words with 'so-called', or questioning the appropriateness of these terms in other ways. Right-wing activists also emphasise that their party upholds left-wing values that their opponents fail to embody.[31] This comes through in the following statement:

> **Benedek:** [. . .] Well, it is very often a topic of discussion who can call themselves left-wing or right-wing. Now these well-defined roles have been completely turned around as . . . well, while the official left-wing, or the MSzP and the DK, they call themselves left-wing, liberals, these [roles] are now inverted. Now it is much more the right-wing which does something for the workers, for the agricultural sector, for the industrial sector, and I don't know what else . . . you just have to look at the decisions that have been taken in the recent past. Bajnai, Gyurcsány, these guys are all about money.

MSzP participants also regularly define their opponents as unprincipled. In the example below, one socialist group explains that they struggle to classify the cards because they are unable to identify the values motivating Fidesz. In their eyes, this removes any kind of legitimacy to the position of opponents, thereby making discussions about the differences or similarities between parties irrelevant:

> **István:** I don't think that there is any kind of ideologically motivated politics infusing Fidesz, and therefore they have nothing that we can compare ourselves to.
>
> **Péter:** We can compare the practice and the communication [. . .] Fidesz accuses everybody else of stealing, lying, cheating, but then they steal, lie and cheat even more. So what then?

Later in the introduction to the discussion, another participant concurs:

> **Pál:** I'm quite unable to [classify these], because, as István said, the Hungarian Right has just no principled political stance.
>
> **István:** Then take the practices, what they do.

---

[31] The claim these participants make about 'left-wing' principles reflects a more general discourse of Fidesz's leadership. For instance, the front cover of one of the main pro-Fidesz weekly magazines in the winter of 2013 ran 'Orbán is a real social democrat' (Stumpf, 2013). In some ways, the party represents itself as fusing the 'best' of what both the Left and Right have to offer.

Pál: Well, yes, their practice, but then one can only criticise everything they do. Because [. . .] if we take the previous eight years and compare them, for instance, here there are huge differences. But only in the practices, there are no principles.

Much like right-wing participants, MSzP-Együtt activists would also picture principles as a tool that their opponents use in order to meet their personal interests, a convenient electoral bait that serves more base motives. This idea is made particularly explicit in the following example, where Zoltán is talking about Fidesz's trajectory since the early 2000s:

Zoltán: In my opinion, that was the direction in which the political wind was blowing. They simply . . . they needed a toolbox [to quench] their thirst for power. And that required some demagoguery. So, I think they became what they are just because that was the most comfortable path. They saw that we have a post-socialist, Kádárist, patriarchal society that needs a strong leader figure, and for everything to be free [of charge]. And that requires some ideological nonsense to stuff people's heads with. And they provide this. And let's be honest, it actually works quite well. I believe that for Fidesz . . . for Viktor Orbán and Fidesz, only one thing matters, and that's power [. . .] It doesn't matter what practical political measure is at stake, what principle is at stake, what alliance is at stake . . . if it can be traded for power, then they trade it.

Like their Fidesz–KDNP counterparts, left-wing activists also insist that their opponents do not live up to their own principles – here conservative ones. In the following dialogue, DK participants denounce a weak connection between the economic policies of Fidesz and the values that it claims to stand for:

István: [. . .] If we start looking into whether Fidesz actually functions as a conservative party, I would answer in the negative. From this starting point, I don't know what their values are. I have no idea.

Péter: I don't know either.

István: I'd like to know, but I think this is simply impossible. I'm sure that on paper they would give a nice, textbook definition of what a conservative party is, that they would say Fidesz is a conservative party. But there is no sense in this.

Attribute F: The lack of a common good

Morality as a key political cleavage

The third attribute of pluralist partisanship is tied to a more general belief in the desire and willingness of opponents to further the common good. This entails, at the very least, that the morality of political opponents is taken as a starting point (Indicator 10). This is not the case among Hungarian activists. As shown in Tables 4.2 and 4.3, morality is a highly politicised issue in Hungary: while French participants classify the card 'Public morality' as a topic of disagreement in only 24 per cent of the cases, this number goes up to 74 per cent within Hungarian focus groups. Hungarian activists are also more likely to see themselves as morally righteous, and their opponents as fundamentally corrupt. As shown in Table 6.14, Fidesz participants tend to depict their opponents as fundamentally evil more frequently than their MSzP counterparts (coded MORAL DEFICIENCY) while MSzP participants accuse their opponents of wilfully harming the general interest (coded THREAT COMMON GOOD).

Fidesz activists use historical narratives to question the very character of opponents as flawed, corrupt and immoral – intent on doing harm. They establish a *personal* continuity between the current MSzP and the pre-1989 elite that ruled over a fundamentally wrong, dictatorial regime. This comes through in the following statement:

> **Nándor:** [. . .] But we know, that [those in the] MSzP are the same as those who were hanging people in Budapest in 1918, in 1945,[32] and

Table 6.14: Criticisms by Hungarian participants of their opponents' ability to further the common good (instances coded)

		MSZP-EGYÜTT	FIDESZ-KDNP
MORAL DEFICIENCY	Counts	8	12
	Share of total	13%	34%
THREAT COMMON GOOD	Counts	55	23
	Share of total	87%	66%
Total	Counts	63	35
	Share of total	100%	100%

---

[32] Attila is most likely speaking here about the communist revolution of 1919, which led to the short-lived Hungarian Soviet Republic of March–August 1919, and the 'liberation' of Hungary by Russian Soviet troops in the winter of 1944–5.

everywhere else. They are the same people. There is this Lendvai,[33] who was a censor under communism. She represented the censorship, the communist censorship. And now that she is in Parliament, she is the one who says that, under Orbán, there is no freedom of the press.

While, in the second part of their sentence, this young party member refers to a very specific individual (Ildikó Lendvai), the first part of the sentence describes the *kind of people* that are today in the MSzP. They are described as the descendants of the persecutors and traitors of 1918 and 1945. The ability to persecute and to betray is thereby cast as part of the 'personality type' of the left-winger and is associated with the absence of principled engagement. This is spelled out in the following statement by a Fidesz partisan:

> **Zsólt:** In the long run, as a general rule, a right-wing person finds interest in public life, their disposition is to think in terms of the common good. The difference with a left-wing person is that the left-wing person is more generally an individualist who has no respect for the collective, and who is capable of hating anybody [. . .] As a result *they have no ideological engagement* that would link them to their party, or to a certain side of the political spectrum. [my italics]

As seen in Chapter 4, Fidesz participants establish a strong equivalence between concern for the common good and the defence of national interest. The Left's dedication to the EU, as a result, is seen not only as a form of disregard for the idea of nation but also for the common good more broadly. As in the following example, the MSzP's attachment to Europe is described as a treacherous allegiance to foreign powers and likened to the previous regime's links with the USSR:

> **Iván:** The defence of national interests is not something they aim for. On the contrary, take Viktor Orbán with the media law . . .[34]
>
> **Sándor:** They just represent foreign interests.

---

[33] Ildikó Lendvai worked for the Central Committee of the Hungarian Communist Party handling cultural matters from 1984 onwards. In this capacity, her functions did involve limiting the possibility for publication of works considered a threat to the party. She then became an MSzP politician and served as party leader between April 2009 and July 2010.

[34] On 10 March 2011, the European Parliament issued a resolution expressing concern over Hungary's new Media Law of 22 July 2010 (European Parliament, 2011). On 19 January 2011, Viktor Orbán was in Strasbourg to defend the Media Law in person in front of the European Parliament.

Iván: The representation of foreign interests, yes. We have already talked about this – Moscow, now foreign multinational firms and other foreign interests are what they defend [. . .]

Virág: They are not interested in the nation, only in their own interests . . .

MSzP transcripts also include examples of activists presenting their opponents as intrinsically immoral. Zoltán, a young Együtt participant, asserted: 'We just don't agree with them, because they are barbarians.' In Fidesz groups, the common good was defined in partisan, nationalist terms, and opponents depicted as foreign traitors. In left-wing groups, participants define the common good as respect for fundamental democratic principles, and their opponents as authoritarians. In the following statement, a young MSzP activist depicts their own party as a model of democratic virtue and Fidesz as dictatorial:

Levente: So they abused their position of strength. As Laci said, when between 1994 and 1998 the MSzP had . . . or rather the MSzP–SzDSz coalition had a two-thirds majority, they did not use this opportunity to govern the country in an authoritarian fashion. They could have done it,[35] but principles were more important back then. It was more important for the MSzP to prove that it is not a surviving inheritor of the party state, but a modern, Western European–style social-democratic party. And not a nostalgic leftover from the Kádár era. That was the important thing back then. Whereas for Fidesz what matters is to demonstrate that there is only them, to capture power for themselves solely, and this they don't even hide.

This equation between the poor morality and the authoritarianism of opponents is also apparent in the following dialogue, where Együtt participants speak of Fidesz as lacking the 'moral urge' to take their opponents' opinion into consideration:

---

[35] A year after having obtained a two-thirds majority in 1994, the MSzP–SZdSz coalition raised the threshold for new constitutional drafting from a two-thirds parliamentary majority to a four-fifths one; the requirement for constitutional amendments, however, remained a two-thirds majority. One of the first constitutional amendments of Fidesz was to lower the threshold for constitutional redrafting back to a two-thirds majority.

Zsofi: And Fidesz doesn't feel the need to ask for the opinion of others, because they have the majority to make the laws. It wouldn't be politically comfortable to negotiate with anybody, and because they are sufficiently strong themselves, they don't need it. And they don't feel the moral urge, let's say, to have exchanges with the representatives of the other 3 million voters, because they feel just fine on their own, which is logical anyway . . .

Ábel: And there is a difference between the Left and the Right, because there was a time in 1994 when the Left had a two-thirds majority, but they had the courtesy to require a three-quarters majority, or rather a four-fifths majority, for the laws that today require a two-thirds majority.[36] But this political culture doesn't exist on the Right. And they haven't made the same gesture towards the Left.

Left-wing activists have regularly condemned the undemocratic practices of their opponents since 2010, but they fall short from condemning Fidesz as intrinsically disloyal. The following dialogue is a good example of this restraint. Here Együtt participants point to the fact that they did agree with many of the policies set forward by the previous Fidesz government (1998–2002), thereby admitting that their opponents are capable, in principle, of contributing to the common good:

Pálko: If you'd asked me three years ago . . . I also hated Fidesz then, but I would have said that on EU-related questions we completely agree. And now it's not the case, so . . . I don't know. And I haven't changed, it's the [Fidesz] government . . .

Béla: And there are some more questions like this. Under the previous Fidesz government, there were also some problems with these questions, with their social policies also, but they were not extremists at that time. Obviously, I'm not saying that . . . I mean they were always a classical right-wing party, in favour of a small state, a low share of redistribution, but [it was] nothing like now. There wasn't this extreme . . . [. . .] So for me, if they had continued to follow this line, then [. . .] I wouldn't have that big of a problem [with them] and disagreements would be limited to specific, local questions. So the whole big understanding of . . . I mean they made a full U-turn, not only when it comes to the EU, but in many other domains as well [. . .]

---

[36] See p. 166, fn. 35.

The absence of a 'national minimum'

As emphasised in Chapter 4, Hungarian participants have great difficulties identifying any ground for agreement with opponents on the different issues they discussed. Yet, as shown in Chapter 5, they struggle to identify the value-systems and policy choices that distinguish them from opponents. There appears to be something more fundamental in this opposition, which has to do with the absence of a supra-partisan community grounded in shared principles. Hungarian partisans cannot disagree on the nitty-gritty of policy, because this would first require that they agree on some basic ideas on the nature of the political community and its basic principles. In several instances, Hungarian participants regretted this absence of a 'national minimum' in Hungary:

> **Tamás:** In my opinion, the main problem with Hungarian politics is that there is no 'national minimum'. Those things on which both sides would agree. In practice this does not exist.
>
> **Author:** A 'national minimum'?
>
> **Olivia:** That is there is no such . . .
>
> **Tamás:** A level . . .
>
> **Gábor:** There is no point in common.
>
> **Olivia:** No [such] themes, on which a common . . .
>
> **Tamás:** [Something] that is shared. On which [parties] aren't torn apart. Something on which they could come together, a shared view. Unfortunately, that doesn't exist. I think that on this, Hungarian politics stands out [as compared to] Europe [as a whole].

Whenever participants refer to the more specific principles and values that they believe parties should ideally share, they also point to the fact that it is not them, but their opponents, who fail to uphold them. This is arguably the key problem of Hungarian politics because there is no agreement on the principles that anchor the political community as a whole, these principles themselves, rather than their interpretation and practical implications, become the object of political contestation. As expressed in the following dialogue, Fidesz participants view nationalism as an ideology that should be endorsed by the political community as a whole. Zsolt is referring to a 2004 referendum on whether Hungarian speakers living outside Hungary's borders for several generations should acquire citizenship. They are also indirectly arguing that the only legitimate way of answering the question 'who we are' is through an ethno-nationalist lens (in contradiction with Indicator 9):

> **Zsolt:** There are some fundamental principles that shouldn't be used in the political arena for one's own gain . . .
>
> **Márk:** Consensual . . .
>
> **Zsolt:** . . . that shouldn't be a topic of political debate, because we know that casting them as topics of debate causes damage [to these principles], that [our opponents] are trying to diminish their value. For instance, the referendum on dual citizenship,[37] this is not a contentious question, because it is not even a question [. . .] Making the question 'who we are' into a political one, it is like hijacking one part of the country. Even if the person doing it is in our ranks, that's tough.

To this extent, Fidesz participants establish an equivalence between the political community and an ethnocultural understanding of the nation, and therefore between a concern for the common good and the defence of national interests. This idea takes root, again, in a certain interpretation of history. Fidesz participants depict the communist regime as a time when Hungary's 'national spirit' was crushed and forced to go underground and see their current opponents as having carried over this disregard for the nation into the twenty-first century. This narrative is clear in the following example, in which Tamás is talking about life under communism:

> **Tamás:** The context then excluded the notion of nation. This question didn't exist under socialism. Those who haven't lived through

---

[37] In 2004, a referendum was initiated by the World Association of Hungarians on whether or not to facilitate the acquisition of Hungarian citizenship by Hungarian speakers living outside Hungary's borders for several generations. The MSzP, then in government, argued against the motion on the basis that this would also grant social and political rights to individuals that do not effectively take part in the country's day-to-day political and social life. Fidesz argued in favour on the basis that these populations are 'ethnic' Hungarians and have been deprived of their citizenship only because of adverse historical circumstances – the redrawing of the Austro-Hungarian Empire's borders under the 1920 Treaty of Trianon. At the time, the referendum was lost by a close margin. In May 2010, the new Fidesz government changed the Hungarian citizenship law in this direction. Following its entry into force in January 2011, the MSzP changed its position and apologised publicly to Hungarians abroad for having opposed the modification of the citizenship law in 2004.

that period, and I haven't, but I have read and learned about it, cannot imagine how different the thinking was at that time. In France, both sides fight for the nation. I've been told that, and I studied it too. But in Hungary, this is quite different. The roots are really different. This whole thing has very different foundations. Because the idea of the nation is really an emotional one.

MSzP-Együtt participants also claim that their opponents contest principles that should, in fact, be held in common, and that it is therefore up to Fidesz to change and join them in upholding these values. However, the principles that MSzP-Együtt participants place in this category form part of a more generally accepted definition of the common good in liberal democratic societies: a respect for the rule of law, human rights, and fundamental constitutional principles more generally. In the following statement, for instance, a young MSzP participant argues that this common basis was lost in the last decade. It is clear that, in their mind, Fidesz bears responsibility for this loss:

> **Levente:** It would be good, if fundamental values, those basic values that were still alive in Hungarian political life before 2006–8, those that concern democracy, Europe, [state] independence . . . those values characteristic of European civilization, that everybody accepted before 2010 or 2006 . . . if we could hold these values in common again, if we would not have to discuss whether we should opt for a one-party system, or whether we should remain a multi-party system . . . I think it is a terrible, huge tragedy that Hungary has fallen so low [. . .]

Key Findings

There are important variations in the extent to which partisans display respect for political pluralism, both across and within the two countries under study. Overall, French partisans display a far more respectful attitude towards their political opponents. They tend to focus on their practices rather than their intentions when they criticise adversaries, but also recognise and sometimes declare as legitimate their opponents' principles. In addition, they show signs of belief in the morality of their opponents, and thus view the common good as a set of principles and objectives that partisans share, regardless of their political orientation. Importantly, each attribute of this pluralist political discourse holds together. French partisans hold back from 'motive-cynicism' because they view their opponents as guided by principles rather than base intentions. Because they recognise that their opponents act out of conviction, they also see them as concerned for the common good. Conversely, they can accept disagreement as legitimate, because they know that what ties partisans together is greater than what sets them apart.

Partisanship in Hungary could not be more different. Party members repeatedly engage in motive-cynicism and regularly deny that their opponents hold any principles at all. They engage in motive-cynicism, frequently accusing their opponents of being motivated by the desire for material gain or personal power. They frequently deny that their opponents endorse any kind of value system and depict them as fundamentally devoid of principle. Finally, they often directly accuse their opponents of being a threat to the common good and imply that they are outside the sphere of common political morality. Again, these attributes of anti-pluralist partisanship hold together: to suspect the intentions of opponents amounts to denying their principled nature, and if opponents act purely out of self-interest rather than principle, it follows that they are intrinsically immoral. From the extracts included towards the end of this chapter, it is clear that Hungarian partisans have no common understanding of the principles that bind their community together: what sets them apart is much greater than what binds them together.

In both countries, however, partisans on the Left show greater adherence to pluralist principles than those on the Right. UMP participants are not only more critical, but also more regularly target the sincerity of their opponents' position. While right-wing activists in France recognise that opponents defend certain principles, references to socialist ideology were themselves part of a critical stance. These ideas are qualified at best as delusional, at worst as a convenient political tool to gain votes regardless of the detrimental consequences for society as a whole. To this extent, right-wing partisanship in France carries a technocratic belief according to which there is a single yet obvious path to the common good, which opponents cannot perceive because they are blinded by their own ideology. This is a form of holism, but of a *benevolent* form: UMP seek to convince their opponents that they are in the wrong, not to eliminate them. PS activists, on the other hand, show more exemplary respect for political pluralism: they explicitly emphasise that they share a community of values with opponents, recognise their principled commitments, and therefore their legitimacy. In this process, they explicitly acknowledge that, in a democratic society, different parties will hold different understandings of common fundamental values.

More controversially, MSzP partisans could be defined as more pluralist than Fidesz activists. Right-wing activists in Hungary argue that their partisan ideas about the political community, anchored in ethno-nationalism, should be shared by all. In this process, they also fail to recognise the partial nature of their own beliefs. They take as the primary focus of their criticism the identity of opponents as heirs of the communist regime, thereby more fundamentally questioning the intrinsic morality of their opponents. Those who disagree with Fidesz are necessarily anti-national and have no legitimacy to govern. If these principles were to triumph, this would necessarily mean foreclosing political debate. This is also holism, but of a more aggressive and *intolerant* form than found among UMP partisans.[38] MSzP activists, on the other hand, take the undemocratic practices of their opponents as a focus of criticism, all the while recognising that their opponents adopted different practices in the past and are therefore not intrinsically evil. By categorising their opponents as undemocratic, MSzP participants paint Fidesz as ill-intentioned and unprincipled. However, the principles that they argue every party should adopt – a separation of powers, respect for constitutional essentials and human rights – would not foreclose partisan contestation if they were adopted by all. In other words, MSzP partisans do not argue in favour of a specific interpretation of key principles but defend an accepted constitutional framework within which all orientations, including those of pluralist opponents, could express themselves.

---

[38] Ethno-nationalism is by definition *culturally* anti-pluralist in terms of its lack of acceptance of minorities within the political community. But, in theory at least, it may not be incompatible with the political pluralism defended in this book – partisans who strive for the 'congruence of nation and state', as formulated by Mudde (2007), can in principle accept that others hold different yet legitimate political views from their own. Fidesz develops a particular brand of anti-pluralist nationalism, where opponents themselves are cast as foreign entities rather than legitimate members of the national political community.

7
Democracy in Partisan Custody

This book started with a theoretical ideal of democratic partisanship, building on the principles that democratic theorists expect parties to uphold. Having studied the discourse of French and Hungarian party members, I return to my initial research questions. *Is democratic partisanship a realistic ideal? Can partisans be both cohesive and pluralist?* and *Under what conditions are democratic forms of partisan identity likely to emerge?*

The discursive variations I find across countries, and between Left and Right, carry implications for students of political parties, theorists of partisanship and citizens concerned with the future of democracy. I start with an overview of my results, and what these say about partisanship as a democratic practice, focusing on the role of partisans as both agents of democratic change and products of their context. The second main section goes back to the theoretical ideal of democratic partisanship in light of my results. I argue against the commonplace association of partisanship and intransigence in democratic theory, while interrogating how the dependence of democratic partisanship on context should impact our normative expectations of parties. The final section returns to the political developments that first motivated this book, ideological convergence and partisan polarisation, and discusses some paths forward for partisanship in a time of democratic crises.

Democratic Partisanship as an Empirical Practice

This study provides evidence that partisanship as a real-world, democratic practice is both a pillar of liberal democratic systems and a product of specific cultural and economic conditions. From an empirical perspective, variations at the micro-level of partisan identity resonate with widely documented changes at the macro-level of party systems: there is a relationship between the extent to which party members in

France and Hungary meet standards of democratic partisanship, and the democratic performance of the organisations they belong to. The results confirm the pivotal role of parties as agents of democratic change, and the importance of political norms in informing the way parties act when in power. The variations uncovered also suggest democratic partisanship is context-dependent: it is only likely to emerge under specific conditions, with a history of open political competition and relaxed constraints on governmental agency facilitating democratic forms of partisan discourse. These empirical results highlight the frailty of liberal democracy itself, given its dependence on context-bound, democratic partisan agency.

The democratic agency of partisans

Shades of democratic partisanship

The three empirical chapters show important variations in democratic partisanship both within and across countries. Overall, the discourse of French partisans resonates with both standards: they are not only able to justify their own positions in an ideologically cohesive manner, but they also express greater respect for their opponents and thus for political pluralism. In turn, Hungarian partisans often struggle to unpack their own normative commitments, and how these translate into distinct policy packages – all the while expressing greater animosity and lesser respect for their political opponents.

There are also variations in democratic partisanship according to political affiliation within each country. The Left in both France and Hungary suffers from relative lack of cohesiveness, albeit with variations. In France, PS partisans display *ideological dissonance*. They know in theory what should distinguish their organisation from opponents, and their commitment has a strong normative grounding. But, in practice, they stumble on their party's lack of agency in power and de facto similarities with the ways in which their opponents govern. There is a strong misfit between what partisans believe their party should defend and what their party actually stands for. In Hungary, this lack of cohesiveness takes a more extreme form, which can be labelled as *ideological confusion*. Unlike PS participants, MSzP partisans have great difficulties identifying the core values that they believe in, or the ways in which they expect their organisation to act in power. They miss an ideal roadmap against which to assess their party's governmental practices. They are also the least cohesive of all four parties under study.

On the right side of both party systems, partisanship lacks relative pluralism rather than cohesiveness. UMP participants display a soft form of *benevolent holism*. They do not systematically question the intentions of opponents, deny their principled nature or orientation towards the common good. Yet, they still hold the technocratic belief that politics is about finding the right technical means to reach uncontroversial ends. Disagreements are rooted in the error and ideological blindness of opponents rather than in different appreciations of fundamental principles. UMP partisans certainly tolerate their opponents. But in their ideal world the PS would see reality as it is and agree with the UMP, thus leaving little room for political pluralism. But this also means left-wing partisans can, in theory, be convinced. To this extent, a pluralist debate is still warranted in the hope of eliminating disagreement in an ideal future.

In Hungary, right-wing party members display a more aggressive form of *intolerant holism*. For Fidesz activists, nationalism and concern for the common good are indistinguishable: they defend the view that there is a single, valid definition of the common good that they alone stand for. While, for UMP party members, opponents disagree because they are mistaken, in Hungary, Fidesz activists root disagreements in questions of morality. If opponents do not defend the same ideas as them, it is because they are fundamentally immoral – deep down, they do not care about public life. In such a situation there is no reason to even tolerate opponents, as these cannot be convinced: it is what they are, not what they think, which is at stake. As a result, Fidesz partisanship appears as the least pluralist of all four types considered here.

From democratic partisanship to liberal democracy

The strengths and weaknesses of democratic partisanship I found at the micro-level of party activity identity resonate with the democratic performance of the parties they identify with. These parallels provide cautious support for the empirical relevance of the theoretical model of democratic partisanship developed in Chapter 2, according to which the norms carried by political parties determine in part their contribution to democracy and, in turn, the vitality and endurance of liberal democracy itself.

Variations in the cohesiveness of partisanship across the different groups studied resonate with the theoretical expectations laid out in Chapter 2. Cohesive partisanship is most likely to sustain the *democratic* dimension of liberal democracy. This quality allows parties to fulfil their key function of intermediation between citizens and the state, providing a platform with which citizens can identify and thus exercise a form of collective self-rule. This assumption aligns with findings from Chapter 5 that right-wing partisanship is relatively more cohesive both in France and Hungary.

In both countries over the past two decades, right-wing parties have had a stronger electoral momentum and right-wing ideas a stronger hold on public opinion. Despite difficult recent years, the UMP has maintained a strong electoral lead of 10–15 points on the PS in past elections and has safeguarded part of its membership base. Taken together, parties from the Centre Right (*En marche!*, *Union des démocrates et indépendants*) to the Radical Right (*Rassemblement national*) have gathered absolute majorities in most French elections since 2012. This is also the case in Hungary, where Fidesz has built strong grass roots in the 2000s and earned two-thirds majorities in 2010, 2014 and 2018. In contrast, left-wing platforms generally fail to convince in both countries. The French Centre Left (PS, *Generations*), green (*Les Verts*) and Radical Left (*France insoumise*) took together less than a third of the vote in 2017 and have barely fared better since. The Hungarian MSzP has faced even more dismal results.[1]

My results provide grounds to argue that the contemporary success of right-wing platforms takes root, in part, in their relative ability to deliver more cohesive platforms: they can respond to the necessities of government while remaining true to foundational norms. In turn, the electoral vagrancies of the French and Hungarian Left have roots in an identity crisis. Neither PS partisans nor MSzP activists achieve a balance between remaining true to certain core values while adapting to a changing world. This provides a weak base for the democratic mobilisation and representation of citizens. Importantly, the democratic gains and losses associated with partisan cohesiveness seem largely *relative* to what other platforms in a given party system have to offer. Fidesz is less cohesive than the UMP, yet its capacity for mobilisation remains strong given the near absence of cohesive internal competition. Left-wing partisanship in France is more cohesive than in Hungary, but given its weakness vis-à-vis other parties, the PS's capacity for mobilisation is also limited.

Variations in pluralist respect across different groups also resonate with the theoretical expectations laid out in Chapter 2. Pluralist partisanship is most likely to sustain the *liberal* dimension of liberal democracy. Partisans who refrain from publicly disrespecting political opponents

---

[1] For a detailed discussion of macro-level changes in the French and Hungarian party systems, see Chapter 4.

will also be more likely to uphold constitutional settlements, and refrain from manipulating them to their own advantage. In turn, when mainstream partisans consider opposition as fundamentally evil, they will also see it as morally acceptable to limit the capacity for nuisance of other parties through institutional change. This assumption aligns with findings from Chapter 6 that pluralist commitments are generally weaker in Hungary, but also weaker in both countries among right-wing parties compared to left-wing ones.

Over the past ten years, Hungary under Fidesz rule has become one of the model examples of democratic backsliding, defined as the 'state-led debilitation or elimination of any of the political institutions that sustain an existing democracy' (Bermeo, 2016, p. 5). As developed in Chapter 4, these changes have involved Fidesz drafting an entirely new constitution to its own advantage, turning independent guardrails such as the media and judiciary into partisan machines, and considerably enlarging the scope of its executive power. The classic view on such authoritarian changes is that party elites are self-interested actors who, if insufficiently constrained by effective institutional safeguards, will abuse the power they are given (Herman, 2016; Herman and Muirhead, 2020). The results of this study suggest a more nuanced and perhaps more troubling conclusion. Party elites abuse power not only because they can, but because they inherit from an organizational culture where such forms of institutional domination are considered as acceptable and even necessary to further higher goods. The rank-and-file party members I interviewed did not personally benefit from the actions of Fidesz, yet they still believed that the good of their country was best served by the complete triumph of their own organisation. Where any mainstream party carries such a holist vision of politics, it is only a matter of time before democratic institutions themselves come under attack. Conversely, the endurance of liberal democracy in France is not solely a function of institutional design – in fact, France's hyper-presidentialism would make its institutions particularly prone to abuse of power. Constitutional settlements are supported by partisans who put their opponents' right to disagree above their own convictions, and therefore do not consider abuse of power as a legitimate course of action.

Pluralist commitments may be stronger in France than in Hungary, yet they are generally weaker among right-wing partisans. This again squares with what we know of the contemporary landscape of party politics in Europe, where threats to pluralism have mostly come from the right wing of the political spectrum (Crum, Oleart and Overeem, 2023). In line with these trends, the French mainstream Right has experienced a radical shift in the past two decades, adopting increasingly intolerant positions towards minorities and harsher positions on law and order. In this process, the Centre Right has shown growing willingness to accommodate the radical-right RN through policy mirroring and to abandon the 'cordon sanitaire' strategy previously enforced by all parties (Berezin, 2013; Godin, 2013; Haegel, 2012, pp. 239–97).[2] While the UMP itself has not engaged in abusive legalism when it was last in government (2007–12), it has actively contributed to the legitimisation of a political force which, if it were to come to power, would represent a challenge to the continued integrity of democratic institutions in France (Ivaldi, 2016). In defining this strategy, ideological proximity between the parties' leaderships and electorates (Gougou and Persico, 2017, pp. 317–18) has weighed more heavily than concern for the long-term faith of political pluralism.

Partisanship as a product of context

Democratic partisanship can emerge and endure in the real world of politics. But the strong variations I uncover also suggest that democratic partisanship is determined by context and will emerge only under specific circumstances. Partisans are shaped by the specific economic, historical and social environments in which they evolve. In the following sections, I analyse the structure of constraints and opportunities that fall on French and Hungarian partisans and contribute to shape their discourse. Through studying the ways in which party members interpret specific dimensions of their immediate context, I draw conclusions on how this context, in turn, impacts their representation of the world. As discussed in Chapter 3 (pp. 55–7 and 61–3), I consider two categories of relevant factors: first, the cultural 'toolkit' that partisans have at their disposal in formulating their claims; and second, the exogenous events – political, economic or social – that parties do not fully control yet need to respond to.

Democratic history and cultural resources

The discourse of partisans in both countries suggests that country-specific cultural resources can be more or less favourable to the development of cohesive or pluralist claims. Differences in the history of French

[2] Since 2011, the UMP has adopted the *ni–ni* (neither–nor) strategy in the second round of both local and national elections: in a situation where the party's score is too low to make it into the second round, and PS candidates are faced with RN ones, the party's position is to encourage their voters to vote neither for the Left nor for the Radical Right – and thus effectively to abstain. Previously, the UMP would side with the PS candidate in a run-off situation with a far-right opponent.

and Hungarian party competition go a long way towards explaining the relative strength of democratic partisanship in France and its relative weakness in Hungary.

Although French partisans refer to their country's past far less than Hungarian activists, France's long history of Left–Right competition is a constant subtext in the discourse of party members today and plays a role in furthering relative ideological cohesiveness and pluralist respect. The discourse of party members suggest that the general categories of 'Left' and 'Right' (White, 2011a), born in revolutionary France, have until recently retained a strong, albeit changing, significance in the country's political history (Gauchet, 1996). In 2013, Left and Right still served as key resources for partisans' positioning. In turn, party members are the carriers of this extended memory of free democratic competition.

In France, the established nature of the Left–Right dichotomy services the cohesiveness of partisan discourse. This is clear of the normative condition, as both political traditions are firmly grounded in a corpus of established ideas, values and traditions that have been associated with certain types of policy solutions over time (Bobbio, 1995; Lukes, 2003). Finally, Left and Right do not exist as autonomous political registers: they exist only as a dichotomy, each grounding its own meaning in opposition to the other (Dyrberg, 2005). This also facilitates partisan cohesiveness, providing party members with cues on how to differentiate their platforms from those of their opponents.

But the historical opposition between Left and Right is also an opportunity for respectful partisan discourse, and thus pluralist commitments. As seen in Chapter 5, French participants share a framework within which to understand the terms of partisan disagreement. Both PS and UMP groups define the key features of the left-wing and right-wing traditions in similar ways. Many of their accounts are fairly neutral: political disagreements are described in comparable terms by one or the other group. Arguably, the established nature of these political identities enables respect: each group of partisans sees opponents in light of a certain political tradition, tradition which is itself attached to a series of values and principles recognised by all. While off the cuff partisans may sometimes doubt the intentions of their opponents or question their commitment to the common good, these attitudes are tempered by a deeper regard for the wider tradition within which the action of their opponents is grounded. As Dyrberg insists, this is why the Left–Right dichotomy may be considered a democratic ideology:

both poles are necessary counterpoints to each other and are thus in a relation of equality (Dyrberg, 2005).

In contrast, Hungarian partisans carry the legacy of a recent authoritarian history. This context helps explain the relatively weaker ideological cohesiveness in the discourse of Hungarian party members, specifically on socio-economic issues. A short history of open debate on these questions means that the policies and ideas generally associated with the left-wing and right-wing traditions of thought are less neatly circumscribed. Left and Right do not prescribe well-defined roles for political parties, precisely because neither the nationalist nor the socialist tradition has had to take part in regular alternation in power before 1989 and therefore systematically defend their ideas against the criticism of opponents. In the absence of a history of free competition, neither political tradition learned how to make partial claims about the common good.

Authoritarian legacies also act as a constraint on respect for pluralism in Hungary. The memories of partisans are of either their own camp being repressed, or their own camp dominating others. Partisans have a limited experience of treating each other as political equals, and instead largely reproduce the 'us versus them' narrative of pre-democratic times. They still describe opposition as a threat to the common good. At a deeper level, it is also apparent that the foundations of the political community are still contested. In the past century, Hungary had three different regimes in which the ruling elite unilaterally proclaimed that it held the truth on how to advance the good of the country. Hungarian parties have had very little time to suggest, contest and negotiate what they have in common with their political opponents, what the supra-partisan political community actually looks like. This contributes to Fidesz and MSzP activists having a fundamentally different reading of what the terms of Hungarian political competition are. Contrarily to French partisans who understand Left and Right in broadly similar ways, they have no shared frame of understanding. Fidesz partisans see party competition as opposing the foreign to the national, the communist to the anti-communist. MSzP partisans see party competition as opposing the democratic to the authoritarian, modernity to backwardness.

Importantly, historical legacies may also help explain greater cohesiveness on the Hungarian Right than on the Left. The discourse of MSzP participants is arguably constrained by the recent authoritarian past of their own party. Hungary's time under Soviet domination tainted a longer and broader tradition of socialist thought in the collective memory.

For the MSzP, committing to democracy and market liberalism in the 1990s meant distancing themselves from this authoritarian past. This has left activists little ground in which to anchor their identity. Partisans on the Left see themselves as the champions of democratic principles and institutions, but their authority to advocate these principles is largely compromised. The post-communist Left carries the guilt of past perpetrators, with no past to take pride in. This also means that party members today have few ideas to promote, fewer policies to link to these ideas, and lack certainty on what sets them apart from their opponents.

Conversely, political history offers Fidesz activists more favourable resources for forming a cohesive discourse. While the tradition of nationalism and social conservatism they inherit from also oppressed otherness in the interwar era, this past is easier to romanticise than socialist times, for a number of reasons. First, Horthy's rule corresponds to the only period of time prior to the late twentieth century when the country was independent from foreign powers. Second, this history was taught in a very selective fashion after World War II, the anti-Semitism of the interwar era – and Hungary's participation in the Holocaust especially – being largely absent from the school curriculum or public debate during socialism. Third, both nationalism and Catholicism were repressed under Soviet domination, providing these traditions with a rebellious, countercultural edge in Hungarian post-socialist society. This historical background is central to the discourse of Fidesz participants, which is all the more remarkable that they were politically socialised after 1989. Party members on the Hungarian Right regularly allude to a time when, in the name of the abstract, foreign principles of socialism, nationalist feelings and religious sentiment were suppressed, and in turn link their own party to a tradition of resistance against the communist regime. Not only does this give temporal anchorage to Fidesz's nationalist platform, but it also provides party members with a blueprint to talk about the present. This is most clear when they compare the socialists' past collaboration with foreign powers to their current support of the EU. This allows Fidesz participants to defend their own policies as grounded in the national interest and their opponents' position as embodying foreign, abstract principles adverse to the Hungarian nation.

This historical context also provides Fidesz party members with greater opportunities for anti-pluralist discourse. They express the resentment of the dominated victim and ground their convictions in the memory of past injustices. They picture their opponents as carrying an oppressive, foreign tradition that is not worthy of respect. But they are fighting a hegemony that disappeared twenty-five years ago, in a contemporary context where the socialist ideal has little practical relevance. Against these ghosts of the past, they declare the supreme legitimacy of a nationalist understanding of the common good, one that had no right of expression before 1989. The terms of the partisan opposition are therefore themselves contested, as this narrative cannot be shared by the MSzP: it does not recognise itself in this oppressive tradition, nor does it pride itself in carrying its memory. Fidesz's framing is perceived by left-wing activists as a form of injustice, a disloyal attack against the MSzP. This situation is, in turn, not conducive to MSzP partisans respecting the Fidesz, and its ideas.

Exogenous factors

Historical legacies are not the sole shapers of partisan discourse, however: activists are also constrained by exogenous factors in their contemporary environment, as they need to adapt political traditions to their present context (see Chapter 3, pp. 55–7). Political, economic and social phenomena beyond the full control of parties may be more or less favourable to democratic forms of partisanship. These exogenous factors do not necessarily impact the discourse of left and right-wing partisans in the same way, given activists make sense of these changes with different political traditions in hand.

French and Hungarian partisans inherit different historical legacies, but their domestic politics are exposed to the same processes of internationalisation – with comparable economic and political incentives weighing on their governments (see Chapter 3, pp. 61–3). This context was central to the group discussions and structured left- and right-wing political discourse, albeit in very different ways. Right-wing partisans in both countries made sense of this context more easily, but the way they read these events also emboldened their anti-pluralist discourse.

UMP partisans frame positively the necessity for governments to consider the current laws of the market in a globalised context. Their foundational values provide a blueprint for reading the context of increasing economic interdependence among European nations and for defining a model of governance on this basis. According to the party members I talked to, governments should be pragmatic in their approach to economic policymaking and accompany rather than resist the global trend towards market liberalisation. In developing this argument, they make good use of their available cultural toolkit. According to Lukes, the main characteristic of the Right across time and space is to defend the social necessity of respecting timeless laws – the divine right of kings in pre-democratic times, the laws of the market today (Lukes, 2003).

This worldview helps UMP activists to make sense of financial globalisation or European economic integration – and thus to develop a cohesive discourse on this basis.

PS participants refer more frequently and more directly than UMP participants to the impact of external constraints on the economic policy of national governments. But they struggle to give meaning to this context in light of their values. PS participants inherit left-wing ideals according to which 'timeless laws' serve those in power and contribute to increasing inequalities (Lukes, 2003). They are at pains, however, to justify their party's response to globalisation on the basis of these values. External constraints on governmental action explain why, according to PS members, their party cannot align its policies with left-wing ideals. But even when they do not accept this state of affairs, PS participants are mostly unable to suggest an alternative set of governance practices. While the current economic context is an opportunity for right-wing partisans to develop a cohesive discourse, on the Left this context is an obstacle partisans struggle to overcome.

How UMP partisans read this economic context also feeds into their anti-pluralism. As shown in Chapter 6, they regularly resort to a technocratic logic of expertise to justify their claims: according to them, the reality of economics, rather than political ideology, dictates the necessity of liberalisation and state disengagement. Such a stance, however, is also conducive to a benevolent form of holism. UMP partisans often argue there exists a well-defined set of appropriate means to reach established and undisputed societal goods. They also position their own party, doing away with 'ideology', as most able to find the proper means to solve common problems. Globalisation offers UMP participants evidence to defend that traditionally left-wing positions on social equality, public services and state interventionism are unrealistic and delusional. UMP partisans are then a short step away from arguing that, if the PS still holds these positions, it is for base motives rather than out of concern for the common good.

While PS participants do not embrace this neoliberal logic, they are worried about the tendency of their own party to do so. PS partisans defend the necessity of political disagreement in democratic societies but believe it to be increasingly absent in their own party system – in large part because their party adopts the ideas and practices of its opponents. The preoccupation of PS members with themselves, their concern about their party's incapacities, also impedes their effective criticism of the UMP. PS members are in some way more respectful, but this is in part because they do not engage to the same degree in unpicking their opponents' stances.

In Hungary, external constraints on policymaking are also key in explaining differences of cohesiveness on the Left and the Right. Overall, Fidesz party members make sense of the weight of external constraints more successfully than their opponents but take the very opposite path to UMP party members. Their historical emphasis on national sovereignty is coherent with an oppositional posture towards the EU. Their party has rhetorically chosen demarcation over integration within the global economy, and thus resolutely positioned itself on one side of the new divides created by globalisation (Kriesi et al., 2008). Party members defend the national economy and culture against external threats, and depict their opponents as favouring foreign, multinational corporations instead. By establishing a clear parallel between the past USSR domination and the EU's current influence, Fidesz partisans tie together the past and the present. They reactivate a century-long narrative of national victimhood, all the while stressing the importance of political agency in an age of nation-state decline (Csehi and Zgut, 2020).

MSzP activists, on the other hand, struggle to make sense of these changes. Their party largely embraced integration within the global economy all through the 1990s and 2000s. They allied with the liberal SzDSz from 1994 to 1998 and were instrumental in deconstructing welfare security nets during this period (Grzymala-Busse, 2002). From 2002 to 2004, they presided over the country's accession to the EU, and, after the 2007 financial crisis, implemented the programme of austerity pushed by international creditors. Crucially, however, none of this is a source of pride for MSzP partisans. To go even further, it is not always clear that the MSzP activists I talked to were aware of their party's role in their country's conversion to market liberalism. They maintain the pro-European integration outlook which justified much of these reforms, but rarely defend economic liberalisation or privatisation for its own sake. Similarly to Fidesz discourse, cultural resources and contemporary events interact, but here to the detriment of MSzP cohesiveness. The MSzP largely relinquished its socialist heritage but could not fully embrace neoliberalism in its place. It conducted reforms to align with the demands of international actors, eager to show its commitment to democratic and capitalist values. But the party also failed to provide justifications for these decisions beyond references to a necessary 'return to Europe'. Now that Hungary has effectively joined the international political community, with all the social costs involved, MSzP partisans are left with very little else to fight for.

Further research would be needed to strengthen the empirical conclusions in this section. The theoretical framework of democratic partisanship outlined in Chapter 2, as well as the methodology discussed in Chapter 3, can form the starting point for future empirical studies. More research is needed into how democratic norms compare across different countries and at different levels of the same party organisation – supporters, party members and elites. The indicators could serve to multiply cases, but also to analyse different types of party data, including social media messaging, elite speeches or televised debates. This type of data would allow further testing of a number of claims developed in this book: that the discourse of party members provides a good indication of the norms within which the party socialises them, that similar norms structure the party's public messaging, that the democratic performance of parties is dependent on these norms, and, finally, that democratic partisanship itself is largely a product of the historical and contemporary context within which it develops.

Back to the Ideal of Democratic Partisanship

The theoretical foundations for this study take root in a thriving literature on the normative merits of partisanship and its supportive role in liberal-democratic systems. This book has made the abstract standards of democratic theory amenable to empirical study and put forward one of the first systematic explorations of the real-world relevance of these normative ideals. In the following sections, I ask what my results say about the ideal of democratic partisanship. I first argue that democratic partisanship is an attainable ideal and show that my results belie the common association between partisanship and intransigence. I then ask whether the context-dependent nature of democratic partisanship justifies lowering our normative expectations.

An attainable ideal? The complementarity of cohesiveness and pluralism

It is commonplace for political theorists to place partisan conviction at odds with pluralist ethics The association of partisanship with sectoral interests, divisiveness and intransigence is as old as the first writings about political parties in the eighteenth century, with authors such as Bolingbroke, Hume or Madison seeing parties at best as an unavoidable yet nefarious by-product of free government (Ball, 1989; Rosenblum, 2008). These negative associations largely persist in the second half of the twentieth century, and to this day. Minimal theories of democracy placed parties centre stage in the post-war era, but only as groups of self-interested elites seeking votes and power (Skinner, 1973; Pateman, 2007 [1970]).

Deliberative democratic thought has largely shunned parties, positing that these contravene some of the basic principles of reciprocal regard and flexible preferences that form its bedrock (van Biezen and Saward, 2008). While an important literature in democratic theory has, in the past decade, aimed to rehabilitate parties as democratic agents, even this school of thought admits to a tension between partisan identity and tolerance for opposition. One of the aims of this study was precisely to focus on the articulation of partisan cohesiveness and respect for pluralism, and interrogate whether these two standards for good partisanship in the literature are, in fact, at odds with each other. I asked, more broadly, whether the ideal of democratic partisanship – combining cohesive justification and respect for opposing views – was in fact a realistic one with roots in empirical practice (see Chapter 2).

The results of this study support the assumption that, under certain conditions, democratic partisanship is an attainable ideal in the real world of party politics. First, partisans judge party politics by very similar standards to those set out by democratic theorists (see Chapter 4, pp. 83–96). The activists I met in both countries see the partisan qualities of cohesiveness and pluralism as necessary components of a democratic society and regret their weakness within their own polity. In France, PS partisans perceive the lack of programmatic cohesiveness of their own party and regret this state of affairs. Without using the terms of pluralism or cohesiveness, Hungarian activists also see that hatred of opponents brings deadlock. They wish for more substantial debates with opponents and yearn for a spirit of greater compromise. Democratic partisanship has real-world relevance to the extent it is also an ideal for partisans themselves.

Second, the discourse of some party members, specifically in France, shows strong, real-world resonance with the standards of democratic partisanship. A number of participants in this study displayed a strong capacity for justifying their political positions alongside respect for their political opponents. I argue in the next paragraphs that the relationship between the different attributes of democratic partisan discourse goes, in fact, beyond simple compatibility. In many ways, ideological cohesiveness and respect for pluralism are complementary, if not symbiotic. This is applicable both to the dynamics of partisan identity at the individual level (cohesive partisans are more likely to be pluralist, and vice versa) and to the dynamics of partisan identity in relation to opponents (partisans with democratic opponents are more likely to behave in democratic ways, and vice versa).

At the level of individual partisans, the interviews offer evidence that a cohesive worldview serves partisans in their respectful criticism of political opponents. French partisans do not attack their opponents on their intentions or accuse them of being morally deficient at least in part because they do not need to do so in order to oppose them. They know what they stand for, have firm ideas on their own values and policies, and are fully aware of how these differ from those of their opponents. They can afford to put forward a constructive, justified indictment of their opponents without resorting to disrespectful arguments.

However, this positive relationship can also be seen to function in reverse: respect calls for cohesiveness. It is also because opponents are part of a common political space and worthy of respect that they should be opposed with strong and justified arguments. Respected opponents cannot simply be dismissed: they deserve to be opposed with a convincing set of values and policies. The fact that French partisans agree on fundamental principles and see their opponents are committed to the common good encourages their formulation of cohesive claims. This common base focuses the scope of partisan claims: knowing this, partisans can set aside moral arguments and compete over rival interpretations of foundational values and on the means necessary to further these in practice.

Cohesiveness and pluralism are also complementary in relation to the democratic qualities of opponents: a good opposition calls for reciprocal regard. In France, partisans treat opponents respectfully in part because their opponents are worthy of respect: they are principled in their engagement, develop sound policies on this basis and are broadly loyal to the liberal democratic framework. The fact that opposition discourse is cohesive also makes it all the more important that partisans develop normatively grounded and policy-based responses to counter them effectively. If they are to be defeated, convincing opponents need to be opposed, not looked down on.

Crucially, *lack of* cohesiveness and pluralism also appear to work together in the Hungarian context. At the level of individuals, uncertainty around foundational values can encourage forms of disrespect. Hungarian partisans have very little else to oppose their adversaries than accusations of immorality. With no clear set of values on which to ground their opposition and no clear set of policies to suggest as alternatives, it is tempting to focus on corruption scandals or the personality of adversaries. With confused notions over the values and policies that they themselves stand for, it is easier to accuse opponents of being immoral and to engage in negative campaigning.

In turn, weak respect for opponents also impedes the development of cohesive claims. If partisans see themselves as the only legitimate representatives of the political community, they will see very little need to justify why this is the case. It then becomes sufficient for them to assert their moral superiority. By the same token, when opponents are considered as fundamentally immoral, they do not deserve to be addressed with alternative, coherent accounts of the common good. They can simply be dismissed.

Again, these logics play out in relation with opponents: when one mainstream actor is anti-pluralist or lacks cohesiveness, this encourages opponents to mirror this behaviour. This is clearly part of the downward spiral occurring in Hungary. Ideologically vague opponents may encourage disrespect. When Fidesz participants, for instance, call their opponents unprincipled and lacking fixed commitments to a series of values, they are not only being disrespectful – they are also describing a political reality. The MSzP's confusion over its own identity is not only an important constraint on Fidesz's pluralist potential, but it also removes the necessity for Fidesz to counter its proposals with stronger ones. This negative dynamic plays out even more strongly for MSzP partisans. The anti-pluralism of the MSzP appears to be largely reactive and points to the difficulties of developing a respectful discourse towards a fundamentally disloyal and undemocratic actor.

The key trade-off here may be less between cohesiveness and pluralism than between two fundamentally different types of partisan disagreement: based on ideas and policies, or on identity and morality. Ideas and policies are up for debate and subject to reasoning, thus encouraging good justification in the context of adversarial relations with persuadable opponents. Identity and morality are non-negotiable absolutes, thereby fuelling scornful assertion rather than measured justification. Partisanship, however, does not need to follow the latter path. By focusing on how they think differently from opponents, rather than on fundamental differences in moral worth, partisans can embrace both cohesive forms of justification and respectful opposition.

A fair ideal? Balancing normative goals and attention to context

While the ideal of democratic partisanship is attainable, this research suggests it is only likely to materialise under very specific cultural, political and economic conditions. Cross-national variations in cohesiveness and pluralism highlight the importance of these factors. A history of open party competition and relaxed constraints on state agency facilitate democratic forms of partisan discourse. As just seen, partisans also tend to mirror the qualities, or faults, of their opponents. While democratic partisans encourage respectful and cohesive opposition in France, the corrupt practices and incoherent discourse of opponents largely contribute to lower the bar for democratic partisanship in Hungary.

Where does the conditionality of democratic partisanship leave our normative ideals? Should we still expect that partisans in adverse conditions uphold democratic standards? The following sections examine two main challenges to normative theorising that arise from the conditionality of democratic partisanship. First, that the standard of democratic partisanship is Western-centred, excessively universalist, and therefore inapplicable beyond first-wave democracies. Second, the related, yet slightly different claim that democratic partisanship becomes a naive, if not a dangerous, ideal when applied to parties that are structurally disadvantaged in backsliding contexts.

A Western ideal? The question of cultural sensitivity

Theories of democratic partisanship are anchored in the Western European and American experiences of party system development. My results caution against taking for granted the cultural and structural preconditions of our theoretical models and call for greater attention among theorists to the structural limits of partisan agency. For some, my findings could also call into question the contexts within which the standard of democratic partisanship can legitimately be applied. Can Hungarian partisanship be assessed with these standards, given their roots in Western political thought and history? Using this line of questioning, Fidesz elites have regularly accused the EU of imperialism for holding Hungary accountable to the model of liberal democracy and, in this process, failing to acknowledge Hungary's specific heritage (Csehi and Zgut, 2020; Isaac, 2017).

I cautiously maintain that it remains relevant to study democratic partisanship in non-Western contexts, under certain conditions. This requires seeing political culture not as a static, immutable characteristic of a given countries, but as a body of norms that changes incrementally as political actors make sense of current events with the help of past scripts. In this understanding, democratic norms are not a fundamental trait of certain cultures and an entirely foreign concept for others. Depending on their direction, processes of cultural change may just as well lead to the failure of historically established democratic regimes (the USA today being a case in point; see McCoy et al., 2018), as to the gradual consolidation of nascent democracies. Partisans are, to this extent, not fully determined by the structures within which they operate. They have agency in how they interpret the past and their current environment, and this interpretation, in turn, shapes the political regime they contribute to. This also means that, while partisanship is shaped by culture, the faith of democracy is not culturally predetermined in any given polity.

In line with the above, using the standard of democratic partisanship in non-Western contexts requires some evidence that liberal democracy as an ideal resonates with the history and struggles of citizens – that the ideal is in a process of reappropriation on the ground. In this specific case, the concept of liberal democracy is foreign neither to the history of post-communist Europe generally nor to Hungary in particular. At the European periphery, the country still inhabits the same geographical space as first-wave Western democracies, with important cross-cultural influences. Hungarian twentieth century history is riddled with examples of democratic struggle, and many Hungarians today still hold dear the liberal-democratic ideal. They have triggered episodic democratic revolutions in the past two centuries, the key dates of 1848, 1956 and 1989 echoing major uprisings elsewhere in Europe. Since the end of the Cold War there also exists a widespread aspiration to 'return to Europe' in post-communist states. Ample survey data shows that, to this day, support for European integration in high in Hungary (Hvg.hu, 2020), and an above EU-average share of the Hungarian population identifies with EU citizenship (81 per cent against 71 per cent) (Eurobarometer, 2022b).

Hungarians today also still aspire to democratic rule. In 2017, 78 per cent of survey respondents in Hungary considered democracy as a good or very good way of governing their country, against 81 per cent of French respondents in the same survey (Wike, Simmons, Stokes and Fetterolf, 2017). Recent Eurobarometer data shows that Hungarian citizens see it as one of the European Parliament's key missions to protect democracy, human rights and the rule of law in the EU – in proportions comparable to the European average (Eurobarometer, 2022a). Given Fidesz's repeated two-thirds majorities since 2010, it is likely that comparable support for European integration and democracy in Hungary and the rest of Europe hides starkly different realities. Yet, these numbers still suggest that the 'will of the Hungarian people' is far more complex and ambivalent on these questions than Fidesz leaders like to suggest.

Finally, this book provides powerful testimony that democratic partisanship is not solely a series of abstract, universalist principles devised by political theorists, but an ideal that partisans themselves can hold dear – and this even in societies with little history of democratic opposition. While partisan discourse in Hungary lacks cohesiveness or pluralism, the activists I met there still aspire to these qualities. The fall of the Soviet bloc has opened, for the first prolonged period of time in the country's history, a free confrontation of ideas about the common good. It has also revealed the problems associated with parties lacking a shared basis. The young Hungarian partisans I interviewed are learning from the contemporary political context and are contributing to changing the culture they are part of. Hungarian partisans do fall short of recognising the responsibility of their own party in the dynamics that are eroding liberal-democratic institutions. But they still have a capacity to make a lucid diagnosis of the pathologies of contemporary partisanship in their own country and therefore to take a first step towards their resolution. Hungarians' historical experience of democratic struggle and their present-day support for democratic values gives us reasons to continue to hold their mainstream partisans accountable to liberal-democratic standards.

A naive ideal? The question of power imbalances

My findings raise another thorny normative challenge: whether it is legitimate to hold partisans accountable to the norms of democratic partisanship when they are faced with fundamentally disloyal, undemocratic actors. I argue in the affirmative, on the condition that said partisans are still in a position to access political power, and can therefore be considered as part of mainstream politics. In 2013, Hungary was still classified by academics and international rating agencies as a democracy, and the Centre Left had been in power three short years before my interviews. To this extent, and despite backsliding at the time of my fieldwork, the MSzP still had a claim to political power and therefore specific responsibilities attached to its mainstream status (see Chapter 2, pp. 17–18).

Today, the situation is quite different. The balance of power has resolutely shifted towards Fidesz, the conservative party that has won three two-thirds majorities in a row at the time of publication, and this largely thanks to its capture of the state. The new institutional landscape has durably undermined the chances of opposition forces winning in the immediate future. Given this process of systematic disempowerment, it would be difficult to classify the MSzP as a mainstream party today, and therefore to hold it accountable to the norms of democratic partisanship. The development of a cohesive and pluralist platform in this context of skewed competition is made considerably more difficult for opposition parties, a form of imbalance that was already starting to be visible at the time of my interviews. First, these reforms complicate the display of respect for pluralism, which would entail left-wing activists acting as if the Fidesz government were principled, well intentioned, and striving towards the common good. Second, these reforms have a direct impact on the ability of the opposition to develop a cohesive discourse – a clear programme of government, linked to well-defined values and contrasting with the political offer of opponents.

From a normative perspective, there are therefore good reasons to relax our standards for partisans who are in a position of systematic disadvantage and to justify 'negative' forms of reciprocity against the perpetrators of democratic backsliding (Schedler, 2020, pp. 6–7). To this extent, minimally understood liberal-democratic institutions are a necessary, preliminary framework to use the standards of democratic partisanship, with different expectations applying in authoritarian regimes. White and Ypi, for instance, theorise the virtues of revolutionary partisanship required 'to fight the injustice of an oppressive regime', acknowledging the need, in certain circumstances, for a more radical contestation of structures of power which does away with the 'ethics of compromise' that they otherwise advocate (White and Ypi, 2016, p. 164).

This same logic, however, does not apply in institutional contexts that remain free and fair, even where mainstream parties are faced with disloyal opponents. The mainstreaming of anti-pluralist populism in countries with competitive elections has made such situations increasingly widespread (Herman and Muldoon, 2018a). The US Democratic Party and France's *En marche!*, for example, are today faced with opponents that would likely fail on most of the standards of democratic partisanship developed in this book. As I show in the next section, if the objective of opponents is to defend democracy in these situations, and their institutional access to power is not fundamentally restricted, the norms of democratic partisanship are still the right means to this end.

The Future of Party Democracy

I started this book with the assumption that, as observers of the political world, we gain from employing an explicitly normative vocabulary, one which characterises precisely the democratic limitations of political parties today. With this vocabulary and what I learned from applying it in France and Hungary, I return in this final section to the developments that motivated this study: the political apathy fuelled by party cartelisation, and the polarising impact of populism.

I find a link between weak cohesiveness and anti-pluralism at the micro-level of party identity: not only do cohesiveness and pluralism tend to work hand-in-hand as qualities attached to individual partisans, but these qualities also work in relation to opponents: cohesive and pluralist partisans also call for cohesive and pluralist opposition. These dynamics shed light on the democratic trajectory of European party systems today. In the following paragraphs, I draw some cautious parallels between these findings at the micro-level of partisan identity, and the interdependence of various guises of ideological vacuity and anti-pluralism at the macro-level of European party systems. These dependencies also offer some way forward for reviving democratic forms of partisanship in the future and, thereby, liberal democracy itself.

The structure of populism itself is one of the most obvious manifestations of weak party ideologies and anti-pluralism working in concert. In its most problematic iterations, populism appears to cumulate all the features of undemocratic partisanship. As many authors have pointed out, anti-pluralism is a key feature of populist political speech (Mudde, 2007; Müller, 2016; Stanley, 2008). Right-wing populists, especially, focus on the ill-intentions of opponents, bent on defending the private interests of elites rather than the common good of the people, deny their principled nature, and defend the conviction that they alone can represent the political community. When László Kövér, co-founding member of Fidesz and speaker of the National Assembly of Hungary, declares that 'the current opposition is not part of the Hungarian nation', he is only slightly more bluntly anti-pluralist than former US President Donald Trump according to whom critical media are 'enemies of the People' (Glasser, 2019; Szily, 2020).

Yet, in line with the findings from this study, populism also tends to lack a cohesive political ideology. Beyond the normative commitment to a nationalist idea of the political community, few radical-right populists provide a justified indictment of how these values can translate into a coherent policy programme. Many scholars prefer to label populism as a 'discourse' or 'style' as a result, and even those who recognise it as an ideology stress its 'thinness' and lack of coherence (Aslanidis, 2015, p. 89). Arguably, populist lack of cohesiveness is related to the anti-pluralist dimension of this phenomenon. Justification is superfluous *because* the populist party is morally superior and obviously more capable than its opponents. This is clearly expressed by Viktor Orbàn, according to whom '[n]o policy-specific debates are needed now, the alternatives in front of us are obvious [. . .] for rebuilding the economy it is not theories that are needed but rather thirty robust lads who start working to implement what we all know needs to be done' (cited in Müller, 2016, pp. 26–7). This echoes the premise of the 'Make America Great Again' slogan, according to which Trump's simple presence in the White House could restore the common good, with the meaning of 'greatness' and the steps towards its realisation being left largely unspecified. Echoing the discourse of Hungarian party members, anti-pluralism and ideological vacuity work hand-in-hand to produce particularly undemocratic brands of partisanship.

As discussed above, cohesiveness and pluralism, or their lack thereof, are also shaped in response to opponents. Scholarship has long emphasised that populist, anti-pluralist politics is at least partly a response to weakly cohesive mainstream partisanship. Populism triumphs against the backdrop of weak democratic agency in an era of mass unemployment and ideological convergence (Hay, 2007; Mouffe, 2005a). This is because populists can then easily point to the subservience of opponents to international creditors, the lack of choice they offer, and their inability to make decisive steps to correct the ills brought about by a globalised economy. They mobilise by asserting the primacy of popular sovereignty when opponents have largely given up on this notion and declaring war on those who aim to restrict it.

It is also well-established that the ways mainstream parties have dealt with populist political contenders has nourished rather than halted this negative dynamic. Different forms of anti-pluralism, rather than ideologically cohesive positions, have informed these responses. One dominant reaction has been the moralisation of these actors and their voters, mirroring the anti-pluralism of populist parties themselves. In Europe, especially, populist parties were long treated as essentially illegitimate given their anti-democratic edge (Downs, 2002; Mouffe, 2005). In the 1980s and 1990s, this justified ignoring these political parties and their programmes, rather than offering a constructive rebuttal of their ideas and policies. When radical-right political forces became a more serious electoral threat to right- and left-wing parties in the 2000s, the strategy shifted to accommodation (Bale et al., 2010; Wagner and Meyer, 2016). Mainstream parties adopted stricter positions on immigration and security to retain voters tempted by the Radical Right, all the while continuing to be dismissive towards these forces in their discourse. These strategies have largely failed to halt the rise of the populist Radical Right in most European countries and, according to recent studies, may even have contributed to its success (Krause et al., 2022; Meijers and Williams, 2020).

Technocratic appeals are another, anti-pluralist variant of mainstream responses to the populist Radical Right, with an emphasis on apolitical expertise as a point of contrast to the uninformed decision-making of populist actors. This response also perpetuates an anti-pluralist view of the world, to the extent it argues there exist single-policy solutions to social, political and economic issues which experts can identify and implement (Bickerton and Invernizzi Accetti, 2017; Caramani, 2017). If populism is weak in the executive dimension, with little in terms of a coherent policy programme for government, technocracy also fundamentally lacks the normative basis of partisanship, a corpus of ideas and values that justify the implementation of given policies.

The argument according to which partisans committed to democracy should give up on pluralist standards when faced with disloyal contenders rests on the assumption that this is a more effective strategy. As the findings for this study show, however, partisans do not need to compromise their cohesiveness, and thus their capacity for mobilisation and conviction, in order to defend pluralism as a political principle. Conversely, anti-pluralism is no guarantee that partisans can respond effectively to their authoritarian opponents. Focusing on the moral deficiencies of opponents may in fact distract from building the sound alternatives that are needed in such circumstances. When partisans have little else to oppose their adversaries than accusations of immorality, they risk alienating those convinced by their opponents and turn their own voters away from the polling stations. More fundamentally perhaps, retaliatory 'tit-for-tat' strategies participate in negative spirals of affective polarisation. This nourishes discursive violence and, ultimately, does not protect the integrity of democratic institutions – in fact, it might provide opponents with arguments to undermine them further (Herman and Muirhead, 2021, pp. 374–7; Schedler, 2020, pp. 6–8).

Long-term trends in ideological convergence and populist polarization are, to this extent, fundamentally linked. The Left–Right divide, which carried with it some fundamental norms of pluralism and cohesiveness, is losing its relevance in contemporary Europe, precisely because parties are failing to adapt its meaning to contemporary circumstances. In this process, Western European parties are progressively cutting themselves off from political roots that have been built over more than a century of open party competition, and increasingly engaging in empty, moralistic attacks to substitute for them. The Left–Right dichotomy is being replaced in many places by a new, more democratically dubious opposition between populist and technocratic appeals (Bickerton and Invernizzi Accetti, 2017; Caramani, 2017; Zanotti, 2021). This is obvious in France, where the Left–Right opposition has been relegated to the margins of politics and a new divide has appeared between a populist pole represented by Marine Le Pen's *Front national* and a technocratic one represented by Emmanuel Macron's *En marche!* (Lorimer, 2018). Contemporary dynamics of party polarisation in the USA follow a similar model. Affective polarisation based on negative emotions towards opponents has evolved at a far quicker rate than issue-based polarisation, based in programmatic disagreements (Iyengar, Lelkes, Levendusky, Malhotra and Westwood, 2019; Lelkes, 2016; Mason, 2016). Moral superiority, negative campaigning and personal attacks have partly replaced programmatic party competition (Ansolabehere and Iyengar, 1995; Gutmann and Thompson, 2012; Mansbridge and Martin, 2013).[3] Partisan identities anchored in a commitment to political justification and pluralism are giving way to ideologically vacuous and intolerant forms.

---

[3] Between 1994 and 2016, the proportion of Republicans having highly unfavourable views of their opponents rose from 21 to 58 per cent, and for Democrats from 17 to 55 per cent (McCoy et al., 2018, p. 30). At the same time, however, Republicans and Democrats can agree on policy when they ignore which party has initiated it (Mason, 2018).

There are some troubling parallels, then, between the dynamics of partisanship uncovered in Hungary and more widespread developments in Western European party systems. As Sean Hanley stressed already a decade ago, 'Western Europe may be increasingly converging towards the CEE [Central and Eastern European] model of fragmented, fluid electorates, ideologically rootless parties and pragmatic managerial politicians whose hold on power is disturbed only by periodic populist upsurges at the polls' (Hanley, 2012, p. 795). The effect that anti-pluralist partisanship has on democratic structures will depend in part on how established democracies are in the first place. In newly born democracies such as Hungary, the stakes are certainly higher. The birth of a democratic culture will always be slow and cumbersome, with nascent democratic systems far more vulnerable to radical forms of erosion. In France, as in other established democracies, it will likely take some time before undemocratic forms of partisanship reach democracy's institutional backbone. However, a democratic past is no insurance against backsliding. Given sufficient electoral clout, mainstream parties have the power to rewrite the rules of the democratic game. Constitutional settlements can delay or limit abuse of power, but they cannot indefinitely protect established democracies from the abusive legalism of anti-pluralist majorities. Crucially, the nefarious effects of anti-pluralism on democratic institutions are already being felt in established democracies with populist governments, including in the USA, Italy and Austria (Albertazzi and Mueller, 2013; Levitsky and Ziblatt, 2018; Norris, 2017).

The Hungarian case should therefore serve as a 'cautionary tale' for democrats elsewhere (Komárek, 2014). In the long run, democratic forms of partisanship are necessary to the survival of democratic regimes – neither existing institutions nor a history of democracy can substitute for the democratic agency of those who exercise power. First-wave democracies still gain some stability from their history and have a lot to lose from partisans who cut ties with their roots. Faced with undemocratic actors, democratic partisans should resist the temptation of responding with anti-pluralism, and instead search their own history for values, ideas and policies to which they can give contemporary meaning. In adverse circumstances, partisans committed to liberal democracy still have a responsibility to exercise their agency in its defence.

Appendix 1: Discussion Guidelines

Introduction

Presentation of author and project, guarantee of anonymity, presentation of participants.

'Thank you. I'm going to give each of you twelve cards. Please have a look at them and let me know when you are done.'

(Wait until participants signal that they are done.)

'What I would like you to do is classify the cards according to how much disagreement or agreement you believe there is between the (UMP/Fidesz) and the (PS/MSzP) on these different topics of policy. Feel free to classify them the way you want: in several categories, on a progressive scale, or even not to classify some of them if you think they don't fit your categories.'

If I am asked whether I meant the party in government or their own political ideas: 'We'll start by the parties in government. But during the discussion you can talk about how that may diverge from your own opinions if you wish.'

(Wait until participants signal that they are done.)

Part 1 (approximately 40 minutes)

'Let's start with the topics with most ground for agreement between parties and go towards the more contentious ones. Can someone volunteer to talk about a choice they made?'

Follow-up questions, if necessary:

- 'Do you all agree with what X just said? You should feel free to intervene and to express a different opinion if you feel like it.'
- 'Can you elaborate further? On what specific aspect of this issue do you think there is agreement/disagreement between political parties?'

- 'Please feel free to take up a new topic whenever you feel like you've sufficiently talked about this one.'
- 'So how would you describe the position of your party on this issue?'
- 'So how would you describe the position of your opponents on this issue?'

(Wait for all twelve cards to have been discussed.)

Part 2 (approximately 15 minutes)

'If we consider the classification of these topics overall, do you think, in your personal opinion, that the balance between areas of agreement and areas of disagreement is right between political parties? Do you think that the French/Hungarian political space would need more political disagreement between political parties? Or would France/Hungary rather need less disagreement, and more areas of agreement between political parties?'

(Wait for questions to have been answered by all or most participants.)

Part 3 (approximately 5 minutes)

'Finally, do you often talk with people who are of different political convictions from your own? Can you tell me a bit about these experiences?'

(Wait for questions to have been answered by all or most participants.)

Appendix 2: Coding Guidelines

Definitions and General Process

This appendix describes the coding process by which I analysed the verbatim transcripts of the twenty-eight group discussions. The terms and definitions that I use are those developed in Johnny Saldaña's *Coding Manual for Qualitative Researchers*, a well-accepted reference for the analysis of textual data (Saldaña, 2013). Coding in qualitative analysis may be defined as the process by which codes are associated with portions of text – a word, a sentence or a paragraph – throughout the data. In this context, a code is generally 'a word or short phrase that symbolically assigns a summative, salient, essence-capturing, and/or evocative attribute' (Saldaña, 2013, p. 3) to the portion of data it is associated with. The same codes are used repeatedly, and different codes often used simultaneously throughout the dataset. Counting these occurrences and co-occurrences allows for the identification of recurrent patterns and themes, and thus facilitates the formulation of rules, correlations and explanations emerging from the data. It also allows the identification of variations in these patterns across different groups of speakers.

The coding was carried out using NVivo, a computer-assisted qualitative data analysis software (CAQDAS). Although similar software (Atlas.ti and QDA Miner particularly) can be used to perform quantitative content analysis – for instance through the investigation of statistical regularities in keyword usage, grammatical constructions or word co-occurrences – this research does not rely on CAQDAS to perform coding in an automatised way. NVivo instead performs important functions in the qualitative coding of textual data. First, it facilitates a process traditionally performed with pen and pencil by qualitative researchers: coding is not only accelerated by the use of software, but is also rendered more systematic and accessible for review. NVivo, for instance, would allow for the systematic removal or modification of a given code throughout the dataset and produces a neat display when multiple codes are associated with the same unit of text. Second, once the cycles of coding are complete, connecting codes and identifying patterns in the data are greatly facilitated by the use of such software. NVivo, for instance, performs 'coding queries' to identify portions of texts in which certain codes co-occur and produces hierarchies and networks to display coding systems visually.

While the coding scheme that I applied to transcripts was inspired both by the theoretical framework for this study and the discussion guidelines for the group interviews, the development of any final set of codes is necessarily the result of both inductive and deductive strategies. In the process of coding, I first submitted portions of the data to several phases of what is commonly termed 'initial coding' before applying consistently a final set of codes to the entirety of the data. 'Initial coding' is a common process of textual analysis, during which 'some codes will be merged together because they are conceptually similar; infrequent codes will be assessed for their utility in the overall coding scheme; and some codes that seemed like good ideas [. . .] may be dropped altogether' (Saldaña, 2013, p. 207). In the case of this analysis, I first developed a coding scheme on the basis of my theoretical framework, worked on a small part of the French data, and then consistently applied it to twelve of the French transcripts. The guidelines for coding were then adapted on the basis of their compatibility with the Hungarian data, also through a phase of initial, exploratory coding of a limited number of transcripts from the Hungarian fieldwork. I then applied this final coding scheme to the entirety of the data, and thus recoded 'from scratch' the transcripts that had already been coded.

In extracting results from this coding process, I compared the occurrences and co-occurrences of different codes according to nationality (whether the groups were conducted in France or Hungary) and according to partisan affiliation (whether the groups were affiliated to the PS, the UMP, the MSzP or Fidesz). In this way, it was possible to establish variations in patterns of speech across partisan groupings of different nationalities and political affiliation. In my three empirical chapters, I relied on these numbers and on a large number of examples from the interviews as my primary evidence. In addition, their analysis allowed me to highlight variations in the extent to which different partisan groupings meet the standards established in Chapter 2.

Coding Steps for Each Transcript

In this section I offer an overview of the steps I followed to code each transcript. I list and detail them in chronological order:

Phase 1 – Group characteristics: As a first step, I applied a series of codes to the whole transcript to assign a number of basic attributes to it. This included, for instance, the country in which the interview was conducted (France or Hungary), the party that my participants belonged to (PS, UMP, MSzP or Fidesz) and the type of partisan grouping (for instance a local section of the party, a group of more senior elites from the group organisations, etc.). Coding these general characteristics allowed me to identify patterns of coding and therefore of speech across different types of groups, especially according to participants' nationality and partisan affiliation.

Phase 2 – Comments about instructions: As a second step, I focused on the ways in which my different participants reacted to the distribution of the cards, and the instructions for the discussion more generally. I coded when participants had a positive reaction to the cards, when they asked questions, and, if they did, what types of questions they asked. As I outline in Chapter 4, these reactions were useful in estimating how partisans understand their own political space.

Phase 3 – Justifications for card classifications: The third step focused on the bulk of each interview where participants talked about their card classifications. I applied a series of codes to each substantiated justification for the classification of a given card given by one or several participants. I define a substantiated justification as a claim made in favour of the point covered by each code that is backed up by participants with at least one argument. Each argument or series of arguments would itself go through a series of coding steps:

Phase 3.1 – Cards or topic under discussion: Here I would simply code for the card or topic being discussed. The information collected during this step was mostly used in Chapter 5 on partisan cohesiveness.

Phase 3.2 – Assessments of conflictuality: Second, I would code for the general assessment given by one or several participants on the degree of conflictuality for the topic under discussion – for instance whether they considered it a 'consensual' or a 'conflictual' topic. The information collected during this step was mostly used in Chapter 5 on partisan cohesiveness, but also in Chapter 6 on partisan respect for pluralism.

Phase 3.3 – Justifications for assessments: Third, I would code for the justifications that partisans offered for their assessment of a given topic as either conflictual or consensual, and especially whether they talked about the differences and similarities in the ideas of political parties or in their practices. The information collected during this step was mostly used in Chapter 5 on partisan cohesiveness.

Phase 3.4 – Actors emphasised: Fourth, I would code for the actors that partisans talked about when justifying the consensual or conflictual nature of a given topic: mostly their own party, mostly their opponents, or comparing the platforms of both parties. The information collected during this step was mostly used in Chapter 5 on partisan cohesiveness, but also in Chapter 6 on respect for political opponents.

Phase 3.5 – Knowledge: Fifth, if relevant, I would code for instances when participants either referred to their ignorance of a certain topic to justify their weak ability to justify their position, and instances when participants referred to their particular expertise in a given domain to give credence to their justification.

Phase 3.6 – Judgements of self and opponents: Finally, I would code for the criticisms and judgements that participants formulated against their own party and their opponents in the process of talking about the differences and similarities between party platforms on a given issue. For instance, I would code for instances where participants criticised the practices of opponents, their intentions, or their unwillingness to pursue the common good. The information collected during this step was mostly used in Chapter 6 on respect for political opponents.

Phase 4 – Assessments of the value of political agreement and disagreement: As a fourth step, I moved on to the next stage of the discussion, in which I would ask participants to formulate a normative judgement on the state of partisan conflictuality in their own political system. The information collected during this step was mostly used in Chapter 4.

Phase 5 – Experiences of inter-partisan dialogue: Finally, I would code the last part of the discussion, in which participants would talk about their own personal experiences of inter-partisan dialogue. I coded here for whether participants accounted for negative or positive experiences in this context. The information collected during this step was mostly used in Chapter 4.

Transversal codes – key examples: This series of codes was used throughout the whole coding process, and thus throughout the five phases listed above, to highlight passages from the transcripts that I found particularly striking. These allowed me to make a pre-selection of interesting examples, some of which were translated and integrated into the body of this book.

Codebook

Preliminary remarks

Below I provide the codebook used for the coding process – in other words, I provide definitions for each code that I applied. In theory, this codebook could be used by a third person to recode my data and thus verify my coding. It could also be used to code new interviews conducted according to the same discussion guidelines. Or it could be adapted to analyse partisan identity on the basis of other types of data.

To apply a given code to a portion of text, one needs to make an assessment of the content of this portion of text, and thus to interpret it. This work does not escape this general rule. Undeniably, some of the codes have required more interpretation than others. When participants would pick up the card 'Employment and unemployment policy' and talk about it, the corresponding code could easily be applied. But even in this case, I needed to decide whether the participant had sufficiently developed an argument about this specific card to warrant being coded. Other codes demanded more interpretation. To distinguish, for instance, between cases where participants talked about the ideas of political parties and their practices, for instance, was not always straightforward. This also means that, if the data were to be recoded, it is plausible that I would obtain slightly different results. This would also be the case if someone else were to code the data on the basis of this codebook.

Notwithstanding the above, I am confident that my general results, and especially the general variations in democratic partisanship uncovered, would be verified with subsequent cycles of coding. As shown in this article, the variations found between the patterns of speech of French and Hungarian participants are consistent across all of the indicators considered. The quantitative results from the coding process are also only an indication of trends that have jointly been assessed from a qualitative point of view, drawing on representative examples from different groups. While one could find slightly different numbers, and thus certain variations between different groups to be a bit more or less pronounced with another cycle of coding, I am positive that the general trends I have uncovered would still hold.

Before I detail my codebook, here are a number of guidelines that may help the reader to go through it:

- I proceed in the order of the steps described above, and thus provide definitions for each code applied according to this order.
- Most of the codes I describe here are applied when at least one participant makes a substantiated claim that supports the argument associated with a given code. I define a substantiated justification as a claim made in favour of the point covered by each code that is backed up by participants with at least one argument. When the words 'at least one participant' are associated with a code description, this means that, if other participants backed up the first speaker with the same argument, a single code would be applied to the portion of text relevant to this dialogue.
- When a given code is indented under another code, this means that the former is a 'sub-code' and the latter a 'primary' code. A 'sub-code' is defined as a 'second-order tag assigned after a primary code to detail or enrich the entry, depending on the volume of data you have or specificity you may need for categorisation and data analysis' (Saldaña, 2013, p. 77). To give an example, I applied two different codes depending on whether participants criticised their opponents on their practices or on their intentions. These codes were then primary codes for a number of sub-codes, refining these categories. For instance, the code used for criticisms on intentions has two sub-codes, one applied when participants target their opponents' preoccupation with political interests, and another when participants target their opponents' preoccupation with personal interests.
- I place the mention 'or' in front of codes or subcodes when these are exclusive of each other. On the other hand, I place the mention 'and' in front of codes or subcodes when these can be cumulative.
- After applying a primary code, I only applied a sub-code where these were relevant and therefore applicable. This explains that instances coded for any given cluster of sub-codes may be inferior to the corresponding number of instances coded for their common, primary code.

- Conversely, several sub-codes from a relevant cluster were sometimes applied to any given portion of text. This explains why the cumulative number of instances coded for any given cluster of sub-codes may be superior to the number of instances coded for their common, primary code.
- In line with this last point, it should be clear to the reader that many of these codes have been applied simultaneously to a given portion of text. This is what allowed me, at the end of this process, to identify variations in the patterns of speech of participants according to nationality or partisan affiliations.

Coding guidelines

Phase 1: Group characteristics

These are the codes applied to the entire transcript to assign a number of basic attributes to it.

Phase 1.1: Country
FRANCE (Applies to the entirety of all French transcripts)
or HUNGARY (Applies to the entirety of all Hungarian transcripts)

Phase 1.2: Position on political spectrum
LEFT (Applies to the entirety of all transcripts of group discussions involving members of a party that self-defines as being on the Left in a given national context)
    MSZP/EGYÜTT (Sub-code of LEFT; applies to the entirety of all MSzP or Együtt/PM transcripts)
    PS (Sub-code of LEFT; applies to the entirety of all PS transcripts)
    or RIGHT (Applies to the entirety of all transcripts of group discussion involving members of a party that self-defines as being on the Right in a given national context)
    FIDESZ (Sub-code of RIGHT; applies to the entirely of all Fidesz and KDNP transcripts)
    UMP (Sub-code of RIGHT; applies to the entirety of all UMP transcripts)

Phase 1.3: Type of group
EXECUTIVES (Applies to the entirety of all discussions happening among groups of participants who have local or national responsibilities in the youth party organisation, and know each other through this medium)

Or LOCAL SECTION (Applies to the entirety of all discussions among participants that belong to the same local party or youth party section)

Or PARTY EMPLOYEES (Applies to the entirety of all discussions happening among party employees that know each other through working for the party)

Phase 2: Comments about instructions

These are the codes that focus on the ways in which my different participants reacted to the distribution of the cards, and the instructions for the discussion more generally.

NO CONSENSUAL CARDS (Applied when at least one participant questions the instructions by emphasising that they are not able to find topics of agreement among those discussed)

and/or POSITIVE REACTION (Applied when at least one participant has a positive reaction to the instructions, either through complimenting the author about the card game idea, or making jokes about it)

and/or QUESTIONING CRITERIA (Applied when at least one participant asks questions about the criteria according to which they are supposed to classify the cards. In these cases, participants would generally suggest two possible logics of classification. For instance, one according to their own beliefs concerning what the opposition between Left and Right should be, and the other according to the position defended officially by political parties in the public sphere. Or one according to the ideals or values that political parties defend, the other according to their practices)

Phase 3: Justifications for card classifications

These are the codes applied when participants justified their card classifications. I applied a series of codes to each substantiated justification for the classification of a given card given by one or several participants (see Preliminary Remarks section). Each argument or series of arguments would itself go through a series of coding steps.

Phase 3.1: Cards or topics under discussion

These are the codes applied that describe the cards or topic being discussed.

Equivalent cards in France and Hungary

PUBLIC SERVICE (Applied when at least one participant gives a substantiated justification for their classification of the card 'Public service reform')

EU (Applied when at least one participant gives a substantiated justification for their classification of the card 'EU politics')

MINORITIES (Applied when at least one participant gives a substantiated justification for their classification of the card 'Religious and/or national minorities')

LAW AND ORDER (Applied when at least one participant gives a substantiated justification for their classification of the card 'Law and order')

EMPLOYMENT POLICY (Applied when at least one participant gives a substantiated justification for their classification of the card 'Unemployment and employment policy')

PUBLIC MORALITY (Applied when at least one participant gives a substantiated justification for their classification of the card 'Public morality')

INDUSTRIAL POLICY (Applied when at least one participant gives a substantiated justification for their classification of the card 'Industrial and/or agricultural policy')

TAXATION (Applied when at least one participant gives a substantiated justification for their classification of the card 'Taxation, social policy and redistribution of wealth')

PUBLIC FINANCE (Applied when at least one participant gives a substantiated justification for their classification of the card 'Public debt finance and deficit management')

ENVIRONMENT (Applied when at least one participant gives a substantiated justification for their classification of the card 'Environmental politics')

Cards particular to the French fieldwork

GENDER (Applied when at least one participant gives a substantiated justification for their classification of the card 'Sexual minorities and societal change')

IMMIGRATION (Applied when at least one participant gives a substantiated justification for their classification of the card 'Legal and illegal immigration').

Cards particular to the Hungarian fieldwork

INSTITUTIONS (Applied when at least one participant gives a substantiated justification for their classification of the card 'Institutional reform')

NATION IN POLITICS (Applied when at least one participant gives a substantiated justification for their classification of the card 'The nation in politics')

Common topics that came up in discussions but were not on the cards

CITIZEN ENGAGEMENT (Applied when at least one participant talks about the question of citizen and youth political engagement)

GENERATION (Applied when at least one participant talks about the question of the generations or generational change)

MEDIA (Applied when at least one participant talks about the question of the role of the media in politics)

POLITICAL CULTURE (Applied when at least one participant talks about the question of national political culture)

FOREIGN COMPARISON (Applied when at least one participant talks about political, economic or social developments in other countries as a point of comparison to their own).

HISTORY (Applied when at least one participant talks about the question of the country's history)

OTHER PARTIES (Applied when at least one participant talks about other parties than the two mainstream parties)

Phase 3.2: Assessments of conflictuality

The following codes correspond to the judgements participants make as to whether parties agree or disagree on the issues discussed. Any of these codes are therefore necessarily simultaneously coded with one of the topic codes listed in Phase 4.1.

UNIDIMENSIONAL (Applied when at least one participant develops a categorical argument to classify a given card as a topic of partisan disagreement or partisan agreement. By this I mean that they insist only on either the differences, or the similarities, between the platforms of political parties on this given topic)

CONFLICTUAL (Sub-code of UNIDIMENSIONAL; applied when at least one participant develops a categorical argument to justify partisan disagreement on a given topic; or insist solely on what differentiates their party's positions from the position of their opponents on a given topic)

or CONSENSUAL (Sub-code of UNIDIMENSIONAL; applied when at least one participant develops a categorical argument to justify partisan agreement on a given topic; or insist solely on the similarities between their party's positions and the position of opponents on a given topic)

or MIXED (Applied when at least one participant develops a nuanced argument about their classification of a specific card. By this I mean that they recognise both elements of partisan agreement or disagreement on a given topic or insist both on similarities and differences between the position of their own party and the position of their opponents on a given topic)

Phase 3.3: Justifications for assessments

The following codes correspond to the basis on which participants justify their assessment of the conflictual or consensual nature of a given topic. Depending on the type of assessment made (see 4.2), they are simultaneously coded with a given topic code listed in 4.1 above, and simultaneously coded with the codes CONFLICTUAL, CONSENSUAL or MIXED.

Justifying unidimensional assessments

IDEAS (Co-coded with CONFLICTUAL or CONSENSUAL; applied when at least one participant develops an argument to classify a given card as a topic of partisan disagreement or partisan agreement, insisting mostly on the differences or similarities in the ideas of rival parties to justify their assessment)

WORLDVIEWS (Sub-code of IDEAS; applied when at least one participant develops an argument to classify a given card as a topic of partisan disagreement or partisan agreement, insisting mostly on the more abstract principles, values and normative commitments that bring partisans together or sets them apart on this given topic)

DIAGNOSIS/OBJECTIVES (Sub-code of IDEAS; applied when at least one participant develops an argument to classify a given card as a topic of partisan disagreement or partisan agreement, insisting mostly on the differences or similarities in the types of problems that parties are likely to identify as needing to be solved, or the types of objectives that parties wish to achieve through policy)

PRACTICES (Co-coded with CONFLICTUAL or CONSENSUAL; applied when at least one participant develops an argument to classify a given card as a topic of partisan disagreement or partisan agreement, insisting mostly on the differences or similarities in the practices and policies of rival parties to justify their assessment)

SPECIFIC (Sub-code of PRACTICES; applied when at least one participant develops an argument to classify a given card as a topic of partisan disagreement or partisan agreement, insisting mostly on the differences or similarities in the specific practices of political parties to justify their assessment – e.g. specific policies, laws, political decisions, speeches)

GENERAL (Sub-code of PRACTICES; applied when at least one participant develops an argument to classify a given card as a topic of partisan disagreement or partisan agreement, insisting mostly on the differences or similarities in the general practices of political parties to justify their assessment – e.g. the types of policies, discourses, or ways of doing things of parties)

INVERSION (Co-coded with CONFLICTUAL, when at least one participant develops an argument to classify a given card as a topic of partisan disagreement, insisting on the reversal by mainstream parties of traditional, Left–Right platforms on a given question)

Justifying mixed assessments

CONFLICTUAL IDEAS VS CONSENSUAL PRACTICE (Co-coded with MIXED; applied when, in expressing a qualified judgement as described above, at least one participant insists that there exists on a given topic both differences in the ideas that parties defend, and similarities in the political practice and policies that parties put in place)

or CONSENSUAL IDEAS VS CONFLICTUAL PRACTICE (Co-coded with MIXED; applied when, in expressing a qualified judgement as described above, at least one participant insists that there exists on a given topic both similarities in the ideas that parties defend, and differences in the political practices and policies that parties put in place)

or CROSS-CUTTING DISAGREEMENT (Co-coded with MIXED; applied when, in expressing a qualified judgement as described above, at least one participant insists that parties are internally divided on a given question, or that political oppositions on a given question do not strictly respect traditional lines of inter-party debate)

Phase 3.4: Actors emphasised

The following codes correspond to the actors participants emphasise when they justify the conflictual or consensual nature of the cards that were distributed to them. Any of these codes are therefore generally simultaneously applied with some of the codes listed in 4.1 to 4.3.

SELF-FOCUSED (Applied when at least one participant mainly talks about their own party's ideas or practices when justifying partisan agreement or disagreement on a given topic)

or OPPONENT-FOCUSED (Applied when at least one participant mainly talks about their own opponents' ideas or practices when justifying partisan agreement or disagreement on a given topic) or COMPARISON (Applied when at least one participant develops a comparison between their opponents' ideas or practices and their own when justifying partisan agreement or disagreement on a given topic)

Phase 3.5: Knowledge

These are the codes applied when participants talk about their own ignorance or expertise about a certain topic when discussing it. These codes are thus simultaneous to many of those described above from 3.1 to 3.4.

IGNORANCE (Applied when at least one participant justifies the fact they have little to no justification for their assessments by the fact that they are too ignorant, or lack expertise, about the topic itself)

EXPERTISE (Applied when at least one participant justifies their ability to talk about a given topic, or about the ability of another participant to talk about a given topic, by the fact that they have specific expertise on this same topic – e.g. because of their professional occupation or qualifications)

Phase 3.6: Judgements of self and opponents

These are the codes applied when participants judge their own party and their opponents. Because these judgements were made in the process of talking about the differences and similarities between party platforms on the twelve issues discussed, these codes are simultaneously applied with some of the codes listed in 3.1 to 3.5.

CRITICISM OF OPPONENTS (Applied when at least one participant casts a negative judgement on their political opponents)

FLAWED PRACTICES (Sub-code of CRITICISM OF OPPONENTS; applied when at least one participant casts a negative judgement on their political opponents by emphasising flaws in their practices)

INCOHERENCE (Sub-code of FLAWED PRACTICES; applied when at least one participant casts a negative judgement on their political opponents by emphasising incoherencies in their practices)

INEFFICIENCY (Sub-code of FLAWED PRACTICES; applied when at least one participant casts a negative judgement on their political opponents by emphasising the inefficient nature of their practices, or their lack of realism)

LACK OF POLITICAL WILL (Sub-code of FLAWED PRACTICES; applied when at least one participant casts a negative judgement on their political opponents by emphasising their lack of political will or vision)

IRRESPONSABILITY (Sub-code of FLAWED PRACTICES; applied when at least one participant casts a negative judgement on their political opponents by emphasising their irresponsibility, lack of professionalism or carelessness)

and/or ILL INTENTIONS (Sub-code of CRITICISM OF OPPONENTS; applied when at least one participant casts a negative judgement on their political opponents by denouncing the lack of integrity of opponents' motivations)

POLITICAL INTERESTS (Sub-code of ILL INTENTIONS; applied when at least one participant casts a negative judgement on their political opponents by denouncing the lack of integrity of opponents' motivations, emphasising especially their tendency to pander to certain groups in society to the detriment of others only for electoral purposes or to be driven solely by the desire to be elected or to please their electorate)

PERSONAL INTERESTS (Sub-code of ILL INTENTIONS; applied when at least one participant casts a negative judgement on their political opponents by denouncing the lack of integrity in opponents' motivations, denouncing especially their quest for material gain or the fact that their opponents are driven solely by the desire to further their personal power. Accusations of corruption, nepotism and clientelism fall under this code)

and/or THREAT TO THE COMMON GOOD (Sub-code of CRITICISM OF OPPONENTS; applied when at least one participant casts a negative judgement on their political opponents by denouncing the harmful or threatening nature of their opponents or their opponents' practices with regard to the common good. This includes describing opponents as a 'menace', a 'threat', as being 'destructive' of fundamental values or widely accepted political goods (prosperity, peace, etc.).

and/or MORAL DEFFICIENCY (Sub-code of CRITICISM OF OPPONENT; applied when at least one participant attributes 'immorality', 'amorality' or 'evil' as a defining characteristic of the personality of political opponents)

PRAISE OF OPPONENTS (Applied when at least one participant casts a positive judgement on their political opponents)

SELF-CRITICISM (Applied when at least one participant casts a negative judgement on their own party)

SELF-PRAISE (Applied when at least one participant casts a positive judgement on their own party)

Phase 4: Assessments of the value of conflict and consensus

The following codes relate to the part in the discussion following the justification by participants of their card classification. Here I would ask participants to formulate a normative judgement on the state of partisan disagreement in their own political system.

VALUE OF DISAGREEMENT (Applied when at least one participant develops a substantiated argument emphasising the positive value of disagreement between political parties, or the negative value of excessive agreement between political parties)

VALUE OF AGREEMENT (Applied when at least one participant develops a substantiated argument emphasising the positive value of agreement between political parties, or the negative value of excessive disagreement between political parties)

Phase 5: Experiences of inter-partisan dialogue

This series of codes applied to the last part of the discussion, in which participants would talk about their own personal experiences of inter-partisan dialogue.

POSITIVE or NEUTRAL EXPERIENCE (Applied when a participant accounts in positive or neutral terms for one of their personal experiences of inter-partisan dialogue)

NEGATIVE EXPERIENCE (Applied when a participant accounts in negative terms for one of their personal experiences of inter-partisan dialogue)

Transversal codes: Key examples

This series of codes was used to highlight passages from the transcripts that I found particularly striking. These allowed me to make a preselection of interesting examples from which I selected the passages that were translated and integrated in the body of this dissertation.

KEY FIDESZ (Applied when I found particularly interesting examples in Fidesz transcripts for future use)

KEY MSzP (Applied when I found particularly interesting examples in MSzP transcripts for future use)

KEY PS (Applied when I found particularly interesting examples in PS transcripts for future use)

KEY UMP (Applied when I found particularly interesting examples in UMP transcripts for future use)

References

Abramowitz, A. (2010). *The disappearing center: Engaged citizens, polarisation, and American democracy.* Yale University Press.

Abramowitz, A. I. (2012). Grand Old Tea Party: Partisan polarisation and the rise of the Tea Party movement. In L. Rosenthal and C. Trost (eds), *Steep: The precipitous rise of the Tea Party.* University of California Press.

Albertazzi, D., and Mueller, S. (2013). Populism and liberal democracy: Populists in government in Austria, Italy, Poland and Switzerland. *Government and Opposition,* 48(3), 343–71. doi:10.1017/gov.2013.12

Alexandre-Collier, A. S. (2018). From soft to hard Brexit: UKIP's not so invisible influence on the Eurosceptic radicalisation of the Conservative Party since 2015. In L. E. Herman and J. Muldoon (eds), *Trumping the mainstream: The conquest of democratic politics by the populist Radical Right.* Routledge.

Allern, E. H., and Pedersen, K. (2007). The impact of party organisational changes on democracy. *West European Politics,* 30(1), 68–92. doi:10.1080/01402380601019688

American Political Science Association. (1950). Towards a more responsible two-party government. *The American Political Science Review,* 44(3), 1–96. doi:10.2307/1950999

Ansolabehere, S., and Iyengar, S. (1995). *Going negative: How political advertisements shrink and polarize the electorate.* Free Press.

Anthoula, M., and Ludvig, N. (2017). Three models of democratic self-defence: Militant democracy and its alternatives. *Political Studies,* 0032321717723504. doi:10.1177/0032321717723504

Art, D. (2011). Activists and party development. In *Inside the Radical Right: The development of anti-immigrant parties in Western Europe* (pp. 29–60). Cambridge University Press.

Aslanidis, P. (2015). Is populism an ideology? A refutation and a new perspective. *Political Studies,* 64(1_suppl), 88–104. doi:10.1111/1467-9248.12224

Bachelot, C. (2020). Le PS bouge encore: Anatomie d'une transformation partisane. *La Vie des idées*. Retrieved from https://laviedesidees.fr/Le-PS-bouge-encore.html

Bächtiger, A., and Beste, S. (2017). Deliberative citizens, (non) deliberative politicians: A rejoinder. *Daedalus*, *146*(3), 106–18.

Bale, T. (2003). Cinderella and her ugly sisters: The mainstream and extreme Right in Europe's bipolarizing party systems. *West European Politics*, *26*(3).

Bale, T., Green-Pedersen, C., Krouwel, A., Luther, K. R., and Sitter, N. (2010). If you can't beat them, join them? Explaining social democratic responses to the challenge from the populist Radical Right in Western Europe. *Political Studies*, *58*(3), 410–26.

Ball, T. (1989). Party. In T. Ball, J. Farr and R. L. Hanson (eds), *Political innovation and conceptual change* (pp. 155–76). Cambridge University Press.

Balme, R., Marie, J.-L., and Rozenberg, O. (2003). Les motifs de la confiance (et de la défiance) politique: intérêt, connaissance et conviction dans les formes du raisonnement politique. *Revue internationale de politique comparée*, *10*(3), 433–61. doi:10.3917/ripc.103.0433

Bánkuti, M., Halmai, G., and Scheppele, K. L. (2012). Hungary's illiberal turn: Disabling the constitution. *Journal of Democracy*, *23*(3), 138–46.

Barr, N. A. (2005). From transition to accession. In N. A. Barr (ed.), *Labor markets and social policy in Central and Eastern Europe: The accession and beyond*. World Bank.

Batory, A. (2008). *The politics of EU accession: Ideology, party strategy and the European question in Hungary*. Manchester University Press.

Beitz, C. R. (1989). *Political equality: An essay in democratic theory*. Princeton University Press.

Bekmezian, H. (17 April 2014). 100 députés PS écrivent à Valls pour dénoncer un plan 'dangereux économiquement'. *Le Monde*. Retrieved from http://abonnes.lemonde.fr/politique/article/2014/04/17/100-deputes-ps-ecrivent-a-valls-pour-contester-le-plan-d-economies_4403436_823448.html

Belzile, J., and Oberg, G. (2012). Where to begin? Grappling with how to use participant interaction in focus group design. *Qualitative Research*, *12*(4), 459–72

Benoit, K. (1996). Hungary's two-vote electoral system. *Representation*, *33*(4), 162–70.

Benoit, K. (2003). Evaluating Hungary's mixed-member electoral system. In M. M. S. Shugart and M. P. Wattenberg (eds), *Mixed-member electoral systems: The best of both worlds?* Oxford University Press.

Berezin, M. (2009). *Illiberal politics in neoliberal times: Culture, security and populism in the new Europe*. Cambridge University Press.

Berezin, M. (2013). The normalization of the right in post-security Europe. In A. Schäfer and W. Streeck (eds), *Politics in the age of austerity*. Polity.

Berlin, I. (1969). Two concepts of liberty. In I. Berlin (ed.), *Four essays on liberty*. Oxford University Press.

Berman, S. (2016). The specter haunting Europe: The lost Left. *Journal of Democracy*, 27(4), 69–76.

Berman, S., and Snegovaya, M. (2019). Populism and the decline of social democracy. *Journal of Democracy*, 30(3), 5–19.

Bermeo, N. (2016). On democratic backsliding. *Journal of Democracy*, 27(1), 5–19.

Bickerton, C., and Invernizzi Accetti, C. (2017). Populism and technocracy. In C. R. Kaltwasser, P. A. Taggart, P. Ochoa Espejo, and P. Ostiguy (eds), *The Oxford Handbook of Populism*. Oxford: Oxford University Press.

Birnbaum, P. (1994). *Les Sommets de l'État: Essai sur l'élite du pouvoir en France*. Éditions du Seuil.

Blais, A. (2006). What affects voter turnout? *Annual review of Political Science*, 9, 111–25.

Blier, J.-M. (2008). *Le Combat des chefs*. Éditions du Rocher.

Bobbio, N. (1995). *Left and Right: The significance of a political distinction*. Cambridge: Polity Press.

Bogaards, M. (2018). De-democratization in Hungary: Diffusely defective democracy. *Democratization*, 1–19. doi:10.1080/13510347.2018.1485015

Bolleyer, N., and Bytzek, E. (2016). New party performance after breakthrough: Party origin, building and leadership. *Party Politics*, 23(6), 772–82. doi:10.1177/1354068815626604

Bonotti, M. (2011). Conceptualizing political parties: A normative framework. *Politics*, 31(2), 19–26.

Bonotti, M. (2012). Partisanship and political obligation. *Politics*, 32(3), 153–61.

Bonotti, M. (2014). Partisanship and public reason. *Critical Review of International Social and Political Philosophy*, 17(3), 314–31. doi:10.1080/13698230.2014.886381

Bonotti, M. (2018). *Partisanship and Political Liberalism in Diverse Societies*. Oxford University Press.

Bonotti, M., and Weinstock, D. (2021). Parties, electoral systems and political theory [special issue]. *Representation*, 57(3), 287–400.

Bornschier, S. (2018). Globalization, cleavages, and the Radical Right. In J. Rydgren (ed.), *The Oxford Handbook of the Radical Right* (pp. 212–24). New York: Oxford University Press.

Bourdieu, P. (1993). Public opinion does not exist. In P. Bourdieu (ed.), *Sociology in question*. SAGE.

Bozóki, A., and Kriza, B. (2008). The Hungarian semi-loyal parties and their impact on democratic consolidation. In A. Blasko and D. Januauskiene (eds), *Political transformation and changing identities in Central and Eastern Europe* (pp. 215–42). Council for Research in Values and Philosophy.

Bozóki, A., and Ishiyama, J. T. (eds). (2002). *The communist successor parties of Central and Eastern Europe*. M. E. Sharpe.

Broockman, D. E., and Butler, D. M. (2017). The causal effects of elite position-taking on voter attitudes: Field experiments with elite communication. *American Journal of Political Science*, 61(1), 208–21. Retrieved from http://www.jstor.org/stable/26379502

Bruter, M., and Harrison, S. (2009a). *The future of our democracies: Young party members in Europe*. Palgrave Macmillan.

Bruter, M., and Harrison, S. (2009b). Tomorrow's leaders? Understanding the involvement of young party members in six European democracies. *Comparative Political Studies*, 42(10), 1259–90. doi:10.1177/0010414009332463

Burke, E. (1990 [1770]). Thoughts on the cause of the present discontents. In E. J. Payne (ed.), *Select Works of Edmund Burke* (vol. 1). Liberty Fund.

Callaghan, J., Fishman, N., Jackson, B., and McIvor, M. (eds) (2009). *In search of social democracy: Responses to crisis and modernisation*. Manchester University Press.

Campbell, A., Converse, P. E., Miller, W. E., and Stokes, D. E. (1960). *The American voter*. Wiley.

Caramani, D. (2017). Will vs. reason: The populist and technocratic forms of political representation and their critique to party government. *American Political Science Review*, 111(1), 54–67. doi:10.1017/S0003055416000538

Casal Bértoa, F., and Mair, P. (2010). Two decades on: How institutionalized are the post-communist party systems? *EUI Working Paper*, 3.

Centre d'observation de la société (2022). Abstention: une hausse ni généralisée, ni inéluctable. Retrieved from https://www.observationsociete.fr/modes-de-vie/vie-politique-et-associative/participationvote-2/

Centre for Fair Political Analysis (2013). The anatomy of the Hungarian Right. Retrieved from http://meltanyossag.hu/content/files/Anatomy_of_the_Hungarian_Right_120630.pdf

CEVIPOF (21 January 2018). Baromètre de la confiance politique – Vague 9. *Sciences Po*. Retrieved from https://www.sciencespo.fr/cevipof/sites/sciencespo.fr.cevipof/files/Confiance2018_CAUTRES_clivage.pdf

Chambers, S. (2010). Theories of political justification. *Philosophy Compass*, 5(11), 893–903. doi:10.1111/j.1747-9991.2010.00344.x

Chambers, S. (2018). Human life is group life: Deliberative democracy for realists. *Critical Review*, 30(1–2), 36-48. doi:10.1080/08913811.2018.1466852

Cheurfa, M., and Chanvril, F. (2019). 2009–2019: La crise de la confiance politique. *Baromètre de la confiance politique.* Retrieved from https://www.sciencespo.fr/cevipof/sites/sciencespo.fr.cevipof/files/CEVIPOF_confiance_10ans_CHEURFA_CHANVRIL_2019.pdf

Chong, D., and Druckman, J. (2007). Framing public opinion in competitive democracies. *American Political Science Review*, 101(101), 637–55.

Christiano, T. (1996). *The rule of the many: Fundamental issues in democratic theory*. Westview Press.

Cinar, K. (2019). *Decline of democracy in Turkey*. Routledge.

Ciuk, D. J., and Yost, B. A. (2016). The effects of issue salience, elite influence, and policy content on public opinion. *Political Communication*, 33(2), 328–45. doi:10.1080/10584609.2015.1017629.

Connolly, W. E. (1993). *The terms of political discourse* (3rd edn). Blackwell.

Constant, B. (2010 [1819]). The liberty of the Ancients compared with that of the Moderns. Retrieved from http://www.earlymoderntexts.com/assets/pdfs/constant1819.pdf

Cos, R. (2017). L'évidement idéologique du Parti socialiste. *Mouvements*, 89(1), 22–31. doi:10.3917/mouv.089.0022

Council of Europe (2013). Adopted opinions for 'Hungary'. Retrieved from http://www.venice.coe.int/webforms/documents/?country=17andyear=all

Crespy, A. (2008). Dissent over the European Constitutional Treaty within the French Socialist Party: Between response to anti-globalization protest and intra-party tactics. *French Politics*, 6(1), 23–44.

Crouch, C. (2004). *Post-democracy*. Polity.

Cruickshank, J. (2014). Democracy versus the domination of instrumental rationality: Defending Dewey's argument for democracy as an ethical way of life. *Humanities*, 3(1), 19.

Crum, B., Alvaro, O., and Overeem, P. (eds) (2023). *Populist parties and democratic resilience: A cross-national analysis of populist parties' impact on democratic pluralism in Europe*. Routledge.

Csehi, R. (2019). Neither episodic, nor destined to failure? The endurance of Hungarian populism after 2010. *Democratization*, 26(6), 1011–27. doi:10.1080/13510347.2019.1590814

Csehi, R., and Zgut, E. (2020). 'We won't let Brussels dictate us': Eurosceptic populism in Hungary and Poland. *European Politics and Society*, 1–16. doi:10.1080/23745118.2020.1717064

Daalder, H. (2002). Parties: Denied, dismissed, or redundant? A critique. In R. Gunther, J. R. Montero and J. J. Linz (eds), *Political parties: Old concepts and new challenges*. Oxford University Press.

Dahl, R. A. (1971). *Polyarchy: Participation and opposition*. Yale University Press.

Dalton, R. J. (2008). The quantity and the quality of party systems, party system polarisation, its measurement, and its consequences. *Comparative Political Studies*, 41(7).

Dalton, R. J., and Wattenberg, M. P. (2000). *Parties without partisans: Political change in advanced industrial democracies*. Oxford University Press.

Dani, M. (2013). The 'Partisan Constitution' and the corrosion of European constitutional culture. *LSE 'Europe in Question' Discussion Paper Series*, 68 (November).

de Lange, S. L. (2012). New alliances: Why mainstream parties govern with radical right-wing populist parties. *Political Studies*, 60, 899–918.

Delage, V. (2021). La conversion des Européens aux valeurs de droite: France, Allemagne, Italie et Royaume-Uni. *Fondation pour l'innovation politique (Fondapol)*. Retrieved from https://www.fondapol.org/etude/la-conversion-des-europeens-aux-valeurs-de-droite/

Dinas, E., Georgiadou, V., Konstantinidis, I., and Rori, L. (2013). From dusk to dawn: Local party organisation and party success of right-wing extremism. *Party Politics*, 22(1), 80–92. doi:10.1177/1354068813511381

Disch, L. (2011). Toward a mobilization conception of democratic representation. *American Political Science Review*, 105(01), 100–14.

Disch, L. (2015). The 'constructivist turn' in democratic representation: A normative dead-end?. *Constellations*, 22(4), 487–99.

Disch, L., van de Sande, M., and Urbinati, N. (eds). (2019). *The constructivist turn in political representation*. Edinburgh University Press.

Dovi, S. L. (2007). *The good representative*. Blackwell.

Downs, A. (1957). *An economic theory of democracy*. Harper & Row.

Downs, W. M. (2002). How effective is the cordon sanitaire? *Journal of Conflict and Violence Research*, 4(1), 33–51.

Druckman, J. N. (2004). Political preference formation: Competition, deliberation, and the (ir)relevance of framing effects. *American Political Science Review*, 98(4), 671–86.

Dryzek, J. S., and Holmes, L. (2002). *Post-communist democratization: Political discourses across thirteen countries*. Cambridge University Press.

Duchesne, S., and Haegel, F. (2004). La politisation des discussions, au croisement des logiques de spécialisation et de conflictualisation. *Revue française de science politique*, 54(6), 877–909. doi:10.1017/S0007123407000014

Dyrberg, T. B. (2005). The democratic ideology of Right–Left and public reason in relation to Rawls's political liberalism. *Critical Review of International Social and Political Philosophy*, 8(2), 161–76. doi:10.1080/13698230500108850

Ehrhard, T. (2016). Le Front national face aux modes de scrutin: entre victoire sous conditions et influences sur le système partisan. *Pouvoirs*, 157(2), 85–103. doi:10.3917/pouv.157.0085

Enyedi, Z. (2015a). Paternalist populism and illiberal elitism in Central Europe. *Journal of Political Ideologies*, 21(1), 9–25.

Enyedi, Z. (2015b). Plebeians, citoyens and aristocrats, or Where is the bottom of bottom-up? The case of Hungary. In H. Kriesi and T. Pappas (eds), *European populism in the shadow of the Great Recession* (pp. 235–51). ECPR Press.

Enyedi, Z. (2016). Populist polarisation and party system institutionalization: The role of party politics in de-democratization. *Problems of Post-Communism*, 64(4), 1–11.

Enyedi, Z., and Linek, L. (2008). Searching for the right organisation. *Party Politics*, 14(4), 455–77.

Eurobarometer (2022a). Hungary factsheet, EP Autumn 2021 Survey: Defending democracy | empowering citizens. Retrieved from https://europa.eu/eurobarometer/api/deliverable/download/file?deliverableId=80193

Eurobarometer (2022b). Hungary factsheet, Standard Eurobarometer 96.3 – Winter Eurobarometer 2021–2022. Retrieved from https://europa.eu/eurobarometer/api/deliverable/download/file?deliverableId=81548

Eurobarometer Interactive (2020). Trust in political parties. Retrieved from https://ec.europa.eu/commfrontoffice/publicopinion/index.cfm/Chart/index

European Parliament (2011). Resolution on the Media Law of Hungary. Retrieved from http://www.europarl.europa.eu/sides/getDoc.do?pubRef=-//EP//TEXT+TA+P7-TA-2011-0094+0+DOC+XML+V0//EN

European Parliament (2013). Report on the situation of fundamental rights: Standards and practices in Hungary ('Rui Tavares Report'). Retrieved from http://www.europarl.europa.eu/sides/getDoc.do?pubRef=-//EP//TEXT+REPORT+A7-2013-0229+0+DOC+XML+V0//EN

Evans, G., and Tilley, J. (2012). How parties shape class politics: Explaining the decline of the class basis of party support. *British Journal of Political Science*, 42(01), 137–61. doi:10.1017/S0007123411000202

Evans, G., and Whitefield, S. (1993). Identifying the bases of party competition in Eastern Europe. *British Journal of Political Science*, 23(4), 521–48.

Evans, G., and Whitefield, S. (1995). Social and ideological cleavage formation in post-communist Hungary. *Europe-Asia Studies, 47*(7), 1178.

Ezrow, L., and Xezonakis, G. (2011). Citizen satisfaction with democracy and parties' policy offerings. *Comparative Political Studies, 44*(9), 1152–78.

Fiorina, M. P. (1999). Extreme voices: The dark side of civic engagement. In T. Skocpol and M. P. Fiorina (eds), *Civic engagement in American democracy*. Brookings Institution Press.

Flett, K. (ed.) (2007). *1956 and all that*. Cambridge Scholars.

Fourquet, J., and Gariazzo, M. (2013). *FN et UMP: Electorats en fusion?* Retrieved from https://www.ifop.com/wp-content/uploads/2018/03/616-1-document_file.pdf

Fowler, B. (2004). Concentrated orange: Fidesz and the remaking of the Hungarian centre-right, 1994–2002. *Journal of Communist Studies and Transition Politics, 20*(3), 80–114. doi:10.1080/1352327042000260814

François, A., and Phélippeau, E. (2018). Party funding in France. In J. Mendilow and E. Phélippeau (eds), *Handbook of political party funding*. Edward Elgar Publishing.

Freedom House. (2020). Dropping the democratic facade. *Nations in transit*. Retrieved from https://freedomhouse.org/report/nations-transit/2020/dropping-democratic-facade

Furedi, F. (2005). *The politics of fear: Beyond Left and Right*. Continuum.

Gallagher, M., and Marsh, M. (2004). Party membership in Ireland: The members of Fine Gael. *Party Politics, 10*(4), 407–25. doi:10.1177/1354068804043906

Galston, W. A. (2002). *Liberal pluralism: The implications of value pluralism for political theory and practice*. Cambridge University Press.

Galston, W. A. (2005). *The practice of liberal pluralism*. Cambridge University Press.

Galston, W. A. (2013). The common good: Theoretical content, practical utility. *Dædalus, 142*(2), 9–14.

Gamson, W. A. (1992). *Talking politics*. Cambridge University Press.

Ganghof, S. (2016). Reconciling representation and accountability: Three visions of democracy compared. *Government and Opposition, 51*(2), 209–33.

Gauchet, M. (1996). Left and Right. In P. Nora and L. D. Kritzman (eds), *Realms of memory: Rethinking the French past*. Columbia University Press.

Gerring, J., and Yesnowitz, J. (2006). A normative turn in political science? *Polity, 38*(1), 101–33. doi:10.2307/3877092

Giddens, A. (1994). *Beyond Left and Right: The future of radical politics*. Polity.

Giddens, A. (1998). *The Third Way: The renewal of social democracy*. Polity.
Glasser, S. B. (2019). The 'enemies of the people' have a few questions for the president. *The New Yorker*. Retrieved from https://www.newyorker.com/news/letter-from-trumps-washington/the-enemies-of-the-people-have-a-few-questions-for-the-president?mbid=social_facebookandutm_brand=tnyandutm_source=facebookandutm_social-type=ownedandutm_medium=social
Godin, E. (2013). The porosity between the mainstream Right and Extreme Right in France. *Journal of Contemporary European Studies*, 21(1), 53–67.
Goetschel, P., and Morin, G. (2007). Le Parti socialiste en France: Approches renouvelées d'un mouvement séculaire. *Vingtième Siècle. Revue d'histoire. Presses de Sciences Po*, 4(96), 3–9.
Gofas, A., and Hay, C. (2007). Varieties of ideational explanation. In A. Gofas and C. Hay (eds), *The role of ideas in political analysis: A portrait of contemporary debates*. Routledge.
Gougou, F., and Persico, S. (2017). A new party system in the making? The 2017 French presidential election. *French Politics*, 15(3), 303–21. doi:10.1057/s41253-017-0044-7
Greskovits, B. (2020). Rebuilding the Hungarian Right through conquering civil society: The Civic Circles movement. *East European Politics*, 36(2), 247–66. doi:10.1080/21599165.2020.1718657
Grubera, O., and Bale, T. (2014). And it's good night Vienna. How (not) to deal with the populist Radical Right: The Conservatives, UKIP and some lessons from the heartland. *British Politics*, 9(3), 237–54.
Grzymala-Busse, A. (2002). *Redeeming the communist past: The regeneration of communist parties in East Central Europe*. Cambridge University Press.
Grzymala-Busse, A. (2003). Redeeming the past: Communist successor parties after 1989. In G. Ekiert and S. E. Hanson (eds), *Capitalism and democracy in Central and Eastern Europe: Assessing the legacy of communist rule* (pp. 157–81). Cambridge University Press.
Grzymala-Busse, A. (2007). *Rebuilding Leviathan: Party competition and state exploitation in post-communist democracies*. Cambridge University Press.
Grzymala-Busse, A. (2019). The failure of Europe's mainstream parties. *Journal of Democracy*, 30(4), 35–47.
Gutmann, A., and Thompson, D. F. (2010). The mindsets of political compromise. *Perspectives on Politics*, 8(4), 1125–43.
Gutmann, A., and Thompson, D. F. (2012). *The spirit of compromise: Why governing demands it and campaigning undermines it*. Princeton University Press.

Haegel, F. (2012). *Les Droites en fusion. Tranformations de l'UMP*. Les Presses de Sciences Po.

Hall, P. A., and Taylor, R. C. R. (1996). Political science and the three new institutionalisms. *Political Studies*, 44(5), 936–57.

Hallowell, J. H. (1954). *The moral foundation of democracy*. Chicago University Press.

Haltinner, K. (2018). Paving the way for Trump: The Tea Party's invisible influence on the 2016 elections. In L. E. Herman and J. Muldoon (eds), *Trumping the mainstream: The conquest of democratic politics by the populist Radical Right*. Routledge.

Hanley, S. (2012). Book review: 'Origin, ideology and transformation of political parties: East-Central and Western Europe compared'. *Party Politics*, 18(5), 793–95. doi:10.1177/1354068812451390

Harré, R., and Moghaddam, F. M. (eds). (2003). *The self and others: Positioning individuals and groups in personal, political, and cultural contexts*. Praeger.

Harré, R., Moghaddam, F. M., Cairnie, T. P., Rothbart, D., and Sabat, S. R. (2009). Recent advances in positioning theory. *Theory and Psychology*, 19(1), 5–31. doi:10.1177/0959354308101417

Harré, R., and Van Langenhove, L. (1999). *Positioning theory: Moral contexts of intentional action*. Blackwell.

Hay, C. (2007). *Why we hate politics*. Polity Press.

Hegedüs, D. (2019). Rethinking the incumbency effect: Radicalization of governing populist parties in East-Central-Europe. A case study of Hungary. *European Politics and Society*, 20(4), 406–30. doi:10.1080/23745118.2019.1569338

Herman, L. E. (2016). Re-evaluating the post-communist success story: Party elite loyalty, citizen mobilization and the erosion of Hungarian democracy. *European Political Science Review*, 8(2).

Herman, L. E. (2017). Democratic partisanship: From theoretical ideal to empirical standard. *American Political Science Review*, 111(4).

Herman, L. E., and Muirhead, R. (2020). Resisting Abusive Legalism: Electoral Fairness and the Partisan Commitment to Political Pluralism. *Representation, FirstView online*.

Herman, L. E., and Muirhead, R. (2021). Resisting abusive legalism: Electoral fairness and the partisan commitment to political pluralism. *Representation*, 57(3), 363–83. doi:10.1080/00344893.2020.1744701

Herman, L. E., and Muldoon, J. (2018a). Populism in the 21st century: From the fringe to the mainstream. In L. E. Herman and J. Muldoon (eds), *Trumping the mainstream: The conquest of democratic politics by the populist Radical Right*. Routledge.

Herman, L. E., and Muldoon, J. (2018b). *Trumping the mainstream: The conquest of democratic politics by the populist Radical Right*. Routledge.

Herman, L. E., and Saltman, E. M. (2014). Hungary's one way ticket to the EU. *Books and ideas*. Retrieved from http://www.booksandideas.net/Hungary-s-One-way-Ticket-to-the-EU.html

Hobolt, S., and Tilley, J. (2018). Divided by the vote: Affective polarisation in the wake of Brexit. *Paper presented at the 2018 ECPR Standing Groups, SGEU Conference* (13–15 June).

Hofstadter, R. (1969). *The idea of a party system: The rise of legitimate opposition in the United States, 1780–1840*. University of California Press.

Hollande, F. (2012). Discours du Bourget. Retrieved from http://tempsreel.nouvelobs.com/politique/election-presidentielle-2012/sources-brutes/20120122.OBS9488/l-integralite-du-discours-de-francois-hollande-au-bourget.html

Hooghe, M., and Stolle, D. (2003). Age matter: Life-cycle and cohort differences in the socialisation effect of voluntary socialization. *European Political Science*, 3(2), 49–56.

Hungarian Parliament. (1989). Act No. XX of 1949 (as amended). Retrieved from http://lapa.princeton.edu/hosteddocs/hungary/1989-90 per cent20constitution_english.pdf

Huntington, S. P. (1991). *The Third Wave: Democratization in the late twentieth century*. University of Oklahoma Press.

Hvg.hu. (2020). Medián: Rekordon a magyar EU-tagság támogatottsága. Retrieved from https://hvg.hu/itthon/20201209_median_rekordon_eu_tagsag_tamogatottsag

Hyman, H. H. (1969). *Political socialization: A study in the psychology of political behavior* (1st paperback edn). Free Press.

Ignazi, P. (2017). *Party and democracy: The uneven road to party legitimacy*. Oxford University Press.

Invernizzi Accetti, C., and Zuckerman, I. (2016). What's wrong with militant democracy? *Political Studies*, 65(1_suppl), 182–99. doi:10.1177/0032321715614849

Ivaldi, G. (2016). A new course for the French Radical Right? The Front national and 'de-demonisation'. In T. Akkerman, S. L. de Lange, and M. Rooduijn (eds), *Radical right-wing populist parties in Western Europe*. Routledge.

Isaac, J. C. (2017). Is there illiberal democracy? A problem with no semantic solution. *Public Seminar*. Retrieved from chrome-extension://oemmndcbldboiebfnladdacbdfmadadm/http://www.publicseminar.org/wp-content/uploads/2017/07/Isaac-Jeffrey-Is-There-Illiberal-Democracy-Public-Seminar.pdf

Ishiyama, J. T. (1999). *Communist successor parties in post-communist politics*. Nova Science Publishers.
Iyengar, S., Lelkes, Y., Levendusky, M., Malhotra, N., and Westwood, S. J. (2019). the origins and consequences of affective polarisation in the United States. *Annual Review of Political Science*, 22(1), 129–46. doi:10.1146/annurev-polisci-051117-073034
Jowitt, K. (1992). *New world disorder: The Leninist extinction*. University of California Press.
Kantar-Soffres-One Point. (2017). Baromètre d'image du Front national. Retrieved from http://fr.kantar.com/opinion-publique/politique/2017/barometre-2017-d-image-du-front-national/
Kateb, G. (1981). The moral distinctiveness of representative democracy. *Ethics*, 91(3), 357–74.
Katz, R. S. (2006). Party in democratic theory. In R. S. Katz and W. J. Crotty (eds), *Handbook of party politics*. SAGE.
Katz, R. S. (2014). No man can serve two masters: Party politicians, party members, citizens and principal–agent models of democracy. *Party Politics*, 20(2), 183–93. doi:10.1177/1354068813519967
Katz, R. S., and Mair, P. (1995). Changing models of party organisation and party democracy: The emergence of the Cartel Party. *Party Politics*, 1(1), 5–28.
Katz, R. S., and Mair, P. (2009). The Cartel Party thesis: A restatement. *Perspectives on Politics*, 7(4), 753–66.
Keith, B. E., Magleby, D. B., Nelson, C. J., Orr, E. A., Westlye, M. C., and Wolfinger, R. E. (1992). *The myth of the independent voter*. University of California Press.
Kirshner, A. (2014). *A theory of militant democracy: The ethics of combating political extremism*. Yale University Press.
Kitschelt, H. (1995). Formation of party cleavages in post-communist democracies. *Party Politics*, 1(4), 447–72. doi:10.1177/1354068895001004002
Kitschelt, H. (2006). Parties and political intermediation. In K. Nash and A. Scott (eds), *The Blackwell Companion to Political Sociology*. Blackwell.
Kitschelt, H., Markowski, R., Mansfeldova, Z., and Toka, G. (1999). *Post-communist party systems: Competition, representation, and inter-party cooperation*. Cambridge University Press.
Komárek, J. (2014). Waiting for the existential revolution in Europe. *International Journal of Constitutional Law*, 12(1), 190–212. doi:10.1093/icon/mou004
Kovarek, D., and Soós, G. (2017). Hungary: Cut from the same cloth? A comparative analysis of party organisations in Hungary. In B. Kosowska-Gąstoł, K. Sobolewska-Myślik, and P. Borowiec (eds), *Organizational*

structures of political parties in Central and Eastern European countries (pp. 185–208). Jagiellonian University Press.

Krause, W., Cohen, D., and Abou-Chadi, T. (2022). Does accommodation work? Mainstream party strategies and the success of radical right parties. *Political Science Research and Methods*, 1–8. doi:10.1017/psrm.2022.8

Kreuzer, M., and Stephan, I. (2003). France: Enduring notables, weak parties, and powerful technocrats. In J. B. a. J. Zeiss (ed.), *The political class in advanced democracies: A comparative handbook*. Oxford University Press.

Kriesi, H., Grande, E., Dolezal, M., Helbling, M., Höglinger, D., Hutter, S., and Wüest, B. (2012). *Political conflict in Western Europe*. Cambridge University Press.

Kriesi, H., Grande, E., Lachat, R., Dolezal, M., Bornschier, S., and Frey, T. (eds). (2008). *West European politics in the age of globalization*. Cambridge University Press.

Krueger, R. A. (1998). *The focus group kit* (vol. 2, Planning focus groups). SAGE.

Lachat, R. (2011). Electoral competitiveness and issue voting. *Political Behavior*, 33(4), 645–63.

Landau, D. (2013). Abusive constitutionalism. *UC Davis Law Review, FSU College of Law, Public Law Research*, 189 (Paper No. 646).

Lardeyret, G. (2006). The problem with proportional representation. In L. Diamond and M. F. Plattner (eds), *Electoral Systems and Democracy*. John Hopkins University Press.

Lawson, K. (ed.) (1980). *Political parties and linkage: A comparative perspective*. Yale University Press.

Le Monde. (2018, May 5). Enquête Cevipof sur Macron: Le chef de l'État perçu de plus en plus à droite. *Le Monde*. Retrieved from https://www.lemonde.fr/politique/article/2018/05/05/enquete-cevipof-sur-macron-le-chef-de-l-etat-percu-de-plus-en-plus-a-droite_5294725_823448.html

Lefebvre, R., and Sawicki, F. (2006). *La Société des socialistes: Le PS aujourd'hui*. Éditions du Croquant.

Lefort, C. (1988). *Democracy and political theory*. Polity in association with Basil Blackwell.

Legrand, B., and Billard, S. (2017). Novices ou aguerris, ces députés de la majorité qui vont compter. *L'Observateur*. Retrieved from https://www.nouvelobs.com/politique/20170619.OBS0953/novices-ou-aguerris-ces-deputes-de-la-majorite-qui-vont-compter.html

Lelkes, Y. (2016). Mass polarisation: Manifestations and measurements [special issue]. *Public Opinion Quarterly*, 80, 392–410.

Levitsky, S., and Way, L. A. (2020). The new competitive authoritarianism. *Journal of Democracy*, 31(1), 51–65.

Levitsky, S., and Ziblatt, D. (2018). *How democracies die*. Crown.

Lewis, P. A. (2002). Agency, structure and causality in political science: A comment on Sibeon. *Politics*, 22(1), 17–23.

Lewis, P. G. (2001). Conclusion: Party development and democratization in Eastern Europe. In P. G. Lewis (ed.), *Party development and democratic change in post-communist Europe: The first decade* (pp. 199–211). Frank Cass.

Lewis, P. G. (2006). Party systems in post-communist Central Europe: Patterns of stability and consolidation. *Democratization*, 13(4), 562–83.

Lijphart, A. (2012). *Patterns of democracy, government forms and performance in thirty-six countries* (2nd edn). Yale University Press.

Linz, J. (1978). *The breakdown of democratic regimes: Crisis, breakdown, and reequilibration*. Johns Hopkins University Press.

Lorimer, M. (2018). 'Ni droite, ni gauche, Français!' Far-right populism and the future of left/right politics. In L. E. Herman and J. Muldoon (eds), *Trumping the mainstream: The conquest of democratic politics by the populist Radical Right*. Routledge.

Lukes, S. (2003). Epilogue: The grand dichotomy of the twentieth century. In T. Ball and R. Bellamy (eds). Cambridge.

Macedo, S. (1990). *Liberal virtues: Citizenship, virtue and community in liberal constitutionalism*. Clarendon.

Maiguashca, B., and Dean, J. (2017). Corbyn's Labour and the populism question. *Renewal, A Journal of Social Democracy*, 25(3/4).

Maiguashca, B., and Dean, J. (2018). Corbynism, populism and the reshaping of left politics in contemporary Britain. In G. Katsambekis and A. Kioupkiolis (eds), *The populist Radical Left in crisis-hit Europe*. Routledge.

Mair, P. (2006). Ruling the void? The hollowing of Western democracy. *New Left Review*, 42, 25–51.

Mair, P. (2013a). *Ruling the void? The hollowing of Western democracy*. Verso.

Mair, P. (2013b). Smaghi versus the parties: Representative government and institutional constraints. In A. Schäfer and W. Streeck (eds), *Politics in the age of austerity*. Polity.

Mair, P., and Katz, R. S. (1998). Party organisation, party democracy, and the emergence of the Cartel Party. In P. Mair (ed.), *Party system change: Approaches and interpretations*. Oxford University Press.

Mansbridge, J. J. (2003). Rethinking representation. *The American Political Science Review*, 97(4), 515–28.

Mansbridge, J. J., and Martin, C. J. (eds) (2013). *Negotiating agreement in politics*. American Political Science Association.

Manza, J., and Cook, F. L. (2002). A democratic polity? Three views of policy responsiveness to public opinion in the United States. *American Politics Research*, 30(6), 630–67.

Marková, I. (2007). *Dialogue in focus groups: Exploring socially shared knowledge*. Equinox.

Marks, G., Hooghe, L., Nelson, M., and Edwards, E. (2006). Party competition and European integration in the East and West. *Comparative Political Studies*, 39(2), 155–75. doi:10.1177/0010414005281932

Marlière, P. (2007). *La Mémoire socialiste 1905–2007. Sociologie du souvenir politique en milieu partisan*. L'Harmattan.

Marthaler, S. (2010). *La course au centre*: Policy convergence and partisanship in France, 1981–2002. *French Politics, Culture and Society*, 28(2), 75–95.

Martin, P. (2015). L'avenir du 'tripartisme'. *Revue Politique et Parlementaire*, 1075.

Mason, L. (2016). A cross-cutting calm: How social sorting drives affective polarisation. *Public Opinion Quarterly*, 80(S1), 351–77. doi:10.1093/poq/nfw001

Mason, L. (2018). *Uncivil agreement: How politics became our identity*. The University of Chicago Press.

May, J. D. (1973). Opinion structure of political parties: The special law of curvilinear disparity. *Political Studies*, 21, 135–51.

Mayer, N. (2013). From Jean-Marie to Marine Le Pen: Electoral change on the Far Right. *Parliamentary Affairs*, 66(1), 160–78. doi:10.1093/pa/gss071

McCoy, J., Rahman, T., and Somer, M. (2018). Polarisation and the global crisis of democracy: Common patterns, dynamics, and pernicious consequences for democratic polities. *American Behavioral Scientist*, 62(1), 16–42. doi:10.1177/0002764218759576

McGann, A. J. (2006). *The logic of democracy: Reconciling equality, deliberation, and minority protection*. University of Michigan Press.

McGann, A. J. (2013). Fairness and bias in electoral systems. In J. H. Nagel and R. M. Smith (eds), *Representation – elections and beyond* (pp. 90–113). University of Pennsylvania Press.

Medián. (2020). 2020. júniusi kutatási eredmények *Közvéleménykutatók.hu*. Retrieved from https://kozvelemenykutatok.hu/2020-juniusi-kutatasi-eredmenyek-median/

Meguid, B. M. (2008). *Party competition between unequals: Strategies and electoral fortunes in Western Europe*. Cambridge University Press.

Meijers, M. J., and Williams, C. J. (2020). When shifting backfires: The electoral consequences of responding to niche party EU positions. *Journal of European Public Policy*, 27(10), 1506–25. doi:10.1080/13501 763.2019.1668044

Meisburger, T. M. (2012). Getting majoritarianism right. *Journal of Democracy*, 23(1), 155–63

Mill, J. S. (1991 [1859]). *On Liberty and other essays*. Oxford: Oxford University Press.

Millard, F. (2004). *Elections, parties, and representation in post-communist Europe*. Basingstoke: Palgrave Macmillan.

Miller, W., White, S., and Heywood, P. (1997). *Values and political change in postcommunist Europe*. St. Martin's Press.

Motet, L., Darame, M., and Carriat, J. (2021, March 8). À l'Assemblée nationale, la lente érosion d'un bloc La République en marche de plus en plus fracturé. *Le Monde*. Retrieved from https://www.lemonde.fr/politique/article/2021/03/08/a-l-assemblee-nationale-la-lente-erosion-d-un-bloc-la-republique-en-marche-de-plus-en-plus-fracture_6072382_823448.html

Mouffe, C. (2000). *The democratic paradox*. Verso.

Mouffe, C. (2005a). The 'end of politics' and the challenge of right-wing populism. In F. Panizza (ed.), *Populism and the mirror of democracy*. Verso.

Mouffe, C. (2005b). *On the political*. Routledge.

Mouffe, C. (2018). *For a left populism*. Verso.

Mourgue, M., and Wesfreid, M. (2019). Européennes: Les ministres transfuges des LR affichent leur satisfaction. *Le Figaro*. Retrieved from https://www.lefigaro.fr/elections/europeennes/europeennes-2019-les-ministres-transfuges-des-lr-affichent-leur-satisfaction-20190527

Mudde, C. (2007). *Populist radical right parties in Europe*. Cambridge University Press.

Mudde, C. (2016). The study of populist radical right parties: tTowards a fourth wave. C-Rex Working Paper Series, Center for Research on Extremism, University of Oslo (1).

Muirhead, R. (2006). A defense of party spirit. *Perspectives on Politics*, 4(4), 713–27.

Muirhead, R. (2014). *The promise of party in a polarized age*. Harvard University Press.

Muirhead, R., and Rosenblum, N. L. (2006). Political liberalism vs. 'the great game of politics': The politics of political liberalism. *Perspectives on Politics*, 4(01), 99–108.

Muirhead, R., and Rosenblum, N. L. (2012). The partisan connection. *The Circuit*, 38.

Müller, J.-W. (2011). The Hungarian tragedy. *Dissent*, 58(2).
Müller, J.-W. (2015). Should the EU protect democracy and the rule of law inside Member States? *European Law Journal*, 21(2), 141–60.
Müller, J.-W. (2016). *What is Populism?* University of Pennsylvania Press.
Müller, J.-W. (2017). Populism and constitutionalism. In C. R. Kaltwasser, P. A. Taggart, P. O. Espejo and P. Ostiguy (eds), *The Oxford Handbook of Populism*. Oxford University Press.
Narud, H. M., and Scare, A. (1999). Are party activists the party extremists? The structure of opinion in political parties. *Scandinavian Political Studies*, 22(45–65).
Norris, P. (1995). May's law of curvilinear disparity revisited. *Party Politics*, 1, 29–37.
Norris, P. (2010). *Democratic deficit: Critical citizens revisited*. Cambridge University Press.
Norris, P. (2017). Is Western democracy backsliding? Diagnosing the risks. *The Journal of Democracy*, April.
Norris, P. (Ed.) (1999). *Critical citizens: Global support for democratic government*. Oxford University Press.
Norwegian Helsinki Committee. (2013). Democracy and human rights at stake in Hungary: The Viktor Orbán government's drive for centralisation of power. Retrieved from http://nhc.no/filestore/Publikasjoner/Rapporter/2013/Rapport_1_13_web.pdf
Offe, C. (2004). Capitalism by democratic design? Democratic theory facing the triple transition in East Central Europe. *Social Research*, 71(3), 501–28.
Orbán, V. (2014). Speech at the Free University and Student Camp in Băile Tuşnad, Romania. Retrieved from http://www.kormany.hu/hu/a-miniszterelnok/beszedek-publikaciok-interjuk/a-munkaalapu-allamkorszaka-kovetkezik. English translation at: http://budapestbeacon.com/public-policy/full-text-of-viktor-orbans-speech-at-baile-tusnad-tusnadfurdo-of-26-july-2014/
OSCE. (2011). Analysis of the Hungarian media legislation. *Tallinn University for the Organisation for Security and Co-operation in Europe (OSCE), Office of the Representative on Freedom of the Media*. Retrieved from http://www.osce.org/fom/75990?download=true
Palonen, E. (2006). *Reading Budapest: Political polarisation in contemporary Hungary*, unpublished PhD thesis. University of Essex.
Palonen, E. (2009). Political polarisation and populism in contemporary Hungary. *Parliamentary Affairs*, 62(2), 318–34.
Pateman, C. (1971). Political culture, political structure and political change. *British Journal of Political Science*, 1 (July), 291–305.

Pateman, C. (2007 [1970]). Recent theories of democracy and the 'classical myth'. In M. Saward (ed.), *Democracy: Critical concepts in political science* (vol. 3). Routledge.

Pech, L., and Scheppele, K. L. (2017). Illiberalism within: Rule of law backsliding in the EU. *Cambridge Yearbook of European Legal Studies*, *19*–347. doi:10.1017/cel.2017.9

Perrin, A. J. (2006). *Citizen speak: The democratic imagination in American life*. University of Chicago Press.

Piketty, T. (2014). *Capital in the twenty-first century*. Harvard University Press.

Plattner, M. F., and Diamond, L. J. (eds) (1996). *The global resurgence of democracy* (2nd edn). Johns Hopkins University Press.

Poguntke, T. (2002). Party organizational linkage: Parties without firm social roots? In K. R. Luther and F. Müller-Rommel (eds), *Political parties in the new Europe: Political and analytical challenges*. Oxford University Press.

Political Capital. (2013). New electoral system in the home stretch: An analysis of the effects of the new Hungarian electoral procedure law and the campaign finance law. Retrieved from http://www.valasztasirendszer.hu/wp-content/uploads/PC_New_Electoral_System_In_The_Home_Stretch_20130723.pdf

Przeworski, A. (1999). Minimalist conception of democracy: A defense. In I. Shapiro and C. Hacker-Cordón (eds), *Democracy's value*. Cambridge University Press.

Rawls, J. (2001). *Justice as fairness: A restatement*. Belknap Press.

Rawls, J. (2005). *A theory of justice* (original edn). Belknap Press.

Rémond, R. (1982). *Les Droites en France* (4th edn). Aubier-Montaigne.

Rokkan, S., and Lipset, S. M. (1967). *Party systems and voter alignments: Cross-national perspectives*. Free Press.

Roland, G. (2002). The political economy of transition. *Journal of Economic Perspectives*, *16*(1), pp. 29–50.

Rose, R., and Mishler, W. (1998). Negative and positive party identification in post-communist countries. *Electoral Studies*, *17*(2), 217–34.

Rosenblum, N. L. (1998). *Membership and morals: The personal uses of pluralism in America*. Princeton University Press.

Rosenblum, N. L. (2008). *On the side of the angels: An appreciation of parties and partisanship*. Princeton University Press.

Rosenblum, N. L. (2014). Partisanship and independence: The peculiar moralism of American politics. *Critical Review of International Social and Political Philosophy*, *17*(3), 267–88. doi:10.1080/13698230.2014.886385

Rosenblum, N. L. (ed.) (1989). *Liberalism and the moral life*. Harvard University Press.

Rothschild, J., and Wingfield, N. M. (2000). *Return to diversity: A political history of East Central Europe since World War II* (3rd edn). Oxford University Press.

Ryn, C. G. (1978). *Democracy and the ethical life: A philosophy of politics and community*. Louisiana State University Press.

Saldaña, J. (2013). *The coding manual for qualitative researchers* (2nd edn). SAGE.

Saltman, E. M. (2012). Who can save the Left in Hungary? *Transitions Online [online]*. Retrieved from http://www.tol.org/client/article/22923-who-can-save-the-Left-in-hungary.html

Saltman, E. M. (2014). *Turning right: Contemporary political socialization of the Hungarian youth*, unpublished PhD thesis. University College London.

Sartori, G. (1976). *Parties and party systems: A framework for analysis*. Cambridge University Press.

Saward, M. (2010). *The representative claim*. Oxford University Press.

Scarrow, S. E. (2006). Party subsidies and the freezing of party competition: Do cartel mechanisms work? *West European Politics*, 29(4), 619–39. doi:10.1080/01402380600842148

Scarrow, S. E. (2015). *Beyond party members: Changing approaches top Partisan mobilization*. Oxford University Press.

Scarrow, S. E., and Gezgor, B. (2006). *Trends in party membership and membership participation*. Paper presented at the Annual Meeting of the Midwest Political Science Association, Chicago.

Schattschneider, E. E. (1960). *The semisovereign people: A realist's view of democracy in America*. Transaction Publishers.

Schedler, A. (2020). Democratic Reciprocity*. *Journal of Political Philosophy*, 29(2), 252–78. doi:10.1111/jopp.12232

Schensul, J. J., and LeCompte, M. D. (eds). (1999). *The ethnographer's toolkit*. AltaMira Press.

Scheppele, K. L. (2018). Autocratic legalism. *The University of Chicago Law Review*, 85, 545–62.

Schmidt, V. A. (2008). Discursive institutionalism: The explanatory power of ideas and discourse. *Annual Review of Political Science*, 11(1), 303–26.

Schmitter, P. C., and Karl, T. L. (1991). What democracy is . . . and is not. *Journal of Democracy*, 2(3), 75–88.

Schumpeter, J. A. (1956 [1942]). *Capitalism, socialism, and democracy*. Harper and Row.

Shapiro, I. (2018, 12 March). Democratic competition: The good, the bad and the ugly. *American Academy in Berlin*. Retrieved from https://www.americanacademy.de/event/democratic-competition-good-bad-ugly/

Shapiro, I., and Green, D. (1994). *Pathologies of rational choice theory: A critique of applications in political science*. Yale University Press.

Sikk, A. (2005). How unstable? Volatility and the genuinely new parties in Eastern Europe. *European Journal of Political Research*, 44(3), 391–412. doi:10.1111/j.1475-6765.2005.00232.x

Skinner, Q. (1973). the empirical theorists of democracy and their critics: A plague on both their houses. *Political Theory*, 1(3), 287–306. doi:10.2307/190588

Sniderman, P. M., and Theriault, S. M. (2004). The structure of political argument and the logic of issue framing. In W. E. Saris and P. M. Sniderman (eds), *Studies in Public Opinion* (pp. 133–65). Princeton: Princeton University Press.

Slothuus, R., and Bisgaard, M. (2021). How political parties shape public opinion in the real world. *American Journal of Political Science*, 65(4), 896–911. doi:https://doi.org/10.1111/ajps.12550

Sözen, Y. (2019). Competition in a populist authoritarian regime: The June 2018 dual elections in Turkey. *South European Society and Politics*, 24(3), 287–315. doi:10.1080/13608746.2019.1688515

Stanley, B. (2008). The thin ideology of populism. *Journal of Political Ideologies*, 13(1), 95–110.

Startin, N. (2022). Marine Le Pen, the Rassemblement National and breaking the 'glass ceiling'? The 2022 French presidential and parliamentary elections. *Modern & Contemporary France*, 30(4), 427–43. doi:10.1080/09639489.2022.2138841

Steiner, J. r., Bächtiger, A., Spörndli, M., and Steenbergen, M. R. (2004). *Deliberative politics in action: Analyzing parliamentary discourse*. Cambridge University Press.

Stille, A. (2013). The justice minister and the banana: How racist is France? Retrieved from https://www.newyorker.com/news/daily-comment/the-justice-minister-and-the-banana-how-racist-is-france

Strom, K. (1990). A behavioral theory of competitive political parties. *American Journal of Political Science*, 34(2), 565–98. doi:10.2307/2111461

Stumpf, A. (2013, 4 December 2013). Orbán igazi szociáldemokrata. *Héti Válasz*. Retrieved from http://valasz.hu/itthon/orban-igazi-szocialdemokrata-71003/

Suiter, J., Farrell, D. M., Harris, C., and Murphy, P. (2021). Measuring epistemic deliberation on polarized issues: The case of abortion provision in Ireland. *Political Studies Review*, 14789299211020909. doi:10.1177/14789299211020909

Sunstein, C. R. (2002). The law of group polarisation. *Journal of Political Philosophy*, 10(2), 175–95. doi:10.1111/1467-9760.00148

Swidler, A. (1986). Culture in action: Symbols and strategies. *American Sociological Review*, 51(2), 273–86.

Szikinger, I. (2001). Hungary's pliable constitution. In J. Zielonka (ed.), *Democratic consolidation in Eastern Europe. Vol. 1, Institutional engineering*. Oxford University Press.

Szily, L. (2020). Kövér: Az ellenzék nem a magyar nemzet része. *444.hu*. Retrieved from https://444.hu/2020/04/29/kover-az-ellenzek-nem-a-magyar-nemzet-resze

Tavits, M., and Letki, N. (2009). When Left is Right: Party ideology and policy in post-communist Europe. *American Political Science Review*, 103(04), 555–69. doi:10.1017/S0003055409990220

Thompson, D. F. (1987). *Political ethics and public office*. Harvard University Press.

Thurber, J. A., and Yoshinaka, A. (eds). (2015). *American gridlock : The sources, character, and impact of political polarisation*. Cambridge University Press.

TNS-Sofres. (2015). Baromètre d'image du Front national. Retrieved from http://www.tns-sofres.com/sites/default/files/2015.02.16-baro-fn.pdf

United States Commission on Security and Cooperation in Europe (2013). Helsinki Commission hearing on 'The trajectory of democracy – why Hungary matters'. Retrieved from < http://csce.gov/index.cfm?FuseAction=ContentRecords.ViewDetailandContentRecord_id=539andRegion_id=0andIssue_id=0andContentType=H,BandContentRecordType=HandCFID=26361986andCFTOKEN=c913fa608e26bcce-DF0375B6-9908-1777-4C6667FC43655A4F >

Urbinati, N. (2000). Representation as advocacy: A study of democratic deliberation. *Political Theory*, 28(6), 758–86.

Urbinati, N. (2006). *Representative democracy: Principles and genealogy*. University of Chicago Press.

van Biezen, I., and Poguntke, T. (2014). The decline of membership-based politics. *Party Politics*, 20(2), 205–16.

van Biezen, I., and Saward, M. (2008). Democratic theorists and party scholars: Why they don't talk to each other, and why they should. *Perspectives of Politics*, 6(1), 21–35.

van der Hout, E., and McGann, A. J. (2009). Liberal political equality implies proportional representation. *Social Choice and Welfare*, 33, 617–27.

van Haute, E. (2011). Who voices? Socialisation process and ideational profile of discontented party members. In E. van Haute (ed.), *Party membership in Europe: Exploration into the anthills of party politics*. Éditions de l'Université de Bruxelles.

Varol, O. O. (2015). Stealth suthoritarianism. *Iowa Law Review*, *100*, 1673–742.

Vassalo, F., and Wilcox, C. (2006). Party as a carrier of ideas. In R. S. Katz and W. J. Crotty (eds), *Handbook of party politics*. SAGE.

Vegetti, F. (2019). The political nature of ideological polarisation: The case of Hungary. *The Annals of the American Academy*, 6 (January).

Venice Commission, and OSCE/ODIHR. (2012). Joint opinion on the act on the election of members of Parliament of Hungary. Retrieved from http://www.venice.coe.int/webforms/documents/default.aspx?pdffile=CDL-AD per cent282012 per cent29012-e

Vigogne, L. (2020). En 2019, Les Républicains ont dénombré seulement 58000 adhérents. *L'Opinion*. Retrieved from https://www.lopinion.fr/edition/politique/en-2019-republicains-ont-denombre-58-000-adherents-209895

Wagner, M. (2008). Debating Europe in the French Socialist Party: The 2004 internal referendum on the EU constitution. *French Politics*, *6*(3), 257–79. doi:10.1057/fp.2008.9

Wagner, M., and Meyer, T. M. (2016). The Radical Right as niche parties? The ideological landscape of party systems in Western Europe, 1980–2014. *Political Studies*, *65*(1_suppl), 8–107.

Weltman, D., and Billig, M. (2001). The political psychology of contemporary anti-politics: A discursive approach to the end-of-ideology era. *Political Psychology*, *22*(2), 367–82.

White, J. (2009). The social theory of mass politics. *The Journal of Politics*, *71*(01), 96–112.

White, J. (2011a). Left and Right as political resources. *Journal of Political Ideologies*, *16*(2), 123–44.

White, J. (2011b). *Political allegiance after European integration*. Palgrave Macmillan.

White, J. (2014). Transnational partisanship: Idea and practice. *Critical Review of International Social and Political Philosophy*, *17*(3), 377–400. doi:10.1080/13698230.2014.886386

White, J. (2015a). The party in time. *British Journal of Political Science*, *47*(4), 851–68. doi:10.1017/S0007123415000265

White, J. (2015b). When parties make peoples. *Global Policy*, *6*(S1), 106–14. doi:10.1111/1758-5899.12233

White, J. (2021). What kind of electoral system sustains a politics of firm commitments? *Representation*, 57(3), 329–45. doi:10.1080/00344893. 2019.1624601

White, J., and Ypi, L. (2010). Rethinking the modern prince: Partisanship and the democratic ethos. *Political Studies*, 58(4), 809–28.

White, J., and Ypi, L. (2011). On partisan political justification. *American Political Science Review*, 105(02), 381–96.

White, J., and Ypi, L. (2016). *The meaning of partisanship*. Oxford University Press.

Wike, R., Simmons, K., Stokes, B., and Fetterolf, J. (2017). Democracy widely supported, little backing for rule by strong leader or military. *Pew Research Centre*. Retrieved from https://www.pewresearch.org/global/2017/10/16/democracy-widely-supported-little-backing-for-rule-by-strong-leader-or-military/

Wolkenstein, F. (2015). A deliberative model of intra-party democracy. *Journal of Political Philosophy*, 24(3), 297–320. doi:10.1111/jopp.12064

Wolkenstein, F. (2016a). *Deliberative democracy within political parties*. (24), London School of Economics and Political Science. Retrieved from http://dx.doi.org/10.1111/jopp.12064 (3)

Wolkenstein, F. (2016b). A deliberative model of intra-party democracy. *Journal of Political Philosophy*, 24(3), 297–320. doi:10.1111/jopp.12064

Wolkenstein, F. (2016c). Intra-party democracy beyond aggregation. *Party Politics*, 24(4), 323–34. doi:10.1177/1354068816655563

Wolkenstein, F. (2018). Democracy, transnational partisanship and the EU. *JCMS: Journal of Common Market Studies*, 56(2), 284–99. doi:10.1111/jcms.12590

Wolkenstein, F. (2019). *Rethinking party reform*. Oxford University Press.

Wolkenstein, F. (2022). What is democratic backsliding? *Constellations*, 1–15. doi: 10.1111/1467-8675.12627

Yanow, D., and Schwartz-Shea, P. (2006). *Interpretation and method: Empirical research methods and the interpretive turn*. M. E. Sharpe.

Young, I. M. (2000). *Inclusion and democracy*. Oxford University Press.

Zanotti, L. (2021). How's life after the collapse? Populism as a representation linkage and the emergence of a populist/anti-populist political divide in Italy (1994–2018). *Frontiers in Political Science*, 3. doi:10.3389/fpos.2021.679968

Index

References in **bold** refer to a table.

activists
   political professionalisation in France, 68–9
   as a study group, 45–7
Antall, József, 114

Bajnai, Gordon, 9 n.4, 76

cartel-party thesis, 68
Chirac, Jacques, 70, 100 n.4, 106 n.11
Civic Circles movement, 75
civic engagement
   abstention rates in France, 67
   achievement of normative goals, 27–8
   for the common good, 23
   concept, 23
   conditions for political engagement, 23–4
   defiance against mainstream parties, 66–8
   disengagement with formal politics, 3–4, 24
   of independents, 23–4
cohesiveness *see* ideological cohesiveness
common good
   absence of a supra-partisan community in Hungary, 168–70
   civic engagement for, 23
   depoliticisation of morality, 145–7
   ideological cohesiveness and, 8, 26, 28
   lack of a shared sense of in Hungarian partisans, 164–70
   morality in Hungarian partisan discourse, 164–7
   normative grounding, 26
   and the political community, 37
   political contexts, 24, 25, 30
   political pluralism and expressions of, 17, 31–2, 35–9, 40, 133, 145–51
   recognition of supra-partisan community by French partisans, 148–51
   shared objectives for a common good, 149–51
constitutional arrangements
   abusive constitutionalism, 20 n.7, 32 n.13
   constitutional abuse in Hungary, 13, 72, 73, 78, 122, 126, 166 n.35, 177
   constitutional essentials of a liberal democracy, 8, 19, 31, 37
   pluralist partisanship and, 32, 37 n.37, 196
   role of mainstream parties, 20, 21
Corbyn, Jeremy, 6

democracy *see* liberal democracy
democratic partisanship
   definition, 2
   as empirical practice, 173–85
   the ideal of, 8–9, 185–92
   ideological cohesiveness and, 8, 17, 22–30, 40, 77, 175–6
   liberal democracy and, 16, 30–1, 39–43

democratic partisanship (cont.)
  mainstream parties and, 17–18, 20–1
  normative model of, 39–43
  paradox of, 15–16
  repolarisation in, 3, 4
  respect for pluralism, 8, 17, 30–9, 40, 41–3, 176–8
  as Western-centered, 189–91
Demokratikus Koalíció, 76

École nationale d'administration (ENA), 68
Együtt, 76
En marche! 66, 71, 195

fallacy of pure ethical motive, 53–4
Fiatal Demokraták Szövetsége-Kereszténydemokrata Néppárt (Fidesz-KDNP)
  absence of a supra-partisan community in Hungary, 168–70
  abusive legalism, 72–3, 75
  anti-government demonstrations, 1, 76
  Civic Circles movement, 75
  differentiation between parties, 127–9
  intention-related criticism, 152–8, **153**
  intolerant holism, 132, 152–70, 175
  lack of respect for pluralism, 77–8, 188
  media strategies, 80
  morality as a political cleavage, 164–7
  motive-cynicism, 155–8
  nationalistic focus, 74–5, 112–16, 118
  negative image in the Western press, 80
  normative grounding, 112–17, 121, 131
  practice-focused criticism, 153–5, **154**
  programmatic substance, 121–4, **125**
  references to the topics under discussion, 88–9, 113
  responses to exogenous factor, 184
  self-praise, 152
  support base, 75–6
  and the transition to democracy, 72
  unprincipled nature of opponents, 158–63, **159**
Fidelitas, 78
focus groups
  advantages of group discussion, 47–8
  challenges of establishing in Hungary, 80–3

coding scheme, 52–3, 85–6, 98–9, 100, 199–213
democratic value of political agreement and disagreement, 87–95, **89**, **91**
discussion guidelines, 44–5, 51–2, 81, 197–8
participation observation, 78–9
partisan disagreement, 83–7
recruitment of, 48, 79–80
visual prompts, 12, 49–50, 52, 84
France
  benevolent holism, 132–3, 171, 175, 183
  citizen disengagement, 66–7
  consensual, cross-party themes, 86–7
  defiance against mainstream parties, 66–8
  democratic value of political agreement/disagreement, 89–93, **89**, **91**, 108–9, **108**
  electoral system, 59, 60
  exogenous factors, 62–3
  history of liberal democracy, 58
  ideological cohesiveness, 77, 97–111, 129–30
  ideological convergence, 66, 69, 84–5, 108–11, **110**
  institutional incentives, 60–1
  normative grounding for ideological cohesiveness, 98–103, **99**
  obligations of EU membership, 58
  partisan disagreement, 83–7, **86**, **88**
  party system dynamics, 59–60
  political culture, 61, 62, 65–6
  political professionalisation, 68–9
  practice-focused criticism, 133–7
  principled opposition in, 140–4, **140**, **141**, 159
  radical right's growth, 67
  recognition of supra-partisan community, 148–9
  respect for pluralism, 77–8, 132–52, **133**, 170–1, 183
  right-wing drift, 69–70, 71–2, 85, 177–8
  2017 elections, 70–1
  visual prompt research cards, 49, 50
  see also *Parti socialiste* (PS); *Union pour un mouvement populaire* (UMP)

Gaullism, 102 n.8
Génération.s., 71
Gyurcsány, Ferenc, 9 n.4, 76, 77, 84–5, 158 n.28

Hamon, Benoit, 71
holism
　benevolent holism of the UMP, 132–3, 171, 175, 183
　dangers of partisan appeals to, 31
　intolerant holism of Fidesz, 132, 152–70, 175
　recognition of supra-partisan community, 148–9
　rejection of by pluralist partisans, 31, 37–8, 40, 41
Hollande, François, 58, 70, 139 n.11
Hungary
　absence of a supra-partisan community, 168–70
　accession to the EU, 73
　authoritarian legacies, 180–2
　Civic Circles movement, 75
　constitutional abuses, 13, 72, 73, 78, 122, 126, 166 n.35, 177
　cultural concept of liberal democracy, 189–91
　democratic backsliding, 73–4, 75, 177
　democratic consolidation, 72–3, 74
　democratic value of political agreement/disagreement, **89**, **91**, 93–5, 168
　differentiation between parties, 121, 127–9, 130
　electoral system, 59, 60
　exogenous factors, 63, 184–5
　history of liberal democracy, 58, 72–3, 181
　ideological cohesiveness, 85, 97, 111–29, 130–1, 187–8
　institutional incentives, 60–1
　intention-related criticism, 152–5, **153**
　lack of a sense of a common good, 164–70
　liberal breakdown, 1–2
　morality as a political cleavage, 164–7
　obligations of EU membership, 58
　partisan disagreement, 83–7, **86**, **88–9**

　party system dynamics, 59–60
　political culture, 61–2, 65–6, 72
　political polarisation, 74, 87
　political power imbalances, 191–2
　respect for political pluralism, 77–8, 132, 152–8, 171, 172, 187–8
　threat of holism, 152–70
　unprincipled nature of opponents, 158–63, **159**
　visual prompt research cards, 49, 50
　see also *Fiatal Demokraták Szövetsége-Kereszténydemokrata Néppárt* (Fidesz-KDNP); *Magyar Szocialista Párt-Együtt* (MSzP-Egyutt)

ideological cohesiveness
　asymmetrical normative grounding in Hungary, 112–21, 131
　authoritarian legacies in Hungary, 180–2
　for citizen engagement, 22–5
　for the common good, 8, 26, 28
　comparative discourse, 30, 107–8, **107**
　within democratic partisanship, 8, 17, 22–30, 40, 77, 175–6
　differentiation between parties, 29–30, 40, 103
　differentiation between parties in French partisans, 106–7
　differentiation between parties in Hungarian partisans, 121, 127–9, 130, 180–2
　of French partisans, 77, 97–111, 129–30
　of Hungarian partisans, 77, 85, 97, 111–29, 130–1, 187–8
　and the ideal of democratic partisanship, 186–8
　ideological confusion of the MSzP, 98, 130–1, 174
　ideological dissonance on the French Left, 97–8, 100, 108–11, 131, 174
　lack of in populist discourse, 193–4
　Left-Right registers in France, 100–1, 103–6, 107, 111, 179–80
　normative grounding, 25–7, 40
　normative grounding for in France, 98–103, **99**

ideological cohesiveness (*cont.*)
  in policies and measures, 28
  political agency, 28–9
  programmatic substance, 27–9, 40
  programmatic substance of French partisans, 103–6
  programmatic substance of Hungarian partisans, 121–6
  respect for political pluralism and, 185–8, 192–3
  values and fundamental principles, 26–7, 97, 99–100
Ifjúsági Kereszténydemokrata Szövetség (IKSZ), 78
institutions
  abusive legalism, 19, 31, 32
  abusive legalism in Hungary, 72–3, 75, 177
  active democratic support for, 19
  anti-pluralism's impact on, 195–6
  in democratising societies, 21
  institutional context for partisan discourse, 21–2
  see also constitutional arrangements

Jeunes populaires (JP), 78

Kereszténydemokrata Néppárt (KDNP), 9, 58, 72 ; see also *Ifjúsági Kereszténydemokrata Szövetség* (IKSZ)
Kövér, László, 193

Le Pen, Marine, 67, 71, 195
Left-Right dichotomies
  decline of in European politics, 14, 195
  as a democratic ideology, 179–80
  in Hungarian economic policies, 116–17
  ideological convergence in France, 66, 69, 84–5, 108–11, **110**
  Left-Right registers in French ideological cohesiveness, 100–1, 103–6, 107, 111, 179–80
  political identities and, 106–7, 111, 179
  populism's threat to, 195–6

Lendvai, Ildikó, 165
Les Républicains (LR), 59, 70, 77–8 ;
  see also *Union pour un mouvement populaire* (UMP)
liberal democracy
  citizen disengagement's threat to, 3–4
  constitutional essentials of, 8, 19, 31, 37
  democratic function of political parties, 2, 8, 17–18, 20–1, 185–6
  democratic partisanship and, 16, 30–1, 39–43
  the future of party democracy, 192–6
  history of in France, 58
  history of in Hungary, 58, 72–3, 181
  Hungary's cultural concept of, 189–91
  minimalist theories, 5–6, 19, 185
  normative enquiry into, 4–6, 185
  partisan discourse and, 18–22
  populism's threat to, 4
  principle of political pluralism, 30–3
  as a way of life, 19–20

Macron, Emmanuel, 66, 71, 195
Magyar Szocialista Párt-Együtt (MSzP-Együtt)
  absence of a supra-partisan community in Hungary, 168–70
  differentiation between parties, 127–9
  economic mismanagement, 1–2, 76–7
  ideological confusion, 76–7, 98, 130–1, 174
  intention-related criticism, 152–8, **153**
  morality as a political cleavage, 164–7
  motive-cynicism, 155–8
  normative grounding, 112, 117–21, 131
  practice-focused criticism, 153–5, **154**
  programmatic substance, 124–7, **125**
  references to the topics under discussion, **88–9, 113**
  responses to exogenous factor, 184
  structural weaknesses, 76–7
  support base, 75
  unprincipled nature of opponents, 158–63, **159**, 188
mainstream parties *see* political parties
Mitterrand, François, 137

Mouvement des jeunes socialistes (MJS), 71, 78
Muirhead, Russell, 24, 26, 28, 39 n.21, 42

normative political theory, 4–7

Orbán, Viktor, 2, 58, 74–5, 154, 155

Parti socialiste (PS)
  comparative discourse, **107**
  democratic value of political agreement and disagreement, 108–9, **108**, **150**
  depoliticisation of morality, 145–7
  funding, 68, 71
  ideological cohesiveness, 99–100, **100**
  ideological convergence, 66, 69, 108–11, **110**
  ideological dissonance, 97–8, 108–11, 131, 174
  intention-related criticisms by French partisans, 134–7, **134**, **135**, 152
  political marginalisation of, 66–7, 71–2
  principled opposition in, 140–4, **140**, **141**
  programmatic substance, 103–4, **104**, 106
  recognition of supra-partisan community, 148–9
  references to the topics under discussion, 86, **88**, **104**, 108
  respect for pluralism, 133, 134–5, **134**, **135**, 151
  responses to exogenous factor, 183
  right-wing drift, 69–70
  2017 elections, 71
partisan discourse
  concept, 8
  cultural context, 21, 57, 178–82, 189–91
  exogenous factors, 22, 56–7, 182–5
  fallacy of pure ethical motive, 53–4
  historical legacies, 180–2
  institutional context, 21–2
  liberal democracy and, 18–22
  political culture, 22, 55–6
  problem-identification narratives, 26
  structural factors, 54–7

partisanship
  definition, 16, 44
  liberal democracy and, 16
  normative enquiry into, 5, 7
  partisans as agents of democratic change, 54–5
  responsibilities of, 7–8
pluralism *see* respect for political pluralism
polarisation
  concept, 6
  in Hungary, 74, 87
  partisan agreement/disagreement, 83–7
  perceptions of in France, 83–4
  populist (re)polarisation, 3, 4
political parties
  as agents of representation, 2, 15, 20–1
  cartel-party thesis and, 68
  defiance against in France, 66–8
  definition, 17, 58
  democratic consolidation in Hungary, 72–3, 74
  democratic function, 2, 8, 17–18, 20–1, 185–6
  normative change, 4–5
  populist polarisation, 3, 4
  proximity to political power, 8
  as state actors, 2, 20–1, 24
  tradition of suspicion of, 15
  Western party system, 3
  see also democratic partisanship; partisanship
political pluralism *see* respect for political pluralism
populism
  anti-pluralism of, 193–6
  concept, 6
  democratic threat of, 4, 193–5
  ideological cohesiveness and, 193–4
  lack of respect for pluralism, 193–6
  polarised party systems, 3, 4
  rise of, 3
  technocratic opposition to, 194, 195

radical right parties
  in France, 67
  Populist Radical Right (PRR), 4
  right-wing drift in France, 69–70, 71–2, 85, 177–8

Rákosi, Mátyas, 117
Rassemblement national (RN; previously *Front national*), 67, 70, 71, 195
Rémond, René, 102 n.7
representation
  key democratic role of, 7, 22–3
  representative-constituent relationship, 19–20
respect for political pluralism
  democratic partisanship and, 8, 17, 30–9, 40, 41–3, 176–8
  depoliticisation of morality by French partisans, 145–7
  in France, 77–8, 132–52, **133**, 170–1, 183
  in Hungary, 77–8, 132, 152–8, 171, 172, 187–8
  and the ideal of democratic partisanship, 186–8
  ideological cohesiveness and, 185–8, 192–3
  intention-related criticism by Hungarian partisans, 152–5, **153**
  intention-related criticisms by French partisans, 134–7, **134**, **135**, 152
  liberal democracy and, 30–3
  motive-cynicism and, 34–5, 133, 134, 142–3, 155–8
  populist anti-pluralism, 193–6
  practice-focused criticism, 33–5, 38, 40
  practice-focused criticism in France, 133–7
  practice-focused criticism in French right-wing discourse, **134**, 137–40, **138**
  principled opposition by French partisans, 140–4, **140**, **141**, 159
  principled opposition in, 35–6, 38, 40
  recognition of a good in common, 17, 31–2, 35–9, 40, 133, 145–51
  recognition of supra-partisan community, 148–9
  rejection of holism, 31, 37–8
  right-wing threat to, 177–8
  unprincipled nature of opponents, 158–63, **159**

Rosenblum, Nancy, 24, 28, 39 n.21

Sarkozy, Nicolas, 70, 100 n.4, 106 n.11, 137 n.8
Societas, 78
SOS racisme, 137
Szabad Demokraták Szövetsége (SzDSz), 1, 2, 72, 76–7

Taubira, Christiane, 139 n.11
Trump, Donald, 193

Union pour un mouvement populaire (UMP)
  benevolent holism, 132–3, 171, 175, 183
  comparative discourse, **107**
  democratic value of political agreement and disagreement, 108, **108**, **150**
  depoliticisation of morality, 145–7
  funding, 68, 71
  ideological cohesiveness, 100–3, **100**
  ideological convergence, 66, 69
  intention-related criticisms by French partisans, 134–7, **134**, **135**, 152
  political marginalisation of, 66–7, 71–2
  practice-focused criticism, **138**, 140
  practice-focused criticism in French right-wing discourse, **134**, 137–40, **138**
  principled opposition in, 140–4, **140**, **141**
  programmatic substance, 103–6, **104**
  references to the topics under discussion, 86, **88**, **104**, 108
  respect for pluralism, 133, 134–5, **134**, **135**, 151–2, 183
  responses to exogenous factor, 182–3
  right-wing drift, 70
  shared objectives for a common good, 149–51
  2017 elections, 71

White, Jonathan, 23, 25–6, 27, 29
World Association of Hungarians, 169 n.37

Ypi, Léa, 23, 25–6, 27, 29